Coaching and Supervising Through Bereavement

This book presents a pragmatic guide for coaches and supervisors working with grief and bereavement, providing both useful case studies and practical techniques to aid professionals in embracing the complexity of working with these topics in a coaching context.

Coaching and Supervising Through Bereavement clearly delineates the boundary between bereavement issues requiring specialist counselling and 'normal' bereavement topics within coaching. It addresses how to coach clients through all different forms of bereavement, not just through death but also other losses such as job loss and relationship loss, and enables coaches to shine a light on their own bereavement journeys for the benefits of themselves and their clients. The authors also offer a guide for coaching supervisors to aid the ethical and emotional support required for their own supervisees and themselves.

This book debunks the myth that bereavement should not be discussed in coaching, and so will be a valuable resource for any practicing coach or supervisor of all levels of experience or expertise.

Julia Menaul has a background in learning and development and is an Association for Coaching Accredited Master Executive Coach with a thriving UK-based coaching supervision practice for coaches and supervisors.

Maggie João has an international career of more than 25 years and holds various coaching credentials (MCC, EIA SP, PMC). She has been a coach supervisor since 2012 and is the author of 14 published books about coaching in various languages.

Coaching and Supervising Through Bereavement

A Practical Guide to Working with Grief and Loss

Julia Menaul and Maggie João

Routledge
Taylor & Francis Group
LONDON AND NEW YORK

Cover image: © Chris Clor/Getty Images

First published 2023
by Routledge
4 Park Square, Milton Park, Abingdon, Oxon OX14 4RN

and by Routledge
605 Third Avenue, New York, NY 10158

Routledge is an imprint of the Taylor & Francis Group, an informa business

© 2023 Julia Menaul and Maggie João

The right of Julia Menaul and Maggie João to be identified as authors of this work has been asserted in accordance with sections 77 and 78 of the Copyright, Designs and Patents Act 1988.

All rights reserved. No part of this book may be reprinted or reproduced or utilised in any form or by any electronic, mechanical, or other means, now known or hereafter invented, including photocopying and recording, or in any information storage or retrieval system, without permission in writing from the publishers.

Trademark notice: Product or corporate names may be trademarks or registered trademarks, and are used only for identification and explanation without intent to infringe.

British Library Cataloguing-in-Publication Data
A catalogue record for this book is available from the British Library

Library of Congress Cataloging-in-Publication Data
Names: Menaul, Julia, author. | João, Maggie, author.
Title: Coaching and supervising through bereavement : a practical guide to working with grief and loss / Julia Menaul and Maggie João.
Description: Abingdon, Oxon ; New York, NY : Routledge, 2023. | Includes bibliographical references and index. |
Summary: "This book presents a pragmatic guide for coaches and supervisors working with grief and bereavement, providing both useful case studies and practical techniques to aid professionals in embracing the complexity of working with these topics in a coaching context"-- Provided by publisher.
Identifiers: LCCN 2022009962 | ISBN 9780367540715 (paperback) | ISBN 9780367540708 (hardback) | ISBN 9781003087502 (ebook)
Subjects: LCSH: Personal coaching. | Executive coaching. | Bereavement. | Grief.
Classification: LCC BF637.P36 M3838 2023 | DDC 158.3--dc23/eng/
20220509
LC record available at https://lccn.loc.gov/2022009962

ISBN: 978-0-367-54070-8 (hbk)
ISBN: 978-0-367-54071-5 (pbk)
ISBN: 978-1-003-08750-2 (ebk)

DOI: 10.4324/9781003087502

Typeset in Times New Roman and Gill Sans MT
by MPS Limited, Dehradun

"Written with grace and sensitivity, this pragmatic and compassionate looks at grief and loss in everyday scenarios from loss of job to crisis of meaning and purpose. This timely wisdom illuminates how to serve your clients and yourself as a practitioner in the coaching industry."

Tammy Turner, *ICF MCC and EMCC Master EIA,*
CEO of Turner International

"Truly fascinating topic to write about and this book by Julie and Maggie is comprehensive and written with love, compassion, and a keen eye for detail to support coaches and supervisors to navigate working with grief and loss and to be better equipped when this topic comes up during sessions. This is an intriguing book and offers tools and lenses to work through in support of clients. A must read for coaches and supervisors as it will improve how you work with these topics for better outcomes for clients."

Zsofia Juhasz, *Executive, Group and Team Coach,*
Coach mentor and supervisor

"This book is an amazing journey through the very sensitive topic of Bereavement, in its many forms. What I love about this book is the care and respect offered to the reader in each section. It is full of information, practical tips and case studies, inviting the reader to reflect and process at their own pace. It is not a definitive guide to the correct responses but an exploration of potential responses and answers for individuals. I believe this book would be a great addition as a must-read for all Coach and Supervision training programs."

Benita Stafford-Smith, *Managing Consultant at BLSS Coaching, and Accredited Coach Supervisor*

"Julia and Maggie have written a highly accessible and practical book, which makes a needed contribution to our profession on this subject. The sharing of relevant theory, their research, and practitioner case studies provides Coaches, Supervisors and Organisations with expert guidance and raises critical questions for professional practice. It could not have come at a better time."

Damion Wonfor, *Founder of Catalyst 14*

"It is a privilege to have made a small contribution to this comprehensive book. Julia and Maggie have made a difficult subject uplifting and exceedingly informative. Both practical and well-researched, it gives real life, relatable case studies throughout. This is an impressive addition to my essential reading list for experienced and student coaches and supervisors."

Marie Faire, *Director at The Beyond Partnership, Executive Coach and Executive Trainer*

"A necessary book on an important topic, reminding us that coaching begins in a shared humanity and for human beings grief and loss are normal experiences. Anchored by case studies and enriched by psychological insights, this is a wise and practical guide offering an extensive box of tools applicable in a range of contexts."

Patrick Hobbs, *Master Executive Coach and Coaching Supervisor*

"Grief and loss are an inherent part of life and growth. This book offers coaches a comprehensive and practical framework to help clients process the various experiences and aspects of loss that life brings their way. This book is a must for every coach who is passionate about helping people reach their fullest potential."

Shiri Ben-Arzi, *Medical Coach, founder of MCI – the Medical Coaching Institute*

For David Thomas Mountford

19.4.1933 – 13.6.2018

Julia Menaul, Coaching Supervisor and Accredited Master Executive Coach

To all coaches and supervisors who help their clients see the sun behind the clouds.

Maggie João, MCC and EIA Senior Practitioner

Contents

Acknowledgements   xiii
Foreword by Eve Turner   xiv

Introduction   1
Health warning 4

PART I
Coaching Through Bereavement   7

1   **The Boundaries of Our Work**   9
Defining coaching 10
Grief in executive coaching 10
Defining counselling 12
Defining bereavement, grief, and loss 13
Types of losses 15
Signs of bereavement 16

2   **The Bereaved Coaching Client**   20
How clients show up 20
    A crisis of meaning 20
    Signs of crisis 22
To coach or not to coach: What do clients need right now? 23
    Showing compassion and empathy: Being a heart
      with ears 23
    Mind your language 26
    A test of faith 27
    What can you offer a client right away? 28

How to contract for a conversation that includes discussing their loss 28
    What is the psychological contract and how does that need to change? 28
  Is coaching the right intervention for the client right now? 29
    Spotting a mental health issue 30
    Functional suffering 31
    Life coaching versus executive coaching and bereavement 31
    The psychological dimensions of executive coaching 32
    Dysfunctional suffering 35
    Mental illness 36
    "They were OK when the coaching started" 37
    Continue, pause, or stop 39
  How other types of loss arrive in coaching 42
    The historical loss 43
    Female clients who have lost babies 44
    Male clients and child death 46
    Loss of job 47
    Relationship loss 49
    Divorce 49
    Loss of health 51
    Carer's grief 52
    Empty nest syndrome 54
    Menopause 55
    Male coaches and menopause 57
    Retirement and ageing 58
    Abortion 59

3 The Bereaved Coach   63
  Self-care for coaches 65
  Serious illness: The ill coach 71
  The dance between coach and client through bereavement 75

4 The Organisational Machine   79
  What does grief in the workplace look like? 79
  Where do organisations go wrong? 79
  Actions for line managers 82
  Considerations for coaches and supervisors 83

What should a coach do if the contract is three-way or
     multi-party contracting? 84
Loss in the system: Grief loss, leavings, endings, and exits 91
Helping your client to process unresolved endings 92

PART II
Supervising through Bereavement   97

5   **Extending the Learning Edge**   99
    What is coaching supervision? 99
    Helping the coach with client bereavement – ethical best
       practice 104
    Helping the coach with bereavement – their own pain, grief and
       loss 109
    How might a supervisor work with a coach experiencing a
       sense of loss? 110
        The immediate response 110
    Resilience building through supervision 114
    When a coach might need therapy 118
    Retriggered loss response 118
    Polishing the personal and professional mirror 120
    The death of a client 124
    Unresolved endings 125

6   **The Changing Lens**   129
    Loss and grief through different lenses 129
    The Lens of the Drama Triangle 129
        Game playing in corporate life 132
        Loss and the Drama Triangle 132
    The Lens of Attachment 134
        Loss and attachment 137
    The Lens of Trauma 139
        Trauma informed coaching 139
        Trauma self 140
        Survival self 141
        Healthy self 142
        Connecting trauma, coaching and loss 142
        The coach's survival self 143
        Is there something more serious with this client? 145
        Suicide risk of client 146

        Suicide bereavement 147
        Post-traumatic growth 150
    The Lens of Neuroscience 150
        What is neuroscience? 151
        Neuroscience and coaching 154
        The Polyvagal theory 155
        The impact of the autonomic nervous system 155
        The grieving brain 156
    Cultural considerations 161

PART III
Practical Guidance and Activities for Coaches and Supervisors   169

7 Tools and techniques to work with grief and loss   **171**
    Activities 171

    Summary   189
    Bibliography   191
    Appendices   193
      Appendix 1 Coaching niches 195
      Appendix 2 Our research findings 197
      Appendix 3 The Global Code of Ethics 205
    Resources   213
    Index   216

Acknowledgements

We would like to thank everyone who helped directly or indirectly with the culmination of this book. First, all our expert reviewers for their useful feedback based on years of wisdom: Benita Stafford-Smith, Damion Wonfor, Marie Faire, Patrick Hobbs, Shiri Ben-Arzi, Tammy Turner and Zsofia Juhasz.

As well as being a reviewer, Eve Turner was instrumental in encouraging us to take a small acorn of an idea generated from the Global Supervisors' Network and turn it into a book, as well as the practical help in connecting us to Routledge and writing our foreword.

Also, a huge thanks to all our brilliant case study writers; all coaches working on the frontline of our profession: Anne Stojic, Carole Davidson, Catriona Hudson, Chris Birbeck, Diane Hanna, Louise Hallett, Lynn Scott, Marie Faire, Roger Williams, Sian Taylor, and Quynh Anh TRINH XUAN.

To all the coaches and supervisors who responded to our research questions, we really appreciated the honesty and experiences shared.

We wouldn't be the coaches and supervisors we are without the clients we have been privileged to serve, and our own supervisors who support us both with great wisdom, compassion, and insight. We salute them all.

An appreciation to Debby Marcy, our wizard VA, who steered us through all the technical guidelines and polished our formatting and grammar.

And finally, to our friends and family who provided inspiration with their stories and support when the writing took over our lives.

Foreword

Bereavement seems inescapable. Most of us may well think first of death of someone close to us which is one of the few certainties for us all. But it also impacts us through many other losses, such as: of a personal or business relationship, divorce, menopause, of connection (through Covid-19), through being a victim of abuse, a takeover of a company we were emotionally invested in, a landscape we cherish, a beloved pet dying, or a species that becomes extinct.

As I sit in my study writing this in late August 2021, I am reminded of a 2,500-year-old olive tree lost in the wildfires in Evia in Greece earlier this month and treasured by local people who described their mourning at the many losses during the widespread destruction (Kissel, 2021). This is the same month that the latest IPCC report has been published describing the impact humanity is having on the climate as a "statement of fact" and the UN Sectary-General António Guterres calling it a "code red for humanity" (McGrath, 2021).

I am aware of my own deep grief and loss at this. Yet accepting our own and others' strong feelings and knowing how to be in the face of bereavement is less clear to many of us, whether we are experiencing and dealing with our own grief and loss or supporting others through theirs. Julia and Maggie encourage us to deal with bereavement with "an empty mind, a full heart, and definitely a non-judgmental approach" and for the coach to be mindful of the process the client is going through "understanding what is going on, not with a judgmental lens, but rather with a compassionate approach, observing all that is emerging for them and how that might impact the way they coach."

This much-needed book's beginnings stem from a LinkedIn post that Julia wrote, shortly after her father died in mid-2018. She wrote about people's varied responses to her bereavement and reflected on how death still seemed a taboo subject, and asked readers to share their experiences. It enabled a conversation that is hugely important.

Julia shared her reflections with a network I was part of, and I remember reading her words: "I have coached many clients who have been recently (or not so recently) bereaved, who are still "struggling" with the death of someone close. I have also supervised coaches trying to deal with a death of a client emotionally, practically and ethically. Some coaches come to supervision never having explored the impact of a close death (particularly at an early age) on them personally and professionally."

Maggie and I were two of those who responded, and I invited Julia and Maggie to run a webinar together for the GSN (Global Supervisors' Network), and they did some original research to inform their sessions. So, thankfully, the seed of the book was sown, on a subject that has been a long-neglected area in the coaching and supervision literature and in training.

And what a wonderful, clearly structured and written addition to the coaching literature this is.. Throughout the text, we are invited to pause, offered practical tips and tools and an abundance of insightful and often moving case studies that illustrate the depth and breadth of this practical text. Its early discussion on functional suffering, dysfunctional suffering, and mental illness, along with its exploration of multiple lenses from trauma to culture, and its dialogue such as on boundary management are liberating in how we can help (ourselves and others) but also perceptive on when we might need to do something different. And the final Part, with practical tools, is a gift to both coaches and supervisors.

I want to end this brief foreword with Julia and Maggie's wise words: "We, coaches, listen; we don't fix." This has never been truer or more needed than here.

Remen describes a demonstration given by Dr Carl Rogers at Stanford University, taken from her beautiful book Kitchen Table Wisdom. She recalls Rogers' words before the therapy session started with one of her doctor colleagues: "Before every session I take a moment to remember my humanity. There is no experience that this man has that I cannot share with him, no fear that I cannot understand, no suffering that I cannot care about, because I too am human. No matter how deep his wound, he does not need to be ashamed in front of me. I too am vulnerable. And because of this, I am enough. Whatever his story, he no longer needs to be alone with it. This is what will allow his healing to begin" (2006: 218). Remen said the session was profound and conducted without Rogers saying a "single word." She concludes the "greatest gift we bring to anyone is our wholeness" and "listening is the oldest and perhaps the most powerful tool of healing" (2006: 219). This new and excellent book in the coaching literature will give us perspective, understanding, tips and tools to listen ever more deeply, to see our clients holistically, offer our presence and "be". It is a must for bookshelves.

Eve Turner
Chair, APECS (Association for Professional Executive Coaching and Supervision);
Founder and lead, Global Supervisors' Network;
Co-founder, Climate Coaching Alliance;
Fellow, University of Southampton and Henley Business School;
Author. August 2021
www.eve-turner.com

References

Kissel, T., 2021. *2,500-Year-Old Ancient Olive Tree Burned Down in Evia Fires in Greece.* [online] GreekReporter.com. Available at: https://greekreporter.com/2021/08/08/evia-fire-greece-ancient-olive-tree-burned/ [Accessed 8 August 2021].

McGrath, M., 2021. *Climate change: IPCC report is 'code red for humanity'.* [online] BBC News. Available at: https://www.bbc.co.uk/news/science-environment-58130705.

Remen, R., 2006. *Kitchen Table Wisdom.* New York: Penguin Group.

Introduction

At some point, bereavement will happen in life, regardless of the nature of the loss: a death of a loved one, a death of a pet, loss of a friendship, relationship, partnership, loss of something material, amongst others.

One might say that the loss from a death of a loved one is much more important than any other loss. But is it really? Isn't this pure judgement? We aren't in the heads, nor the hearts, of the bereaved person and we haven't lived their lives. We are not aware of the bond they had with the person who just died, nor the pet, nor the material thing that disappeared. So, in fact, dealing with bereavement requires an empty mind, a full heart, and definitely a non-judgemental approach.

We know bereavement is something natural in the life cycle, even though it is not easy to face. We also know that bereavement depends on many factors, such as the emotional resilience the individual has; the relationship they had with the person who died or the thing lost; the context currently living in; the support network; past experiences; and future expectations, amongst others.

There isn't a right way to go through bereavement. It is an individual process and there isn't a specific deadline when things will be fixed or back to normal again, if that is even possible. The individual comes out differently from bereavement as well as their relationship with their own self, others, and the world in general. The key resides in the quest of finding their answers to unlock the rebuilding process.

Everyone can become bereaved, but not everyone can access help when bereaved. Whilst many believe that bereavement is territory only for the psychologist and therapist, gradually the world is discovering that coaching through bereavement is a resource that provides a non-judgemental approach as well as helping in defining strategies and methods that create hope and resources for a brighter future.

As this develops and coaching through bereavement becomes a reality within the profession, increasingly coaching supervisors are working with coaches whose clients are bereaved or who are themselves going through bereavement.

DOI: 10.4324/9781003087502-1

Both of us have gone through bereavement of the death of loved ones and we have also experienced coaching and supervising others through bereavement. As we leaned on each other to navigate through these waters, it became clearer that there was a void when it comes to literature relating to coaching and coaching supervision through bereavement. We saw an opportunity, and after many months of more in-depth research, we decided to start writing this book.

The book came alive after several meetings debating the topic from multiple angles, after many articles published in specialised journals and magazines, and after various invitations received from worldwide recognised coaching entities to conduct webinars to groups of international coaches and supervisors. The feedback received from all of them was phenomenal and supported our idea that there was an opportunity to provide the coaching world with more knowledge on this topic. As many coaching professionals age themselves, so do their clientele, and regardless of the fact bereavement doesn't choose an age, we all know that there is a higher likelihood of this topic arising in coaching sessions.

This book intends to shine some light onto this important life topic, as well as providing some ideas and resources to coaching professionals when they come across it in their sessions with their clients.

The main intention of this research is to inform coaches and supervisors of best practices and eventually models they can use when working with clients who are going through bereavement. It is important to provide support to these specialists so they can enhance their skills and competencies in this field and hence, provide a better service to the client.

Our main research findings are based on the following conclusions:

- Bereavement is an individual process and there isn't a right way to go through it or a right time to come out of it.
- Terminology is different from culture to culture.
- Terminology is key to establish the relationship between coach or supervisor and client.
- The fact the coach or supervisor has experienced bereavement him/herself may impact the coaching/supervision relationship.
- The list of best practices to navigate through bereavement includes various topics, from behavioural to rational.
- It is paramount for the coach to understand when they are out of their depth and therefore referencing other professionals or practices is crucial.
- Coaching presence is of extreme importance and needs to be mastered by the professional.

The book will develop in more depth these findings, providing further knowledge and sharing experiences and case studies that will assist the individual coaching professional to work more confidently with their clients about this topic.

In addition to the analysis resulting from these findings, we would also like to bring attention to how the workplace is ready to receive bereaved employees and what are the supporting mechanisms in place.

On the other hand, the book also aims to inform organisations through their HR departments about what a bereaved employee might be experiencing. Any alternative approaches and behaviours considered by employers for bereaved employees, may also be an additional benefit for team effectiveness, safeguarding, and conflict resolution.

However, we now know that grief and loss are not solely confined to feeling bereaved at death, and as James and Friedman (2009) point out there are at least 40 other losses that anyone can encounter during a lifetime. Each one is unique.

We decided early on in this project to focus heavily on case studies written by a wide variety of coaches and supervisors. We felt it was important to hear their stories, their complexity, commonality, and the frequency with which bereavements arrive in the coaching room.

When we went out to our network for help with the case studies, the questions below produced a flow of experiences from coaches of all levels and cultures.

We asked coaches and supervisors to write about:

- How they helped coachees through their own current or historical grief (for example, employee/family/friend death, miscarriages, terminations) during coaching, that is, how did they decide to coach or not to coach?
- How they navigated their own fitness to practise during bereavement (either if personal loss happened for them during the coaching/supervision or if historical grief was triggered in response to some work).
- How they navigated their own fitness to practise during loss of health as a coach or supervisor, such as, informing clients, managing workload, etc.
- Stories of consultancy challenges dealing with employers/sponsors/buyers of coaching around bereavement, and other organisational issues/policies that caused ethical dilemmas for coaches/supervisors.
- Unusual examples of coaching and supervising through other losses that caused significant challenges personally or professionally. For example, changing identity, carers grief, empty nesters, menopause, infertility, childlessness, redundancy/being fired, ill health diagnosis, pets, separation/divorce, family estrangement, lost custody/access.

We will share later some unique research we gathered from this network of coaches and supervisors.

It is our hope you will find these pages interesting and resourceful and that by reading them it will lead you into a reflective mode on how to become a better partner when coaching or supervising your bereaved client.

And who knows? Reading this book might also help you navigate through bereavement when it crosses your own life. We all know it is not a matter of if, but rather a matter of when.

As this book is a practical guide, we have created three icons that will help you smoothly navigate this book:

– promotes the idea of a pause for thought. We suggest you take time to reflect, and maybe even take some notes.

– is for activities you can do with yourself or your clients providing them with a different approach than just questioning and reflecting back.

– this is our little gift to you in the shape of a practical tip.

The case studies

The case studies peppered throughout the book are real situations. However, in some cases, they are an amalgamation of several different scenarios and individuals. In all cases, the names, gender, and other identifying features of individuals have been changed. Any specific organisational references have been removed and only the organisational sector is alluded to in many of the stories for greater anonymity. The terms "he" or "she" are used interchangeably and do not reflect any gender differences unless stated. We have chosen to use the term "client" in a variety of situations as this could refer to a coaching client or supervision client in equal measure. The "sponsor" is the paymaster and usually organisational and could be the line manager, HR department, Learning & Development, or OD Partner. When we specifically refer to a supervision client it will be "supervisee", or a coaching client as "coachee".

Health warning

This book comes with a health warning. Grief, loss, and bereavement in its many forms can be extremely emotive. We dearly hope you will find this book easy to read and useful for your work as a coach and supervisor. However, we want you to please bear in mind that some of the information, and in particular the case studies, may kick off new and unforeseen thinking, feelings, and behaviour for you. Therefore, we ask you to take good care of yourself, use your supervisor for anything that appears incomplete or unfinished so that you experience some loving support that will enable you to grow professionally and personally through examining this universal topic.

Reference

James, J. and Friedman, R., 2009. *The Grief Recovery Handbook, 20th Anniversary Expanded Edition: The Action Program for Moving Beyond Death, Divorce, and Other Losses including Health, Career, and Faith*. New York, NY: Harper Collins.

Part I

Coaching Through Bereavement

This first section starts by presenting several important definitions related to the topic of loss and laying the boundaries of the coaching work in relation to bereavement. Bereavement may be caused by many types of losses we may encounter in our life, and they are not only triggered by the death of a loved one. It explains what the best course of action is when we as coaches face a client who is going through bereavement. It also explores the perspective of the bereaved coach and how important it is to the coach's self-care. Coaching is not only about one person's life, it is about many because the coach touches many lives (some unseen). We can only try to offer our very best.

Chapter 1

The Boundaries of Our Work

Pain and suffering in coaching and supervision (Hobbs, 2019) can show up in coaching in the form of bereavement, infertility issues, mental illness, divorce, etc. but not necessarily as the main focus of the coaching itself. These topics are a part of life but can remain hidden especially in high-pressure corporate situations where people feel it will be perceived as a sign of weakness to even discuss these topics. Coaching is often seen as being about success, so what happens if clients feel they can't bring these topics, and does the coach feel the same in supervision? Being able to talk about failure, inadequacy, and suffering, we believe, is the cornerstone of a good supervision relationship where the coach feels safe to explore these topics for themselves and their clients.

Hobbs also believes that coaches are experiencing more and more clients with the topic of pain, grief, and suffering, as people are more likely now to employ coaches rather than therapists. Could this be because there is less stigma in having coaching? **And are coaches equipped for this and are we as supervisors able to notice this?**

We found ourselves whilst reading the Hobbs's chapter (2019) mentally listing many coachees from our own past work who we would categorise under this theme and then considered how this may be the same for many other coaches, for example, custody battles, a client's son with Autism, supervisee suicide, a coachee with parental death as a child, sexual abuse, serious ill health issues such as Multiple Sclerosis (MS) (Tricarico, 2021), and many cases of marital breakdown.

We will be considering some of these questions and there are many more:

- How comfortable are we with talking about death/bereavement with our clients?
- How much have we worked through our own bereavements to be 'clean and safe' if our clients raise this as an issue?
- What are the emotional, ethical, and moral implications when a coachee dies during coaching?

- How do we help clients if a bereavement happens during coaching, and should we, as part of the contract?
- Where do we draw the line between coaching and therapy when it comes to dealing with bereavement?

Defining coaching

If you are reading this book then it is likely you are a coach, supervisor, or interested/have skills in coaching. We are, therefore, making some assumptions about you and will not go into detail defining coaching. However, here are a few definitions of coaching from others that we like:

> "Coaching is the art of facilitating the performance, learning and development of another."
>
> –Myles Downey (2003)

> "Coaching is the unlocking of a person's potential to maximise their own performance."
>
> –Sir John Whitmore (2017)

> "Coaching is about facilitating the learning required to improve performance but will invariably be about change."
>
> –Peter Bluckert (2005)

Many of the definitions relate to coaching in a corporate or business context and therefore emphasise performance. Performance coaching for executives/managers/leaders can often involve support for balancing work and home life as a conduit for increased effectiveness at work, although not always the central focus of the work. As we will see later, this assumption about the boundaries of a coaching contract can cause confusion for coaches when grief and loss intrude on a specific corporate agenda.

We will also be referring to executive coaching, life coaching, and a myriad of different coaching niches (Appendix 1).

Grief in executive coaching

As a result, is it more acceptable to see life coaches handling loss issues such as bereavement around death than it would be for an executive coach?

Executive coaches can and should pay attention to significant losses impacting their clients even if they are not classic bereavement situations via death. However, even executive coaches will recognise losses such as:

- Loss of trust (in any workplace environment involving employees, bosses, etc.)

- Loss of safety (unsafe feelings can be stirred up during redundancy, retirement, maternity leave, mergers and acquisitions, and anywhere clients experience the uncertainties of change.)

These are all grief issues. They say grief is a broken heart and not a broken brain.

Intellectually we can know that 'something is for the best' but emotionally we may not feel that way.

> ### Julia's coaching case study: Loss of trust
>
> Winston was a middle manager within the public sector. He was part of a coaching programme offered to several managers to help with major organisational change. I was an associate coach. From the very first session, Winston was difficult to warm to and I struggled to make full contact with him. I had initially set out two seats for us, but he went to the opposite end of the room, so I had to follow him there. Over the next three sessions, I challenged his commitment and tried to cut through what was holding him back. He insisted he wanted to do the coaching even when I pointed to his behaviour demonstrating the opposite, that is, being late for/postponing sessions, not doing pre work, giving short brusque answers to questions. I offered him the opportunity to pause or discontinue the coaching. He declined but the same behaviour continued. I had a feeling he was 'running the clock down' in order to tick a coaching box.
>
> Before the last session, I finally managed to speak to the coaching sponsor who told me that the previous year some senior directors had been literally frogmarched out of the organisation due to the uncovering of financial irregularities. One of these directors was Winston's line manager. As part of the ensuing restructure and new management, Winston was identified as a poor performer, which led to him being coached by another coach. Something had happened between Winston and the coach and the contract was terminated. This information had not been shared with me at the start of the coaching programme. I checked back at my original notes for session one with Winston and saw the word "guarded".
>
> At our last session, I asked Winston about what I had heard from the sponsor, and the full story came tumbling out. Unfortunately, his coach had breached confidentiality (in his eyes) which exacerbated what had happened in the organisation. Suddenly I could see that Winston's behaviour was coming from a place of fear and that perhaps the insecurity he felt after suddenly losing his manager with no explanation, then his own position becoming tenuous, had created

> even less trust for him, and so he became even more guarded with me. I had no way of knowing (because he wouldn't tell me) of other unacknowledged or unsettled losses that had happened to Winston which were perhaps impacting the whole efficacy of the coaching.

Defining counselling

> I'm a Grief & Loss Coach. Both coaching and therapy can work for grieving clients. Some of my clients are more drawn to coaching because they want to navigate their grief in an action-orientated way, or because they felt like therapy just isn't working for them. When it comes to knowing when to refer to a therapist, I use my intuition. For example, if there are signs that trauma is present, or when grief becomes complicated. The simple answer is to ask the client what they need rather than feel like you have to figure it out for yourself.
> **Louise Creswick**, www.louisecreswick.com

We are often asked what the difference is between therapy and counselling. Both focus on problem solving or on learning specific techniques for coping with or avoiding problem areas. "Counselling is usually more short-term than therapy. Psychotherapy is more long-term than counselling and focuses on a broader range of issues." (Saling, 2019.)

Like coaching there are many definitions of counselling, so there is potential to get embroiled in a contentious issue here. For our purpose, looking at bereavement, we share some thoughts mainly about the interconnection and boundary with coaching as opposed to purist definitions. Counselling[1] can:

- Explore personal issues and problems through discussion in order to increase understanding or develop greater self-awareness.
- Lead the client toward self-directed actions to achieve their goals.

Coaching is not therapy although it can often feel therapeutic. Many models and techniques are shared between other disciplines such as Transactional Analysis (TA), Neuro Linguistic Programming (NLP), Cognitive behavioural therapy (CBT), and Gestalt, and used in personal and corporate contexts.

Coaching clients may present with issues such as low self-esteem, poor motivation, and work performance issues even though the focus may be setting goals and achieving results within a short to medium-term time frame.

---

1 Coaching and counselling share many core skills. However, professional counsellors work with personal issues in much greater depth than would generally be explored within a coaching context. (www.coachingnetwork.org)

Coaching can sometimes be helpful around raising awareness of these blockages to improved performance but there is a fine line for when the problems are too deeply entrenched, sometimes from childhood and/or trauma, to enable a shift within coaching that will benefit the coachee and the organisation (who may be paying for it).

For most coaching assignments, we are working on the premise that coachees are basically well, whole, and self-aware (although as we mentioned earlier, there can be clients seeking coaching instead of therapy for pride or shame reasons). Some underlying issues may not actually be obstacles to achieving success. After all, none of us is perfect and we all come to coaching with a certain amount of historical baggage. Problems can arise, however, when a coachee becomes stuck and this may mean a therapeutic intervention is necessary. It is possible for a coachee to receive counselling and coaching alongside each other if necessary to their mutual benefit.

As coaches, we need to stay alert to this possibility. Not that we are there to decide what intervention is required, as these are specialist skills, but knowing when to seek help outside our own skill set is crucial.

Some coaches will also be trained counsellors and psychologists themselves so contracting is crucial to define what the relationship is at the start and to change it as the work progresses.

One word about the term "psychologist". In UK law there are several protected titles to protect the public: Registered Psychologist, Clinical Psychologist, Counselling Psychologist, and Occupational Psychologist. Titles that are not restricted by legislation are coaching psychologist, counsellor, and therapist.

In the USA, it depends on the law in a particular state. In some states, the law protects the title. Practitioners can do whatever they want, but they can't call themselves a 'licensed' practitioner without meeting all the formal requirements. In other states, the law prevents practitioners from engaging in the practices of counselling, therapy, or psychology without a license, no matter what the title is.

Throughout the book, we will be using counselling and therapy interchangeably and will not distinguish particular therapies such as psychotherapy, person-centred, cognitive behavioural, or any others when we occasionally recommend some seek a therapeutic intervention instead of coaching.

Defining bereavement, grief and loss

Lots of words become associated with grief that can create confusion. If we have learned false or faulty ideas about what grief means, then this can lead to inaccurate defining which loops back to inaccurate approaches to grief. Grief is still a taboo subject in a time when many other taboos have disappeared within our culture. We have been socialised from an early age, and also societally, that any feelings related to grief are abnormal. Conflict comes from experiencing feelings around grief that are unexpected compared to what you might have been brought up to expect. Grief is not always about sadness. Other emotions can be anger and relief and are completely normal too. We assume how we are socialised about grief applies to others as well.

> My (Julia) paternal grandmother died suddenly when I was twelve years old. I remember my mother being cross that I wanted to go out to play immediately after being the told the news. Later a decision was made that it was deemed inappropriate for me to attend my grandmother's funeral. However, my school was situated on the same road as the crematorium and so I saw the funeral cortege and other members of my family drive past in the big black scary limousines. I now consider that as part of my own unresolved grief and subsequent adult difficulties regarding fear of death. This was over fifty years ago and thankfully we have progressed somewhat in our thinking about involving children in the reality of death and dying. My mother was probably only making decisions for me based on her own socialisation about death and societal norms in 1970s England.

We will explore later how different cultures approach death and what we might learn from those perspectives.

In a general sense, all loss has some level of grief attached to it, as we grieve the passing of something we once knew or took for granted. Bereavement is not just related to death. We can grieve the loss of our identity (becoming an 'empty nester' after years of parenting or even becoming a new parent after the freedom of youth), our relationships (marriage, divorce, separation), our youth (ageing, menopause, ill health), our jobs (redundancy, dismissal).

We are in such a rush sometimes to move into new things that we fail to see that we have not ended what has gone previously. As James and Friedman (2009) point out: "An incomplete past may doom the future". They define grief as: "the conflicting feelings caused by the end of or change in a familiar pattern of behaviour".

We may define bereavement simply as:

- The **sorrow** you **feel** or the state you are in when a **relative or close friend dies**.
- The condition of having been **deprived** of something or someone valued, especially through **death** (or 'robbed of something' in old English).
- A state of intense grief, as after the loss of a loved one; desolation.
- Deprivation or loss by force.
  (João and Menaul, 2019)

Types of losses

For coaches and supervisors, it may mean that one loss can trigger another. A client losing their job can suddenly be confronted with new feelings that seem out of proportion to what has happened but can often surface as unfinished emotions around grief that may go back years. The same could be said for another common loss, divorce. There may be positive feelings of freedom and relief as well as sadness and anger about how the relationship ended (which may not match who did the ending).

Types of Losses listed by James and Friedman (2009) are:

- Death of a spouse or former spouse/family/friends.
- Major health changes – loss of health more than most factors causes people to feel vulnerable leading to loss of safety especially losing the ability to be physically active.
- Start/end of addictions.
- Legal problems.
- Empty nesters.
- Death of a pet.

Some events may seem 'positive' such as:

- Marriage.
- Moving (house/school/workplace) – moving is a major loss for children so as an adult this can get triggered by future moves (Hilpern, 2014).
- Graduation.
- Retirement.
- Holidays.
- Legal problems.

Many of these events although not seen as 'losses' by many people are largely about relationships and grieving for the loss of all relationships irrespective of the circumstances.

We would also add to this list:

- Infertility.
- Childlessness.
- Identity change including gender transition.
- Carer's grief.
- Menopause (possible loss of libido, loss of identity, loss of childbearing capability).
- Redundancy/being fired.
- Family estrangement/lost custody or access.
- Ageing.
- Divorce.

If we take a broad-brush approach to the topic of loss and how we might grieve that loss, then there are many topics that arrive in coaching that have a form of bereavement attached to them, that we may have to handle. According to *The Grief Recovery Handbook* (James and Friedman, 2009) most adults on average have had 10–15 loss experiences in life depending on their age.

The pain of unresolved grief can be cumulative so we may see clients who appear to be 'overreacting' to a loss (in the eyes of others) when in fact it may be a final straw in a long list of previous losses that have never been processed or completed. These emotions are unfinished.

A good example is that it is recognised that divorcees (or anyone who has undergone a separation from a life partner) who do not successfully 'complete' their recovery from loss can go on to report the same mistakes in future relationships. Sometimes "it will create hypervigilant self-protection from further emotional pain" and thus limit future trusting, open, honest new relationships and doom them to failure (James and Friedman, 2009). Grief can also be felt by those who have instigated the separation and divorce.

Nevertheless, many commentators now have a problem with the Kübler-Ross Curve (2009), which we discuss later, in that it has become so famous now that there is an expectation that grievers will go through these stages when it might depend on the type of loss and the uniqueness of the relationship. Denial as a stage is particularly disliked by some, although this could be that by the time counsellors see grievers, they are completely aware of their loss and are not denying it. Also, many grievers do not become angry either, which also looms large on the Curve. Grief specialists also take a swipe at 'closure' particularly for people who have lost others in tragic circumstances and have perhaps been involved in some legal proceedings. Successfully gaining justice for loss does not always lessen the grief and can even be a distraction. The fact of the law does not equate to completing unresolved grief.

What are your losses?

Signs of bereavement

So instead of stages and time frames for recovery, we perhaps need to notice common responses with our clients such as:

- Reduced concentration.
- Sense of numbness.
- Disrupted sleep patterns.

- Changed eating habits.
- Roller-coaster of emotional energy.

Anecdotally these symptoms have been referred to as 'grief brain'.

> *We also have to bear in mind that there should be no expectation that people will 'forget' about their loss in order to 'get over it'. Just because a client wishes to talk about a loss does not signal that it is a problem that they haven't 'got over' and therefore we must rush to medicalise or therapize it in some way. Time by itself doesn't really heal. It really does depend on what you do during that time that makes the difference.*

Projecting our own emotional reaction onto clients can be dangerous too, either because we connect it to our experience of loss, or we pass value judgements on the type of loss and how we would expect people to react. An example is if there has been a loss in tragic circumstances such as suicide or murder. I (Julia) remember being on a webinar and a participant saying her daughter had been murdered the previous year, and I struggled to know what to say, which I knew was not how I normally reacted when people told me about other family deaths.

> *As we discuss later, as part of the biographical enquiry with a client it may be helpful to discover how death was discussed or perceived in families especially if helping a client to deal with a loss that might initially appear unrelated.*

Unresolved grief for any loss is usually about "undelivered emotional communication" (James and Friedman, 2009). This is just as relevant if the loss is a death or a divorce or an unsatisfactory ending to a job.

One area that can easily fit into a coach/supervisor's brief is facilitating the client to give voice to the unsayable. We frequently hear from clients how coaching works because they can verbalise much of what is happening for them. "A story told out loud is an event; the listener is not a passive receiver." (Kaiser and Burley, 2021)

> *Chair work activity from Gestalt coaching or perceptual positions if you have more of an NLP slant is ideal for clients to say out loud something even if a person/relationship is no longer there.*

When we have lost something whether that is a person, a relationship, or a job we can often take up black and white thinking which leads us to create a perspective that is all negative or all positive. James and Friedman (2009) call this "enshrinement or bedevilment".

When we have worked with coachees who are suffering the loss of a difficult ending in an organisation, they can often see only the negative aspects of their time in the job unless specifically asked to focus on what was good about their experience. Using good foundational coaching techniques can be incredibly useful to enable clients to create a more balanced view of their situation. A great question for helping people to find what is incomplete is "What do you wish had been different, better, more/less?"

Holding the space for clients to talk about a variety of losses and connect the dots can be enormously helpful for their long-term resilience and wellbeing. We now know that unresolved loss is cumulative and cumulatively negative and the amount of energy this takes can lead to mental and physical ill health further down the track.

Over recent years there has been a shift from more traditional approaches to bereavement based on western philosophies that emphasised closure, letting go, completing the cycle, accepting death, and saying goodbye. This approach required the griever to sever emotional ties with their loved one as a way of moving on. It is now known that the opposite needs to be true. Many people find they can incorporate their grief into their life (it never disappears anyway, so make friends with it) by actively remembering their loved ones through various activities and rituals which provide meaning and a legacy. So instead of saying goodbye, it's really about saying hello to the (new) relationship. The person dies but the relationship does not. Removing the need to say goodbye removes the feeling of failure for many people when they feel that they are still carrying around their grief when others expect them not to. "A respectful audience can help to keep relationships alive and to honour aspects of that relationship." (Kaiser and Burley, 2021).

Timing is particularly important if a client brings a loss issue to coaching. Unfortunately, there is no set time in which we could say "X time has passed now so you can talk to your client this way or that way".

Everyone is uniquely different, and the best option is to be led by your client.

If they feel open and willing to think about a loss of a person, then some empathic enquiry may give the permission (possibly for the first time ever) to talk it through with someone outside their immediate circle and who has no emotional vested interest.

Now we have defined our terms and started to explore the themes of bereavement, grief and loss and various boundaries between the helping professions, we now move onto assisting the bereaved client.

References

Bluckert, P., 2005. Critical factors in executive coaching – the coaching relationship. *Industrial and Commercial Training*, 37(7), pp. 336–340.

Downey, M., 2003. *Effective Coaching: Lessons from the Coach's Coach*. 3rd ed. New York, NY [u.a.]: Texere.

Hilpern, K., 2014. Moving House and How Children Can Be Affected. *Huffington Post*, [online] Available at: https://www.huffingtonpost.co.uk/2014/08/14/moving-house-and-how-children-can-be-affected_n_7334248.html [Accessed 22 June 2021].

Hobbs, P., 2019. Working in the shadows: pain and suffering in coaching and supervision. In: J. Birch and P. Welch, eds., *Coaching Supervision: Advancing Practice, Changing Landscapes*, 1st ed. Abingdon, Oxon: Routledge.

James, J. and Friedman, R., 2009. *The Grief Recovery Handbook, 20th Anniversary Expanded Edition: The Action Program for Moving Beyond Death, Divorce, and Other Losses including Health, Career, and Faith*. New York, NY: Harper Collins.

João, M. and Menaul, J., 2019. *Coaching and Supervising Through Bereavement*. Coaching Perspectives [Webinar] [online]. Association for Coaching, 4 October 2019.

Kaiser, P. and Burley, C., 2021. Give Sorrow Words – Exploring Grief and Loss in a time of COVID. In: *British Psychological Society*. Available at: [Accessed 23 June 2021].

Kübler-Ross, E., 2009. *On Death and Dying*. 40th ed. London: Routledge.

Saling, J., 2019. *Psychiatry, Psychology, Counseling, and Therapy: What to Expect*. [online] WebMD. Available at: <https://www.webmd.com/mental-health/guide-to-psychiatry-and-counseling> [Accessed 22 June 2021].

Tricarico, E., 2021. *MS May Reduce Life Expectancy and Increase Mortality*. [online] Mdedge.com. Available at: [Accessed 22 June 2021].

Whitmore, J., 2017. *Coaching for Performance*. London: John Murray Press.

Chapter 2

The Bereaved Coaching Client

How clients show up

A crisis of meaning

Sometimes grief and loss (but not necessarily bereavement at a death) show up as a crisis of meaning. Performance coach, Sir John Whitmore (2004), devoted an additional chapter in the third edition of his profession defining book *Coaching for Performance* and labelled it "coaching for purpose and meaning". This was in some part due to the coaching profession responding to clients who were increasingly bringing much bigger existential questions about who they were and what they wanted to do with their lives rather than more specific transactional business performance issues.

As discussed earlier, a crisis of meaning for a client may have been triggered by a current loss but only reflects a more hidden loss that was already lurking there waiting to be examined.

This event like many others can then be framed as part of life's development journey and to see challenges and obstacles as a necessary part of reaching full potential or the higher self.

Figure 1 shows that sometimes coaching clients have travelled far along the horizontal plane before being confronted by a crisis. Most clients we meet are those in the workplace who have pursued the more quantitative aspects of life, for example, status, achievement, money, promotions, marriage, family. They may have never contemplated the meaning of their life. This is recognisably the twenty-first century way of life with its business achievement and success focus.

Often the crisis occurs in midlife but not always.

As shown in the figure another cluster of people who might have a midlife crisis are those who have overdone the qualitative aspects. They probably don't seek a coach and relate to life in general in a lighter way. They can hit a crisis if they go too far along the vertical axis. They may wake up one day and realise they are getting older, they have no partner, no family, no money, pension, or property, and no sense of meaning or any aim in life.

DOI: 10.4324/9781003087502-4

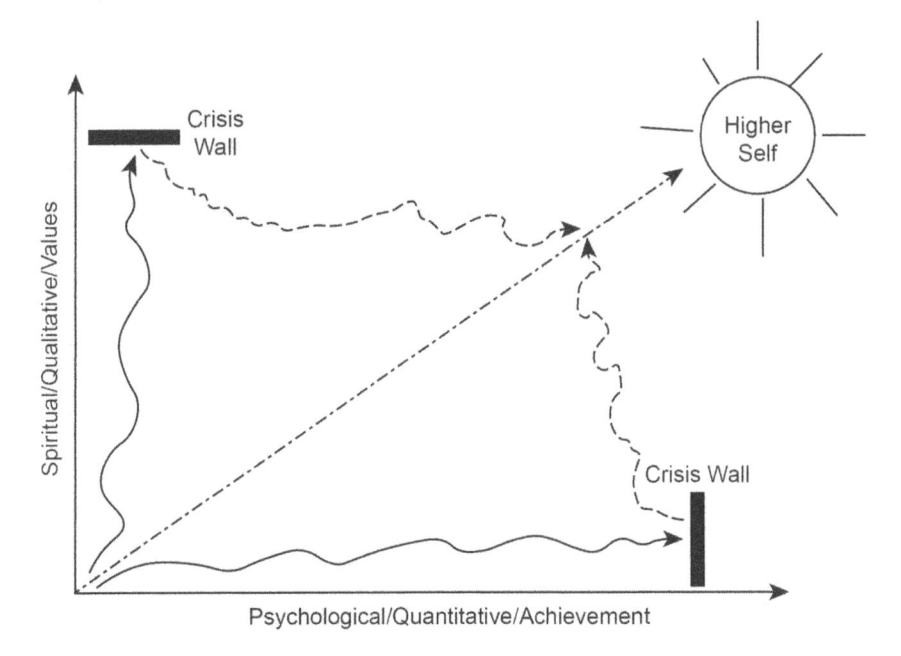

Figure 1 Dimensions of growth: Crisis of meaning. Whitmore (2004).

In, we can see that the journey, once we hit a crisis, is rather like a car happily cruising along a highway with bumper rails on either side. At some point in life, we have a wobble, become unsure of our direction, and hit the guard rail at the side of the road. This makes us veer off across the carriageway toward the midline. The midline is the ideal happiness point that balances our requirements for a spiritual and psychologically balanced journey towards the higher self. However, as we hit the midline many of us overcorrect our steering and go too far the other way. We end up zigzagging backwards and forwards across the midline to try and gain some equilibrium.

> Julia had a client, Jeff, who had a very high-powered executive role in the energy industry and was close to burning out at aged 40, when he was offered redundancy. He said in his own words he was a walking cliché of a midlife crisis. After much soul searching, he decided to leave his job for a more balanced way of life for him and his family by starting his own gardening business. He dreamed of a more instinctive lifestyle in tune with nature that also chimed with his disquiet at working in an industry connected to the climate change crisis. Through coaching we worked on the transition for over 12 months and Jeff got his wish and the coaching ended soon after. Two years later, Jeff contacted me to say

that it had not worked out and he had returned to work in a senior management role for a national charity.

Jeff had found the pace of life too slow and lonely as a gardener (notwithstanding the massively reduced salary). Jeff had overcorrected and therefore had bounced back across the midline, only this time he had not gone all the way back. He had found a role working for a charity that suited more of his "giving back" needs whilst still recognizing his other need for the cut and thrust of business.

Jeff was a perfect example of someone who may spend their life wobbling backwards and forwards over the midline in search of an ideal and ultimate happiness. The trick for him (and all of us probably) is to make the waves in the wobbly line as small as possible rather than great big tsunamis. A series of mini crises is probably what most of us experience and what most coaches must handle regularly.

Whitmore (2004) makes the reassuring point:

> In fact, under almost all circumstances if a coach sticks tightly to non-prescriptive principles and follows the coachee's agenda, little can go wrong. A problem only arises when a coach unaccustomed to extreme outbursts and sudden swings of emotion, panics and intervenes to try to help the person control their feelings.

If you are a supervisor, bear in mind that the same thing could happen for a supervisee and that sometimes the 'crisis' may not belong to the client but to the coach. A few projection questions can sometimes elicit issues such as:

- What does it feel like if you think of your client as being a reflection of you?
- What could it mean if this situation is a reflection of something in you?
- What does this process tell you about yourself? About your client?

Signs of crisis

So, what are the signs of crisis if the client does not specifically refer to a loss event?

You may see, or they may report the following:

- Shock and numbness "being in a daze, walking around like a zombie".
- Overwhelming sadness (lots of crying).
- Tiredness and exhaustion.
- Anger towards someone or the reason for loss.
- Guilt at feeling angry, or something that they said, or didn't say at the time of loss.

All of these signs and symptoms can equally apply to many reactions to loss as well as death.

We will now focus especially on coaching and supervising through bereavement from death as most of the responses and techniques used by coaches and supervisors will be similar. Where there are differences between a death event and other loss events, we will highlight.

To coach or not to coach: What do clients need right now?
Showing compassion and empathy: Being a heart with ears

As we have said already, loss is universal and particularly death. James and Friedman (2009) mention that each person will experience the death of a loved one every 9–13 years. Overlay that onto the other losses we have highlighted and it is, statistically, highly likely that during a whole year of coaching clients, a bereavement event could occur (every day 21 dogs were euthanised in the UK in 2019). For supervisors, that may be more frequent as you may be dealing with the coach's personal losses as well as the client's that they choose to bring.

Given that most people are ill-prepared to deal with loss then often the people we encounter as coaches and supervisors, do not have the right support around them. If we only ask the question, "do you have family and friends to support you?", then this may not actually elicit a full answer.

As a coach, we may be one of the few people our clients feel they can talk to, with the added benefit that we are often **not connected to the loss** that is occurring. Notice we didn't say, **we are not emotionally connected**. It is important to realise that we can all be affected by another's loss. It is how we use this in service to the client that is crucial.

The main problems our clients may have with getting the support for loss they may need are:

- People don't know what to say.
- Others are frightened by a griever's feelings.
- They may change the subject.
- They intellectualise.
- They don't hear.
- They don't want to talk about death.
- They want the griever to keep (a/the) faith.

A key emotional intelligence competency for all coaches is empathy. There is a difference between sympathy and empathy as well as compassion. Saying "I know how you feel" is not useful. Even if you have had a similar loss you cannot know, as all relationships are unique. It may be a comfort to your client that you have also experienced something similar, and you may judge it appropriate to allude to this. However, the sharing of your own bereavement is not going to take away their pain.

As we see in the section on handling clients with suicidal thoughts (Part II), we can become almost paralysed by worry about saying the wrong thing and making it worse. "I know how you feel" is unlikely to make it worse but may not actually help.

Grieving people often say they just want others to listen but what they often mean is that they want to be heard. James and Friedman (2009) say, "Grieving people want and need to be heard, not fixed", and isn't this like coaching? We coaches, listen; we don't fix.

Many coaches say they became coaches to help people. This can lead to empathic overload in some cases and when loss is involved it may lead coaches to neglect their self-care and make poor ethical decisions.

There is a world of difference between empathy, sympathy, and apathy though.

A good analogy is if you see someone who has walked onto a frozen pond and fallen through.

- If you stand back and watch with indifference, the person may drown – apathy.
- If you rush onto the ice without thinking, you may risk your own life too – sympathy.
- If you gradually feel your way onto the ice, until you get close enough to throw a line, they can haul themselves out – empathy.

Empathy is helping another but keeping ourselves safe while we do it.

We allow ourselves to get emotionally close to the other person. We experience their world as if it were our own, without losing the 'as if'. We still maintain our own separateness.

Empathy is **not** imagining how **you** would feel in the other person's situation; it is entering this person's world by listening to them so well that you accurately pick up their thoughts and feelings.

This leads to a core coaching skill of empathic responding that demonstrates that you really understand. This is shown by reflecting back, summarising and paraphrasing with appropriate sensitivity in language that suits your client.

We have heard many coaches say they can find it difficult not to get emotionally involved with the feelings of their clients in their desire to help. We assert that coaches need compassion as opposed to empathy in these situations. Whereas empathy is about **feeling with** another person, compassion is about **feeling for** them.

Some people are often taught from an early age that sad, painful negative feelings are not appropriate. People around the bereaved can often be afraid of the feelings of those who are grieving. As coaches we need to work on being **not** afraid of the feelings of others, but how good are we at looking at our own? In the "Supervising Through Bereavement" section of this book we discuss how valuable it is for coaches to work with their supervisors on exploring their own values and beliefs around big systemic and existential topics as well as developing emotional literacy regarding their own emotions and feelings. This helps to role model a way of being with clients and instills confidence in coaches to tackle emotive situations or as we would say, "Live the message to give the message".

Notice as a coach if you are generally good at staying with emotion but when grief appears (attached to something in particular) you start to intellectualise, then examine where is the fear coming from for you? It might be useful to explore this with your supervisor.

> **Maggie's coaching case study: Visualisation and transformation**
>
> One day one of my clients brought a topic that was bothering her tremendously regarding the loss of her husband from cancer. It was the last image of him she kept seeing in her mind that was troubling her. It was not an image of the last time she had seen him; it was not even of the young handsome man he once was. It was of an ill, fragile, extremely thin man who she carried to the bathroom one morning, who fell on the floor because he was so weak. And it was in that split second when his eyes were closed and when she realised "this is it", he has died.
>
> In fact, this image remained with her, because this is when his weak physical condition hit her in the face and when she really realised "this is it". This was the moment, when she couldn't deny any longer his condition, and that soon he would leave her, and she would be alone.
>
> We worked on many angles about what the image meant to her, the feeling of being alone, the leaving process, what happened immediately before and after that image, played with the image, giving it black and white tones, but what really enabled her to come out of that trance, was the visualisation we worked on based on that image, that he would open his eyes and give her a heart-felt hug and this transformation of this moment into something that she created, brought her peace and made her let go of the original image and hold on to a new image that put her in a better and safer place, developing coping mechanisms that helped her move forward in her bereavement journey.
>
> Once again, as everything in coaching, there isn't a right answer, a right move for the coach to do, or a right tool. What is right is your level of presence and curiosity, of focus on the client, of good intention and care for this person. This stage will most certainly grant you your next move, your next question, your next observation.

Mind your language

Earlier we talked about using language that is appropriate for your client. This can be a tricky area because it could well be that some people may not even be able to say the words death, dead, or dying. This is perpetuated in families as a way of avoiding thinking and talking about it.

Here are some alternative words about death you may be familiar with and you may have you own favourite euphemisms to add:

- Passed/passed away/passed over.
- Being lost.
- He has gone to a better place.
- She left us.
- She has fallen asleep.
- God has taken him.
- Resting in peace.
- Deceased/departed.
- Succumbed.
- Kicked the bucket.
- Gave up the ghost.
- Lost the battle.
- Shuffled off this mortal coil.
- Met his maker.
- Was called home.

Euphemisms can be confusing and lead to dangerous miscommunication. However, we must be sensitive to how someone is grieving after a bereavement and follow their lead.

Julia knows this is a trigger for her as she prefers to use non-euphemistic terms about death, and a client who uses something else may cause interference in her and be an obstacle to her really being present, hearing them and supporting them.

Also, just as there are challenges for many in trying to use non-discriminatory language in diversity awareness, being able to keep up to date on terminology can make us tiptoe around a subject for fear of causing offence. Death is a similar subject that may deskill us through fear.

For example, as part of the research for this book, we discovered it was best not to use the term "committed suicide". We were informed that the word **committed** had historically been connected to criminality, that is, **committing** a crime, and was strongly associated with a time when suicide was a criminal act (and of course it still is in many countries around the globe).

We have now trained ourselves to say, "they took their own life", or "killed themselves".

A test of faith

Clients may also want to talk about their faith in a coaching session and it could be something that has not been raised before in past sessions. Loss can often test people's faith in God or even sometimes make it stronger. Clients may feel they want to explore that as part of their general outpouring about the loss. Like much in coaching this can create real tension for the coach depending on their own faith leanings. Rather like political affiliations, people's religious faith is often deeply embedded and is strongly connected to their value/belief system plus being a part of their identity as a person. For the coach, this is not as straightforward as handling a dilemma where the coach has experienced a similar event to the coachee and how to handle their own prejudices, bias, and emotions around it. Faith can be much more fundamental.

We would therefore urge you to reflect on these questions for yourself:

- *What happens for you as a coach when you have to sit with empathy as a client talks about their faith if you are a non-believer?*
- *What happens if you both have differing views about God possibly from different religions?*
- *What would happen for you if your client is raging at their God and feeling let down by their faith, whilst your faith remains strong?*

These are all questions that cannot be ignored. Coaches cannot rationalise them by insisting that they can be neutral and put their own affiliations aside. Who you are as a coach is in the room with you and your client. If you notice your unease with this, it is safest to handle yourself the best you can in that moment within the session, to be in best service to your client, and then take this question to supervision to explore.

If you are with a client who has just suffered some form of loss, it's unlikely to be helpful for them to indulge in a theological discussion about the merits of whether God exists and why he didn't prevent this dreadful thing from happening. In a future session, you may or may not want to share how you feel about this topic, **if it will be in service to your client**, but that is the same as you would do for any topic where there were similarities between you.

Depending on the client and your relationship (the level of trust and rapport) you may be able to surface your unease to take the heat out of it. This may look something like: "I hear your faith is really important to you and I'm noticing my own unease about being able to support you right now because I don't have any religious affiliations. However, I want to assure you that I'm here for you as support in any way that is useful to you. What do you need from me right now?"

What can you offer a client right away?

Once we move past the idea that we are not 'allowed' to talk about bereavement, grief, or loss, how can we be in service and how do we contract for that when it shows up in the coaching room?

We have to be careful as coaches not to buy into the myths that we have been instilled with at coaching school or we may collude with our clients. We have all worked with clients who like to keep busy as a form of distraction from something emotionally painful. Not examining it doesn't make it go away.

James and Friedman (2009) also list other myths coaches need to take care of colluding with, such as replacing the loss with something else immediately and negatively, insisting on being strong for others, always staying positive, and feeling they must grieve alone or later.

How to contract for a conversation that includes discussing their loss

Contracting is one of the key elements of a good coaching relationship. It is vitally important at the best of times, never mind when someone is suffering loss. When we say contracting, we are mainly talking about the psychological contract with your coachee (or supervisee). You or your client may not have been expecting to go down this route and therefore it's unlikely you will have contracted for a conversation about bereavement, grief, and loss at the very start particularly if the work is within a corporate setting. This contract may have involved performance goals and been agreed in a three or four-way contract with others within the organisation who were looking for results outcomes and a good return on investment from the coaching.

What is the psychological contract and how does that need to change?

Most coaches are familiar with the need to review the coaching and how it is progressing with clients along the way. This can be done solely with the coachee but sometimes involves others in the multi-party contracting. The most common form of contracting or re-contracting happens midway through a programme of coaching where there is a need to have a sense check on how things are progressing.

However, we also revisit the contract at each session when we check in on anything that happened as a result of last session and invite our coachee to pinpoint what they would like to focus on for that particular session. This is usually against the background of the overall aims of the coaching.

If you do this regularly then you are creating a window of opportunity to have a discussion with your coachee about what is front of mind for them in this particular session.

This may be an important invitation, especially for coachees who may feel that it is not appropriate to bring a loss topic. It may stop them even raising the issue and an important opportunity may be missed that could have a significant impact on them and future coaching sessions. Not all clients will signal that something is amiss, for example, by turning up in floods of tears.

This lack of signal from the client is an area of tension for many coaches and came up on one of our bereavement webinar Q&A sessions, with us both giving suggestions.

Participant:	When a client discloses that there has been a significant death in their life (after empathising) what is a sensitive, yet effective opening question to ask to understand where they are at?
Julia:	I would say: "Would you like to talk about it with me here? This is not counselling but at this difficult time it may be helpful to process some of what you are feeling and then perhaps we can allow some time to consider how it may impact on our work together and whether we need to change anything from our original contract. I will be led by you".
Maggie:	Here are a few questions to choose from:

- How can this coaching space best serve you? With that in mind, how would you like this coaching session to be?
- What can I provide you with that is helpful at this moment?
- How do you want to use this session?
- Finding the right words that feel authentic for you as coach is the key.

Is coaching the right intervention for the client right now?

Most coaches as part of their training and experience have key skills that are ideal for a grieving client such as:

- Listening.
- Empathy.
- Compassion.
- Being comfortable with emotions.
- Sitting with not knowing.
- Holding the space.
- Being fully present without the need to solve problems or rescue them.

Spotting a mental health issue

One of the key things that create fear and uncertainty for coaches when being confronted by a client who is suffering loss, is whether the emotional reaction is normal or abnormal and how to spot a mental health issue.

If it is abnormal, how would you know and then what do you do?

Buckley and Buckley (2006) when discussing mental health guidance in coaching are very clear that coaches only have to decide if someone is coachable at that time or not. They are not responsible for diagnosing an alternative intervention if coaching is ended or paused; coaches are not there to diagnose, even if intuitively we may suspect that therapy is what a client needs.

They go onto describe a Venn diagram (see Figure 2) that shows the overlaps between:

- Functional suffering.
- Dysfunctional suffering.
- Mental illness.

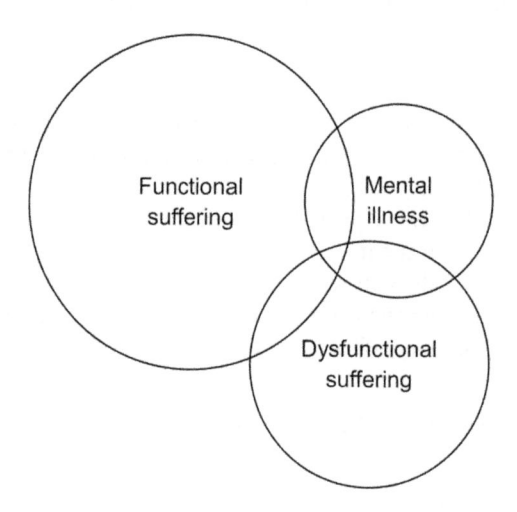

Figure 2 Categories of problems. Buckley and Buckley (2006).

Functional suffering

For our purposes (when focussing on grief and loss in coaching) we will usually see something akin to normal functional suffering. This is the pain associated with an identifiable event such as bereavement. It is almost irrelevant how distressing and horrible it might be for the client because emotional turmoil tends to be a normal reaction expected by most cultures in response to a loss, especially death. It gets a little more complicated when people react strongly to another loss (that may be defined by societal norms) as not being as traumatic as a death. This is where we move into the realms of imposing our own perceptual map of the world onto clients. Someone getting married can still experience a myriad of emotions with an event largely associated with joy, and this doesn't make it abnormal.

If we see upset and distress, no matter how normal it might be, we should not ignore it or rationalise it away. Sometimes it can be about degrees of distress as well as seeing the event through the client's eyes. Julia, for example, has never owned a pet. A very distressed client who becomes upset describing the death of her dog or cat, can make it difficult to calibrate and empathise with, even if intellectually we understand that people can be extremely attached to their pets.

The same can be said for other losses where we judge what we think the client should be experiencing based on our experience. The death of a parent, even when one has entered adulthood can engender a wide mix of emotions. Assumptions about their loss (and the sorrow they may or may not be feeling) cannot be based on our own relationships. There are the people who have been poorly parented and may feel a mix of relief that their parent has gone, guilt/shame or anger for feeling that way or even a sense of grief for the relationship they wished they had had with their parent.

It is best to tread carefully as the common reflex response "I'm so sorry for your loss" may not be appropriate. Keep questions open to areas such as "How are you feeling?" and listen with intense focus not only to the words but the 'mood music' behind those words so that you are led by your client.

Even with a client who cries more than expected in a session, if it only impacts one coaching session rather than a series then it is likely to be viewed as 'normal' by both. Also bear in mind that other life events can be triggers for coach and client such as the coach working with a client who has just suffered a miscarriage and reconnecting with her own lost baby.

Life coaching versus executive coaching and bereavement

Something else to consider is the type of coach you are and the type of coaching you do.

If you see yourself as a life coach, then perhaps there is a stronger sense of normalcy around grief, loss and bereavement in coaching compared to a business coach. However, we would also hope there was a commensurate level of knowledge and skill too for the business coach to be able to make an accurate assessment of their own motivation and ability to be just a listening ear for the client if nothing else.

The psychological dimensions of executive coaching

In executive coaching there can be a blurred line between the organisational context and the life context. Julia remembers as a trainee coach asking what the difference was between executive coaching and life coaching and one witty answer was, "None after session three".

Most executive coaches, when asked, would say they work with the whole person especially as they become more mature as practitioners. So, for example, they may have ostensibly started to work on a leader's public speaking skills but by working at a psychological dimension level start to see a client showing signs of functional suffering because the very act of looking at change in a more systemic way, can highlight the exact change they don't want to make and that "I want to be confident at presenting better" is just an iceberg with the real problem beneath the waterline.

We can also come across clients who have been referred to coaching because of performance issues, poor interpersonal skills, and threat of career derailment but on closer inspection have poor psychological functioning, as in this case study.

Julia's coaching case study: A loss in disguise

Dina worked as a middle-ranking manager for a well-known UK retailer. She had worked there for 15 years, was in her mid-40s, had no partner, and was still living with her parents. After a company restructure, new senior management arrived, and they were not impressed with Dina.

They found themselves handling a lot of bullying complaints from Dina's staff and peers about her brusque manner and poor management style. They were considering the disciplinary route. However, Dina had complained to them that no one had ever questioned her performance before, so the company felt a moral obligation to provide some development coaching for her.

I met Dina and she cried on and off throughout our first two meetings in what I can only describe as a state of shock. I was worried about her physical and mental health by this point (she was going through an early menopause too) and I discussed it with my supervisor. Dina's reactions seemed a form of bereavement. She was suffering sorrow at the loss of a world she thought she knew. Her image and identity as a senior and respected manager had been blown apart by the negative feedback. She was also struggling against the unacknowledged difficulties of menopause and the realisation that she would never have children plus mourning the loss of a life she thought she might have had with a partner, not the one she was facing with elderly parents.

By session three, Dina had got over the shock and had started to move into some sort of acceptance. She was prepared to look at herself not only in the light of her work crisis but also to examine the important and impending transition that would be coming her way over the next few years for herself and her rapidly ageing parents.

I worked with Dina for over a year and saw her blossom from someone so anxious about who she was and what her life entailed that she projected her fears onto others, into someone much happier in her own skin. She is still working at the company 15 years later. As a new coach, this was an early opportunity for me to learn about stepping back from the presenting problem, taking time for some biographical enquiry, and seeing the client holistically, rather than just through the prism of the problem projected onto her by her managers. I remember really making contact with my own emotional impressions of what it would be like to be childless for her, as I had a young son at the time, but also wonder now what I may have missed given that my own roller coaster experience with the menopause was still many years away at that point.

A key part of coach training is working with the Inner Game as espoused by Timothy Gallwey (2000). This is where we work with the client on their outer landscape initially (roles, job descriptions, responsibilities, goals, objectives, relationships), and then dip down below the surface into their inner landscape to explore their values, beliefs, hopes, dreams, defence mechanisms. This inner part is akin to the Reality section if we are using the GROW model (Whitmore, 2004) (Figure 3).

We need to dip below the line long enough to help coachees gain self-awareness and then come back into the outer landscape where the actions may need to take place. This could be another easy way of defining the difference between coaching and counselling. Coaches dip into the inner game just long enough to enable clients to examine their survival self in action and then pop back up to plan changes from their healthy selves. The concept of the survival self and healthy self will be discussed in Part II when we examine the role of trauma and coaching.

However, we need to bear in mind other stakeholders in the system especially working in a corporate context, as it could be important to flag up support elsewhere such as an Employee Assistance Scheme (EAP).

Sometimes change and loss are exacerbated because of problems in the

34 Coaching Through Bereavement

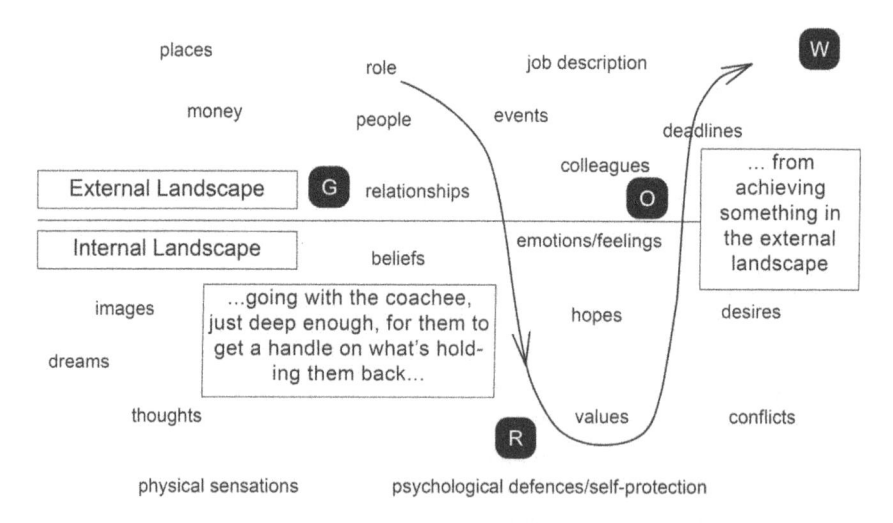

```
      places                         job description              W
              role
   money            people      events
                                            deadlines
                                    colleagues        ... from
  ┌─────────────────────┐                              achieving
  │  External Landscape │ G  relationships    O       something in
  └─────────────────────┘                              the external
  ┌─────────────────────┐             emotions/feelings landscape
  │  Internal Landscape │     beliefs
  └─────────────────────┘
    images    ┌──────────────────────┐
              │ ...going with the coachee, │   hopes    desires
              │ just deep enough, for them to│
   dreams     │ get a handle on what's hold- │
              │    ing them back...          │
              └──────────────────────┘
          thoughts                   values          conflicts
                                R
      physical sensations   psychological defences/self-protection
```

Figure 3 External and internal landscape. Novum/PB Coaching (2014).

system and the system needs to change and not the individual – as amply illustrated by the following case study.

Coach's case study: A peculiar transition

I was asked to coach a newly hired manager and help her take up her position and ensure a smooth transition with her team.

Soon the real situation and needs emerged during the initial meeting with the client and stakeholders. I could feel from the start a certain discomfort in the room. All signs were pointing towards a hidden request behind the official one. We spent five hours delicately peeling off the layers of the unsaid, with myself slowly pushing everyone to open up, whilst managing potential embarrassment from HR and Directors.

The new manager, Sophie, was actually not that new. She had been hired by the previous manager Caroline a year before, to prepare a smooth transition. Caroline was the creator of the department, hired everyone in the team and had managed it for the past 15 years. Initially, she was presented as a revered manager. However, it soon became apparent that when Sophie joined, Caroline shut her out from any piece of information, even locking her drawers and door. Sophie became almost 'transparent'. After nearly a year of 'non-transition' towards the official handover, Caroline made her exit from the organisation. Caroline, then took her own life on Christmas day.

Understandably, this was an incredibly traumatic event for everyone. Behind the shock, which upset the whole organisation, and the grief of her closest colleagues, something else blocked the way to move forward; the obligation by many to remain composed and politically correct. It was finally disclosed that Caroline was actually a tyrant to many, obliging some colleagues to work without a desk, computer, or even an email address, while being the most caring manager to others. All this was happening in plain sight of HR and senior management and because results were somehow always delivered, there was a sort of "omerta" around this situation. Caroline's death fractured it.

Although a psychologist helped the team go through the mourning process, they couldn't move forward. People were not speaking anymore to each other, only to blame or finger point. Activity was semi-paralysed. Transition with the new manager was at rock bottom.

Consequently, there was a need to adjust the planned intervention to incorporate team coaching before Sophie's individual coaching. What turned out to be essential was to create a cathartic space; a secure and safe place for each member of the team, to express in front of others, how they were personally going through this dramatic event. It was OK to be mourning, and in grief, for those who were close to Caroline and who received help from her, as much as it was OK to express relief or anger against Caroline for those who were bullied by her. By engaging this broken team, in listening and understanding each other's pain, which was at different levels, they started a healing process.

Only then, could the team open the door for the next step, and transition work with Sophie, the new manager, could finally begin."

Quynh Anh TRINH XUAN
Executive Coach, MCC
www.exploreandgrow.com

Later, we will look at the organisational machine and how businesses do or don't deal with loss.

Dysfunctional suffering

This can be thought of as when the psychological distress does not have a focus on what is really happening today. Or when the reaction to the event seems considerably greater than what would be normally expected (Buckley and Buckley, 2006).

> Recently when running a short session for internal coaches on attachment theory where a discussion ensued about their respective attachment styles

and how they had been influenced by their parents (particularly mothers) one of the coaches, in her early thirties, became visibly upset and excused herself from the room. At breaktime, after seeking her out it was discovered that her mother had died when she was aged six. She apologised for her tears and said that it wasn't just the discussion about attachment but that she had noticed herself becoming emotional on a number of occasions that month because it was the thirtieth anniversary of her mother's death. As a fairly new coach, she was berating her own "weakness". As there was no contracted arrangement to take this conversation any further; an enquiry about whether she had had any bereavement counselling seemed safest. She had not, but soon realised that doing some recovery work on this would help her coaching practise immensely and was in no way "self-indulgent".

Dysfunctional suffering can show up at any time. It may show itself in a senior high-flying executive who starts to inexplicably underperform after the death of her father, who is ostensibly "not grieving," but is feeling the loss of someone she had been unconsciously trying to impress by overachieving in her career.

Mental illness

The final part of the consideration about whether you should be coaching your client at this time is if it's neither functional nor dysfunctional suffering but bordering on mental illness. Unfortunately, there is a large overlap with the latter and the label is in the domain of medical professionals and not coaches. One of the most common mental illnesses within the population is depression. Many people are on long-term or lifetime doses of anti-depressants, so a question about medication at the contracting stage would alert a coach and possibly be useful data. Sorrow can last many months which is a normal grieving response to a deeply felt loss. These sad feelings can pass eventually which is different than depression, which can envelop a person and last for months and years.

There are four dimensions that are wise for you to cross-check by observing and also by talking through them with your client that will help you understand the signs of depression in a client. Broadly speaking, they can be categorised into thoughts, behaviours, physical signs, and emotions.

Self-criticism, memory and concentration difficulties, procrastination (especially when the client normally doesn't do it), avoidance, unusual outbursts compared to normal self, body signs, sleep deprivation, loss of appetite, passive and sad emotions, self-disappointment, and numbness, are all signs that the client might be facing depression. On their own many of these indicators do not suggest depression but the more of them there are then the chances are higher that a person is heading towards a depressive illness. The American

Psychological Association reported in 2017 (Vinerman, 2017) that 12.7% of the American population is on antidepressants. One analysis found that nearly 15.5 million people have taken antidepressants for more than five years, so statistically speaking there is a high chance that coaching clients are on long-term medication or may require it if depression is diagnosed.

Another thing to consider is Broken Heart Syndrome. As romantic as dying of a broken heart sounds, it is a real affliction and people have been known to suffer chest pain after a bereavement usually due to stress (increased cortisol levels). Often this returns to normal soon after, however, if someone already has an underlying heart condition (known or unknown) then this could trigger a heart attack and therefore should always be taken seriously. Depression may be a symptom of another physical ailment so coaches may want to encourage a coachee to have a medical check-up. Our training as coaches may lead us to look for and notice psychological issues primarily to the detriment of physical ones, so as we discuss later this is an item that should be incorporated into contracting when asking the health and wellbeing question of clients. In fact, in Medical Coaching it is good practice in the contracting piece to ask clients whether they are being monitored by a medical doctor, just to rule out scenarios that might be out of the coaching boundaries. If the coachee has not visited a medical doctor, the coach will strongly recommend it and in some cases might even prioritise this over the Medical Coaching.

> *When considering whether this is functional or dysfunctional suffering remember we only have to decide if coaching is the right intervention for our clients, not if they are suffering a mental illness. We are not there to diagnose. We would talk it through with our clients and raise self-awareness about what they may need at this sensitive time. Often the client decides for themselves that they need counselling and possibly a pausing of the coaching, although both coaching and counselling can run side by side if appropriate, depending on the level of distress and the type of objectives in the coaching. Even in this category clients may be provided with alternative help such as therapy and/or medication which stabilises them enough to continue coaching whilst still under strict medical supervision. As already stated, even a quick check up with their doctor can put both minds at rest. We will discuss later about how much to help a client with accessing therapy once that has been decided.*

"They were OK when the coaching started"

Another factor to consider is what Andrew and Carole Buckley (2006) call "They were ok when I started". Sometimes clients have had previous mental health issues that have been treated in the past which they may or may not tell you about even if you ask it as a specific question in contracting. It could well be that the coaching itself may push clients out of their comfort zone (exactly what's required for most clients) but may fetch past problems to the surface for others. Unfortunately, you won't know until you start working with them. Also, we have to bear in mind that if we stopped coaching someone every time they felt uncomfortable no coaching would ever be completed. What coaches need to consider here is the individual's comfort zone and how it has been meeting their needs so far and their desire to change something via coaching.

Mihaly Csikszentmihalyi (2002) describes the "psychology of flow" as the movement between our comfort zones and discomfort zones and the fine line between something that causes distress (Panic Zone) and the area where we are happy to just coast (Drone Zone) (Figure 4).

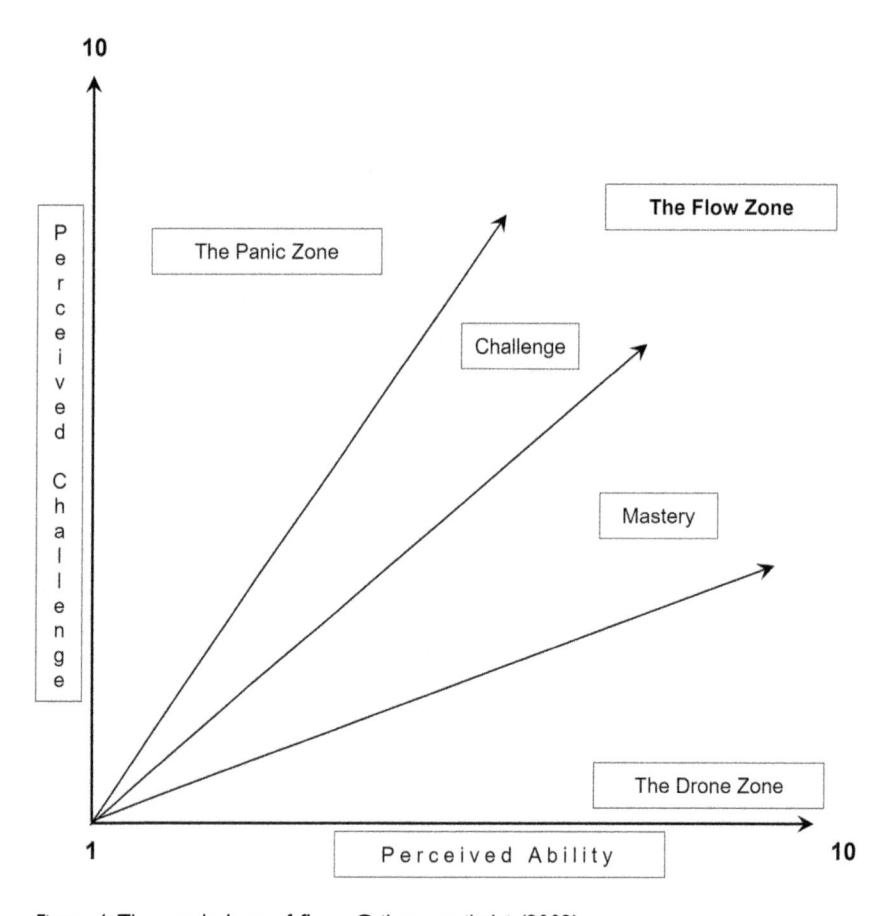

Figure 4 The psychology of flow. Csikszentmihalyi (2002).

1 The Panic Zone
When our perception of the challenge/difficulty we are facing far exceeds our perception of our ability/skill to meet that challenge, we tend to perform in "the Panic Zone". Here, we may find ourselves overcommitted and out of control, feeling either nervous, scattered, and hyper. Or, if we have cut off from those feelings of anxiety and 'shut down' to deal with our fear, we may feel bored, disinterested and apathetic.

2 The Drone Zone
When our perceived ability/skill to handle a situation far exceeds the perceived difficulty of the situation, we may find ourselves in "the Drone Zone". Here, we become lethargic, sluggish, and bored, longing for excitement, and frustrated with doing the same old things, day in and day out.

If you think of life in a typical office environment, you'll quickly recognise those people who are stuck in hyperdrive in the Panic Zone and those who quietly fantasise about their escape while plodding along in the Drone Zone.

3 The Flow Zone
Fortunately, most of us have at least occasionally experienced the calm, focussed energy that comes with performing in the Flow Zone, when we feel 'up to' the challenges that we are faced with.

If your client is already in a discomfort zone when you first meet them then you may have to help them find alternative help. If they move into a discomfort zone during coaching you may have to reassess before deciding whether to pause, stop or find alternatives to coaching.

Continue, pause, or stop

If a bereavement occurs during a coaching programme, do you continue, pause, or stop?

Coaching can be paused if the timing is not right, especially in corporate coaching where the client may not actually be at work after a bereavement. Our role as a coach may be to discuss with them how they may benefit from counselling if it seems that the distress is stopping them from going about their daily business. However, in a more 'straight forward' bereavement scenario, clients may be keen to discuss things that are more action-focused and practical within the coaching, for example, discussing changing relationships around the bereavement especially in families or changing goals and motivation at work given the new dynamic around the loss.

As coach you may need to reflect on what is appropriate right now. This may mean right now in this coaching session with a particular client given their emotions, in this minute. You may have a client very upset/angry and tearful for half an hour who then gathers themselves together and becomes very focused in the next part of the session. Would you continue with them "now" compared to the "now" an hour ago?

We also need to consider "now" in the wider context and this information you may or may not know. This is the mode seven aspect of the seven eyed model that will be discussed in Part II, "Supervising through Bereavement", which may involve reflecting with your supervisor on questions such as:

- *What is happening for them within their family system?*
- *What other losses are occurring?*
- *What other stresses are about?*
- *How are the people around them reacting to or supporting your clients?*
- *What is happening at work that could have an impact (relevant whether this is executive coaching or not)?*
- *Is there major change or uncertainty in their role? What other losses are swirling around for your client and their colleagues?*
- *What is happening in the sector in which they work? What change and uncertainty is on the horizon? What might they lose or gain? For example, redundancies, mergers and acquisitions, privatisation, nationalisation, liquidation.*
- *How might what is happening with your client connect with challenges at a country-wide level, for example, legislation, technology, economic, social, political, environmental.*
- *What impact are global events having on the organisation in which your client (or close family member) works? For example, Covid-19 pandemic, climate change, Black Lives Matter, #metoo movement.*

Answers to these questions will give you a greater sense of whether there is 'too much' for your client to handle right now alongside everything else. We are all familiar with the phrase "the straw that broke the camel's back". Sometimes it's the small event that is reacted to as a displacement of a different loss.

Essentially, the bottom line is that the decision is only three fold:

To continue coaching, stop coaching, or to pause coaching (with the possibility to restart later or run coaching alongside some therapeutic intervention at the same time). If the latter option is chosen, then contracting with your client on what they want to bring from their counselling may be very beneficial to coaching outcomes. Encouraging clients to discuss their coaching in broad terms with the therapist can also be useful. This connecting work can really help to keep boundaries of the work much cleaner, although we would say always defer to the greater knowledge of the therapist if there is any doubt that coaching can continue alongside counselling and keep reviewing and re-contracting with the client.

Julia's supervision case study: Is this a mental health issue?

Marcus was an internal coach working in the Higher Education Sector in the UK and came to supervision so concerned about a manager he was coaching (Doug) that he requested an emergency session. He had discussed Doug before who he felt did a lot of venting in coaching which bordered on "dramatic". Marcus mentioned the Drama Triangle and was worried he was being pulled into a rescue role to Doug's victim stance. Doug kept calling the coaching sessions "counselling" even though Marcus had explained the difference and corrected him many times. When I asked Marcus what the crux of the issue was with Doug, he said that he felt his boundaries were fuzzy and he couldn't find where his boundary was for coaching people on work-based stress and emotions, versus when it was a real mental health issue. The reason Marcus had requested an emergency supervision session was that Doug had "seemed more depressed" than ever, especially about a re-hearing of a promotion panel. Doug was worried he would fail to secure the role again and was concerned about how he would cope, as he was only just getting used to the previous disappointment and this new opportunity was creating (false) hope for Doug. Doug then mentioned in passing to Marcus that he had been suicidal some years ago and then said he would throw himself off a bridge if he didn't get the promotion this time. Marcus was worried by this remark and had not slept much that night. Marcus wanted to think through whether he should inform anyone and what his responsibilities were versus maintaining confidentiality. After exploring whether he thought Doug really was suicidal, Marcus then said no he didn't actually think he was as the remark seem flippant but needed to check this out more directly with him rather than backing away from it.

I sympathised and shared my own feelings about a client who had actually taken their own life many years ago. By the end of the session, he decided to offer Doug an extra coaching call and a pre-meeting with his manager ahead of the promotional board.

Marcus emailed me the next day to say he felt better for talking it through with me, however, when writing up his notes from supervision he had noted a new insight. In the session, I had asked Marcus if Doug reminded him of anyone. Was this connected to some unfinished business, I wondered? Later Marcus had a moment of clarity thinking about whether Doug reminded him of someone. Marcus then admitted that he had had a suicide in his own family, a brother two years previously and although a very different type of person to Doug, he had not made the connection until now. Marcus said, "It seems obvious now it's written in black and white, but I just couldn't see it." Marcus was over sensitised to anyone mentioning suicide because of his past which had led him to jump to conclusions about Doug and turning it into a mental health issue rather than seeing Doug as someone going through a stressful period that could be viewed as functional suffering. At no point had Marcus had any bereavement counselling or other support, so he decided to source a therapist to focus on the loss of his brother specifically.

How other types of loss arrive in coaching

As we saw earlier there are many different types of losses although some are more common in life and therefore in coaching.

Here we cover some of the main ones and discuss how differently a coach needs to work with these topics from a grief and loss perspective compared to how they may have been handled before.

As the Covid-19 pandemic started to unfold across the globe in early 2020, the Harvard Business Review described what many people were experiencing at that time with the aptly named article "That Discomfort You're Feeling is Grief" (Berinato, 2020). It is largely an interview with David Kessler (co-author with Elisabeth Kübler-Ross). He describes the collective grief for a world that has changed, possibly temporarily but probably not. Even if death did not visit us in the pandemic there was a palpable sense of loss of normalcy, loss of connection with others, plus fear of the economic and health toll.

Kessler also describes anticipatory grief which is when we are uncertain about the future and feeling that something bad is heading down the track. Grief can feel like a physical pain as well a mental and emotional pain. With anticipatory grief, we are pessimistically predicting the future and running doomsday scenarios in our heads. Many clients reported imagining people they loved becoming sick, dying, and being unable to see them. Our brains are wired for threat far more than reward, so we are pulled towards this kind of anxious thinking. Encouraging others to not deny these images and feelings but to explore them, talk about them, and subsequently take the heat out of them can lead to a more helpful framing of finding something else to balance it, so both positive and negative are considered. In a coaching or supervision session, calming and bringing a person into the present using a "Pause for Breath" activity is an excellent option, as well the "Triggers" activity. (see "Activities" in Chapter 7 "Tools and techniques to work with grief and loss").

As a coach you will know the power of naming something for yourself as well as your client, that is, "emotions need motion". It also gives a coach an opportunity to encourage clients to sit with that emotion in a safe space rather than fighting the feelings, squashing them down, or finding things to distract oneself. If there is a time limit to this (the length of a session) this helps to contain your client in safety. Sometimes it's the fear of being overwhelmed by the emotion that stops us from letting it in (or out). When Julia talked to her own supervisor, during the Covid-19 pandemic, her fear was that if she allowed herself to cry then she would be sobbing for hours. However, when she did allow herself to weep (because a family photo popped up in a text) she found that it was almost impossible to keep the crying up for any length of time. She noticed that after five or ten minutes there was a natural release, and she felt free to move onto something else, whilst feeling much better because she had not repressed the feeling. We often admonish others for 'bottling up grief' and there is agreement particularly within the trauma community, and now being supported by advances in neuroscience, that denying emotion and dissociating from it keeps it trapped inside the body where it can eventually emerge as a physical illness. One client said she knew she was getting stressed about everything that was happening because her Psoriasis had flared up which she had had since a broken romance over 20 years ago. Van der Kolk in "The Body Keeps the Score" (2015) lists many common ailments that are probably connected to the finding than unfinished emotions or trauma can emerge as post-traumatic stress disorder, attention deficit disorder, chronic fatigue syndrome, skin conditions, hair loss, etc.

As already mentioned, a loss can precipitate a crisis of meaning for people (the Covid-19 pandemic which started in 2020 certainly did this for millions of people), and our clients can be more willing to share the big existential questions they began to reflect on in lockdown.

See Figure 1: "Crisis of meaning" (p. 21)

The historical loss

As we saw earlier dysfunctional suffering shows up when something has triggered "unfinished business" regarding a loss. People then react in the "here and now" as if it was "there and then" (Vaughan Smith, 2019).

Coachees who talk about a bereavement that is quite historical may not have discussed it for many years but come to understand it is impacting on them if a coach is confident enough to allow their client space and time to explore it.

Is there are different approach for a coach to take for a recent and a historical loss?

There isn't per se a different approach, but the coach needs to be very attentive and very present, because the fact that it was so long ago might encourage the coach to unconsciously probe less, delve less deeply, assume more things. And also, it might make the coach turn a blind eye on the importance of referring for more suitable help. The assumption that "it was a long time ago" might be a barrier. The coach in these cases needs to be on top of their game and master the coaching competencies to be even more attentive to the client's cues and not make assumptions that will not help the client.

Female clients who have lost babies

Rather like the statistics for depression, the universality of the death of babies is likely to be in the coaching room implicitly or explicitly for some clients. It may be historical loss in terms of time but the pain of grief at losing a child may be raw no matter how much time has elapsed.

In 2018 in the UK, one in five women had a miscarriage (or stillbirth after 24 weeks). Globally this can be more like one in four of all known pregnancies ending in miscarriage. More babies are miscarried than are carried to full term and some women never know they have miscarried (Starr, 2018). Also, the experience of miscarriage increases the risk of suicide, depression, and anxiety.

The same year in the UK, there were 217,000 terminations of pregnancy. According to the World Health Organisation, worldwide this figure is usually between 40–50 million each year (approximately 125,000 abortions per day) (Worldometer, 2020).

Given these huge numbers it is likely that many of our clients have lost babies (Mazumdar, 2021), but we never hear about it, either because of emotional reasons such as sadness or shame, or feeling that it is not relevant to a conversation in a corporate environment, or it never comes up as part of a client's biography when they are telling us about their life. As we discuss later, this may be even more so for male clients, who because of societal expectations do not feel that their grief is recognised or even expected, and therefore can suffer in silence.

> Maggie recalls a client showing her their Lifeline drawing in session two of the coaching relationship, and the birth of her children was a highlight on her drawing. A premature baby who had died at 6 weeks

was not mentioned at this point. This traumatic event only came to light when she came to a session in tears that one of her close colleagues, who had left only a few weeks before for her maternity leave, had delivered her baby stillborn. The whole department where she worked was shocked and upset but no one knew about the client's history which she found unbearable, and it brought much of her grief to the surface again even though she had lost her baby 15 years previously.

Most of the session was spent talking about her loss, which she found helpful to process her feelings in the 'here and now' about her colleague but also recognising and acknowledging what was arising from 'there and then'. She mentioned some therapy she had had all those years ago which had been useful, although she was now worried and shocked about how unexpectedly distressed she had become. Her description of how her counsellor had helped her sounded positive and until now had served her well. This was an example where a coach can easily panic that they are straying over the boundary into therapy, back off from coaching too quickly and try to push the client into getting more counselling.

However, in this case, her reaction to her colleague's news was entirely normal and could be classed as functional suffering because until this point the coachee had found ways of moving through her grief and had learned to live with it over the years. Showing her a quick drawing based on Figure 5. was useful at this point.

Figure 5 shows that grief doesn't get smaller, but the life circle gets bigger to incorporate it into life. So, grief doesn't go away, you don't get over it but

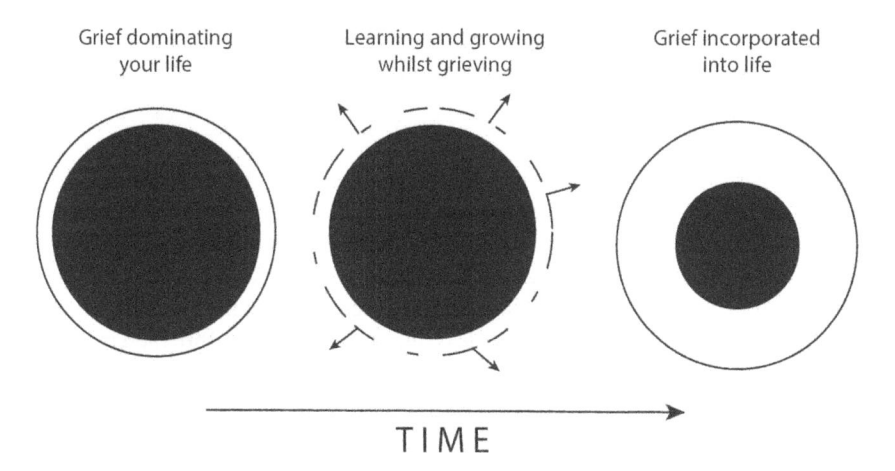

Figure 5 Growth through grief. Menaul (2021).

learn to live with it. Then sometimes something will trigger grief again (birthdays, anniversaries, hearing about other deaths) and it will dominate and fill the circle again (BBC, 2018). However, the circle doesn't remain dark and can become fuzzy and lighter over time even though it is still there.

The client thought it was a great descriptor and that she knew her colleague's loss would affect her for a while but that her "grief-ball" would shrink back again, and as she didn't believe she needed counselling again, we concentrated on how she could resource herself during this difficult time.

A lovely compassion mantra is: "Be kind to yourself in the midst of suffering and it will change". As in this client scenario facilitating some self-compassion was a perfectly acceptable use of coaching time given that developing compassion can be core to many healthy behaviours. A brief introduction to the RAIN acronym developed by Tara Brach (n.d.) provided a framework for the conversation.

> **RECOGNISE**: *Acknowledge what emotions are coming up.*
> **ALLOWING**: *Let thoughts, feeling and sensations be there; just as they are, saying "It's OK let it be".*
> **INVESTIGATION**: *Deepen attention and get curious by asking questions such as "What wants my attention right now? What does this vulnerable place want from me, how am I experiencing this in my body"?*
> **NUTURE**: *Enquire what this hurting place might need. Love? Companionship? Reassurance? Forgiveness?*

From this, the client was able to process her emotions by revisiting her birth story and looking practically what she might do. This involved how to make contact and send condolences to her grieving colleague that felt "at the right level" and how to share something so that it didn't feel "all about me".

It has been said that grief needs to be witnessed and as a coach we are sometimes perfectly placed to act as witness.

Male clients and child death

When Julia discussed this topic with her male supervisor, he said, "Where are all the men in this?" So, if we suspect that many of our female clients have had this sort of loss, then possibly many of the male clients we coach also have stories to tell like this but from a uniquely male perspective. How much more difficult is it for men to talk about something as sensitive as this and why would they? Society may view fatherhood as less important and therefore men may be ignored or sidelined when they have suffered the death of their own child. Also, when the women around them have had a miscarriage or termination, it may be viewed as specifically more of physical (and therefore emotional) issue for the mother. Men may be more unwilling or unable to share the pain they are feeling and keep it bottled up for years. But as we saw earlier the triggers for loss can come in strange and unique ways and that an ending handled badly in another scenario such as redundancy, divorce, retirement, or ill health diagnosis can easily be a trigger for unaired grief and trauma elsewhere. We may not know about it as coaches and indeed our clients may not even be consciously aware of any connection. Tentatively asking about endings, loss, and losing something, can sometimes create insight in unexpected places: "Where else have you lost someone or something?"

The gender of a coach and coachee may throw up lots more complications on such an emotive topic, and both need to be aware of their unconscious bias and limitations when working with clients of either sex when the death of a child arises, especially if there is historic loss for the coach as well as the coachee. Our unconscious bias may extend to underplaying male grief for instance and a female coachee may not only be handling her own grief but also that of her partner.

Loss of job

This is probably the number one loss handled by coaches. Indeed, for some coaches, it is their niche area of work and may be called career/transition coaching, redundancy coaching, outplacement coaching/counselling. Many coaches will be familiar with the pattern of response to job loss although it may vary depending on the reason for the loss. The emotional and psychological fallout from dismissal is often different from forced redundancy or voluntary redundancy, and also retirement (See "Retirement and ageing" later in this chapter).

A form of bereavement and subsequent movement through the Kübler-Ross Curve (2009) can be instantly recognisable with people who have lost their job or even under threat of loss. (This threat could even be seen as anticipatory grief which we mentioned earlier.) Some coachees will already be familiar with the Curve as it has become a staple of change management courses over the last few decades. For the readers who have not yet come across the Kübler-Ross Curve, it is worthwhile to mention that it was developed by Swiss psychiatrist Elizabeth Kübler-Ross in the late 1960s, specifically as the five stages of grief or the five stages of loss, as defence or coping mechanisms to help deal with grief, loss, or change in general.

According to the website of the Elizabeth Kübler-Ross Foundation, the Curve is supposed to be a curved line, and was never meant to be drawn as a straight line nor a step-by-step process. In our opinion, the curved line resembles a wave with all its ups and downs, all the certainties and uncertainties, all the majesty and all its fragility.

Kübler-Ross described this in five stages:

- The first stage she called **Denial**, characterised by a reaction of shock, where the griever doesn't want the status quo to be changed. One of

- the best approaches to take in this stage is to communicate and share the information you have at hand about what has happened.
- The second stage was originally called **Anger**. Later, when the Kübler-Ross Change Curve was introduced, it changed to **Frustration**. Basically, the state is that of disruption, sometimes even fear. Observing and listening to what is going on might sometimes be the best support one can give. Going down the road of arguing with someone who is at this stage, is not the best use of energy for both parties.
- The third stage, according to Kübler-Ross, is **Bargaining**, where the individual enters a state of negotiating with others, themselves, the universe, to get back what presumably was lost.
- The fourth stage or **Depression** is considered the lowest point of the Curve, where the unresourceful state the individual is in has a negative impact on his day-to-day life and stamina.
- The fifth and last stage according to this model is the **Acceptance** stage, where the individual starts to experiment new ways out of the depression loop, starts taking some decisions towards a more positive impact and gives time to explore and test different options. This stage is also the beginning of an integration phase, where the individual is committed to rebuild their projected future and celebrate their wins, as small as they might be.

(David Kessler later proposed a sixth stage of grief called "Finding Meaning" (Kessler 2019)).

Originally this model was first thought to fit the grief scenario, but years later, it has evolved and developed towards a broader concept of change itself often within a corporate setting. Many psychologists and coaches use it with their clients to explore the different types of change one may go through during their life experiences.

This extended Kübler-Ross Change Curve (rather than the grief Curve) has seven stages starting with Shock, Denial, moving onto Frustration, Depression and following with Experiment, Decision to finalise, and finally with Integration.[2]

Coaches may find it worthwhile to revisit this with their clients and it can be a theory that translates well into a practical activity. By laying out a visual or even imaginary curve on the floor of the coaching room, a coach can guide a client through a somatic response and increased awareness of how they felt at various stages, where they are now and visualisation of future stages.

---

2 For more Information, please visit https://www.ekrfoundation.org/

Later we focus on "The Organisational Machine" and how organisations approach bereavement, which can be equally applicable to job loss. In Part II on "Supervising through Bereavement" we examine loss from a systemic perspective and the implications of leavings and endings for our clients.

Relationship loss

One of the casualties of the Covid-19 pandemic was disruption or rupture of people's relationships.

We have both experienced clients (coachees and supervisees) separating from partners and suffering grief and loss during a time when there was already systemic loss whirling around.

> Maggie had two clients during this time who split up with partners; one in a domestic abuse situation which forced her to leave her home under the first lockdown and another being obliged to continue living under the same roof as his partner as restrictions on movement compelled them to be together. On one occasion the latter was attending his supervision session in one room online, as his partner remained in another, dropping his voice to a virtual whisper every time his situation was referenced. Our focus that day was mainly about his own self-care as well as examining his diary for the different types of client work he had, and assessing if he was able to do it. As an internal coach his employer was not aware of his personal situation, and so he felt under pressure to put on a brave face during extremely difficult circumstances. He was a new coach, so encouraged him to consider his fitness to practise obligations and how he might broach this topic with his employer.

Divorce

This is one of the most common losses and one the most frequent losses we may see in coaching and supervision. In 2019 there were 107,000 divorces in the UK and in the USA, it was 750,000. In the Holmes and Rahe Stress Scale (1967), the scale assigns points for various stressful life events. Divorce comes in at second place (73 stress points) and marital separation at third place (65 stress points), being one of the most stressful life events. Death of a spouse being the top stressor. (100 points).

- A score of 300+ suggests a risk of illness.
- A score of 150–299: the risk of illness is moderate (reduced by 30% from the above risk).
- A score of less than 150: there is only a slight risk of illness.

Like empty nest syndrome, divorce can also set off interrelated losses such as financial predicaments, for example losing a shared house/home, relationships with others that were predicated on being a couple particularly with extended family of an ex-partner. Julia has coached someone who not only lost her husband and her house when they separated but also a "realisation of the loss of twenty-five years of her life and the chance to ever have children".

Identity is also an issue particularly after a long marriage. It can take a great deal of adjustment to move from being married to single, calling yourself a divorcee, and for many women a change of name. Changing names after a divorce is a more common problem than many would imagine. Many people have set ideas about whether one should return to a previous or maiden name with all the inherent inconvenience of altering a multitude of ID documents as well as children having a different name than their parent. Family and friends around your divorcing client can also have established notions on name changing which can put undue pressure and stress into an already difficult situation. Problems of access to children after a divorce is also a common topic in coaching. Julia had a male client who brought a huge bag of documents to each coaching session, and when she enquired, he said they were for fighting a custody case in court against his wife over access to his two young children. Whether it was a corporate coaching contract or not, this major life event was certainly a big elephant in the room and forced itself in as part of the agenda because the stress was having such a massive impact on him at home and at work.

As coaches we may make assumptions about gender differences regarding relationship breakdown and what might be the emotional fallout for someone who is choosing to end the marriage versus a partner who has not been the instigator. Even someone instigating a divorce can still suffer grief and loss for the relationship. If we add in the additional complexity of children, then this can be such a major issue that it can easily dominate and derail coaching agendas and may require substantial re-contracting on immediate needs. Coaches can also fall into the trap of seeing this issue through the prism of their own experience. How we have handled our own divorces (or been affected by our parents divorcing) can lure us into unseen bias. It is our belief that supervision is essential for coaches going through divorce.

The possibility of counselling may be a useful conversation to have with a client and marriage guidance counselling is not just for helping couples to patch up relationships. It can be useful to process the grief we have discussed in traditional bereavement. The Kübler-Ross Curve (2009) still has meaning and relevance for the emotional roller coaster of ending a marriage as well as enabling divorcees to reflect on why their marriage didn't work, create a sense of ending, and enable a new way of being that bodes well for future relationships.

If a client has suffered a number of different stressful life events in one year, then this could easily increase their propensity for physical and mental illness. An enquiry about what else is going on in their lives is often fruitful.

Loss of health

This could be the health of the coachee or someone close to them. It could encompass the additional challenges of being a carer.

Loss of health can be temporary or permanent. It is something most of us take for granted. However, our health is one of the core indicators for happiness. Every part of life relies on having good health. If we lose our health, we lose a lot. As coaches we may be confronted with supporting our coachees as they handle differing levels of health issues such as cancer treatment – according to the *British Journal of Medicine* in 2015 (Torjesen, 2015), one in two people will get cancer – where there is a defined level of treatment and support, through to illnesses that impact daily life but have limited diagnosis or little treatment such as chronic fatigue syndrome or autoimmune diseases like MS, Celiac disease, Crohn's disease, Rheumatoid Arthritis. We may also be required to support coachees who have family members with a variety of illnesses that impact on their own lives. Julia had a client who worked in a senior position in the public sector and on his first session told her about his MS because flare-ups could happen at any time, and he was worried about postponing and cancelling sessions at the last minute. The disclosure was also significant because his illness impacted on his coaching objective which was career transition and the limitations his MS would impose on various career options. He shared with me the grief he had experienced on diagnosis with the realisation that it would probably shorten his life. (According to Dr Nina Grytten, men have a 36-year median life expectancy from MS onset, compared with 50 years in the general male population.)

Again, the health and wellbeing question at the start of coaching is crucial to establish mitigating factors for the success of the coaching itself.

Later in the book, we look at the impact of loss for the coach, particularly the ill coach and how this may affect their coaching practice. In Part II, "Supervising through Bereavement", we also pick up some of the practicalities of protecting oneself as a coach should the worst happen.

Another growing niche in coaching is Medical Coaching, which deals with clients who are going through a medical process or crisis be it their own process/crisis or that of someone else who they care about. Founded by Shiri Ben-Arzi, Medical Coaching has grown incredibly across the globe focussing not only on the clients who are also patients, their caregivers (informal and formal) but also on the entire healthcare community including doctors, nurses, and auxiliary personnel. One of the purposes of medical coaching for the healthcare community is to develop programmes that create adherence, communicate in a clearer and more empowering way with patients and colleagues, to focus on self-care for themselves and make their visions, dreams, and goals a reality[3].

Carer's grief

Carer's grief can be unseen. There are 13.6 million carers in the UK (Carers Week, 2020 research report[4]) and an estimated 43.5 million adults in the US have provided unpaid care to an adult or a child in the prior 12 months (Internationalcarers.org, 2021[5]).

Subsequently, we may see recognisable grief from our clients when a loved one dies after a long time of caring duties. "I think we can all relate to how hard it is losing someone, but when you've also been that person's carer it's a double whammy. Your whole identity is changed in an instant." –forum user on www.carersuk.org.

Carers also build up a myriad network of support from professionals, friends, and family. These may come to an end when caring responsibilities end and can leave a void in people's lives. Alternatively, some carers find that previous relationships drop away under the pressure of a heavy caring burden.

> It can also be the loss and grief felt when a way of life has shifted once carer responsibilities have been imposed on them. I (Julia) had a client whose husband had a major car accident that left him in a wheelchair, found that her own life was almost as profoundly affected as his. The loss of her career, her social life, and her identity as a wife and lover rather than a carer is an incredibly difficult life shift.

Carer's grief can also apply to clients who are parents. We may have clients who have parental responsibilities that create more challenges for them because they have children who have special needs around care and/or education.

In some cases, the grief and loss are sudden, for example, death or accident. In others, it is more a creeping awareness as years go by, on what is being lost and will continue to be lost over the years.

Coach Louise Hallett who writes the case study below has advice for coaches and supervisors about working with carers.

- One in nine of the UK's workforce are an unpaid carer. Not all organisations will have a Carer's Policy so self-advocacy and

---

3 For more information visit www.medical-coaching-institute.com.
4 https://www.carersuk.org/images/CarersWeek2020/CW_2020_Research_Report_WEB.pdf
5 https://www.caregiving.org/wp-content/uploads/2020/05/2015_CaregivingintheUS_Executive-Summary-June-4_WEB.pdf

assertiveness are skills many carers find essential to gaining support for their own needs in the workplace.
- Acknowledge the breadth of responsibilities the carer is undertaking.
- Encourage a support network of others in similar positions. There are many organisations and forums available. (See "Resources" list)
- Don't assume the carer has time for 'self-care' routines. A focus on this can feel meaningless and unempathetic. Caring is hard work and often relentless. Basic self-care actions such as healthy food, sleep, and connection with others may be more achievable.
- Professional careers have pathways and financial rewards, but caring roles don't. Hope and a sense of purpose are important factors in sustaining wellbeing in a caring role.

Coach case study: Carer's grief

Kate was a lawyer in her late 40s who requested coaching support to help her decide if she should leave her job, something she was reluctantly considering due to her caring commitments for her young son who had complex medical needs, and her elderly mother.

Kate was finding it incredibly difficult to balance the demands of her role with supporting her son's needs as he was frequently unable to attend school and she recognised she needed to find alternative educational provision for him. She felt that the law firm she worked for were becoming unsympathetic and increasingly annoyed at her last-minute meeting cancellations due to supporting both her son and her mother, and as her husband was often working away during the week the caring responsibilities were falling to her. Kate was feeling overwhelmed by the conflicting demands on her time and energy, and her emotional wellbeing was suffering as a result. She was showing signs of exhaustion and burnout.

With a parallel to my own experience, I was able to approach our session with a strong sense of understanding and compassion, something that Kate recognised and was grateful for.

The resilience that Kate was already demonstrating in her caring roles was evident as she described her daily responsibilities. Reflecting this back to her encouraged her to share her fears and concerns to form some meaning making in her experience. She shared her fears of the impact of the loss of her career and change in circumstances to her personal identity – and the financial implications.

Societal expectations and perceptions of caring roles are complex. Many people feel instinctively that their caring role is unquestionably the right thing for them to do but the changes this brings to their identity, hopes and dreams raises questions such as "will I still be valued by my husband, my family and by society?", "how I re-define my purpose", "what does the future hold for us?" and "how do I ensure I will be financially secure?".

Like many carers, being heard was incredibly important to Kate. Her support network felt 'flaky' as friends were offering advice to "keep up with her career" which resulted in her feeling unacknowledged. Well-meaning advice was incongruent to her own values and very strong maternal instinct to care for her child. She was feeling increasingly isolated as she was withdrawing from others as she not only felt confused, angry, and resentful but also self-critical and guilty that she was experiencing these emotions.

Kate believed that she was facing a black and white situation of keeping her job or giving up work completely. Stress often inhibits creative thinking and coaching offers an opportunity to create ideas and practical solutions that may not have been considered. Kate had also been unwilling to share her personal circumstances with the organisation which had resulted in her feeling trapped into making an 'all or nothing' decision.

Kate began to advocate for herself within the organisation and work with them to find a flexible working solution. Many organisations have a carers policy but for those that do not, many carers find they need to advocate for themselves to ensure legal rights meet their own needs. This requires having to display some disclosure and vulnerability which can be difficult when struggling with a loss of confidence, exhaustion, and uncertainty about the future.

Alongside coaching, a strong support network with other carers in similar situations was recommended for Kate to feel acknowledged and supported.

Louise Hallett
Executive Coach
www.louisehallettcoaching.co.uk

Empty nest syndrome

This is a loss that can often take people by surprise especially if they have been dreaming of having more freedom from years of child-oriented activities and duties. Unfortunately, the loss of offspring as they fly the nest can set off other losses too. It can be easy in coaching to focus on the children leaving and miss the subtleties of what else has changed as a result. Particularly for mothers, this time may coincide with menopause, ageing and a neglected partner relationship after years of parenting (Knight 2019).

Empty nest syndrome can prompt an existential crisis, especially around identity. In our activities at the back of this book is one called "Who are you?". This sits alongside tools on resilience looking at self-esteem and self-confidence. The repeating "Who are you?" question answered by "I am ...." soon unpeels away the labels we give ourselves: wife, mother, parent, nurse, teacher, carer, etc. For many people, this activity can leave them feeling exposed, although at the same time it can sharpen awareness that we are not these labels and that we are more than this. After two minutes of repeating the same question, clients usually arrive at answers such as angry, brave, funny, sad, an idiot, etc.

The "Nine Box Grid" activity which you will find at the end of the book is also useful for a variety of clients and not just empty nesters. Clients who can only fill two or three boxes with kids, partner, work, are going to be in serious trouble if one of these is lost. Resilience occurs when we can lose one or two major parts of our life and still survive because we have six or seven other things to define us.

Empty nesters can certainly show up in coaching as grievers and may go through the same stages on the Kübler-Ross Curve (2009) as those experiencing a death.

Menopause

We've already said that death is still the great taboo. In our experience, some people (mainly women) insist that menopause is the greatest taboo. Menopause is literally the loss of reproductive capability that has physical and emotional aspects with far-reaching consequences. A large percentage of coaches and coachees are women. Another big group of these same women are aged 40–60. We highlight this as a common loss topic because of the amount of women it affects and therefore the regularity with which it will show up either implicitly or explicitly in coaching.

The average age of menopause is 51 although women can start experiencing symptoms of 'the change' during perimenopause from age 40 (early menopause) to 55–60 (late menopause). One in 100 women start to go through menopause before the age of 40 and one in 20 between ages 40 and 45 (Newson, 2021), so statistically speaking we may have some of these women in our coaching and supervision. Menopause is a fact of life that some women will take in their stride with minimal symptoms. For some women, it can be a devastating loss especially if it is early onset and destroys fertility. For those who have suffered fertility issues and/or childlessness throughout their adult life the onset of the menopause can feel like a cruel reminder of what they have missed. Menopause may happen to our clients naturally or as part of other treatment such as cancer or hysterectomy. Like other losses women can have mixed feelings about what they are 'losing' or 'gaining' about this stage of life.

The symptoms of perimenopause can start in the 10–15 years before menopause itself (which is technically the cessation of menstruation). Psychologically this can be a huge life change. Having periods is a big part of women's lives (for better or worse) sometimes for 40+ years (Jones, Eichenwald, and Hall 2007).

The list of perimenopause and menopause symptoms is huge but can be:

- Difficulty concentrating and memory lapses.
- Heart palpitations.
- Hot flushes.
- Insomnia and fatigue.
- Anxiety, irritability, depression, mood swings.
- Weight change.

Notice how similar this list is to the one earlier where we talked about "grief brain". Oestrogen receptors are located all over the body and particularly the brain. A depletion of oestrogen in midlife will therefore have a big impact on memory and mood.

Some symptoms are hormonal and some psychological. Although many physical conditions can lead to mental and emotional problems and menopause can be one of these. Even doctors struggle to separate menopausal symptoms from psychological disorders. Newson (2021) says that the highest rate for suicide for females is among the 50–54-year-old group, precisely the average age of menopause.

Much of this can be happening while other life events create grief and loss, such as caring for ageing parents, experiencing the empty nest, and retirement. These other events can trigger changes in ovarian function and set up a vicious cycle, that is life events affect mood, which affects internal hormones, which exaggerate the mood swings.

Organisations are only just starting to respond by developing menopause polices that acknowledge the stress of this major life change and its impact on women and their careers. Nine out of ten women report that their work has been impacted by menopause. (Menopausesupport, n.d.) 10% of women seriously consider giving up work due to their symptoms.

In the UK, the National Health Service is one of the biggest employers, and females make up 77% of NHS staff, with an average age of 43, so it's a huge issue.

Coachees may present with issues around confidence and low self-esteem or decreased mood and be puzzled about where their previous vibrant self has disappeared to. Asking the age of our client is not intrusive, it is essential for us to sensitively ask a question such as "How much is the menopause impacting on you?" In the same way we would check that our clients are handling the wellbeing basics such as good nutrition, sleep, less caffeine, alcohol, etc. before trying to make other changes in their life, we should consider that some women need to stabilise their hormone situation before gaining a true picture of the challenges they are seeking to be coached on.

Here are some statistics from Menopause Support that highlight that menopause could be impacting coaching objectives and outcomes. (Approximately 13 million women in the UK are either peri- or post-menopausal.)

- Over 60% of women experience symptoms resulting in behaviour changes.
- One in four women will experience severe debilitating symptoms.
- Almost half of menopausal women say they feel depressed.
- A third of women say they suffer with anxiety.
- Women commonly complain of feeling as though they are going mad.
- About 72% of women in work who are going through menopause say they feel unsupported.
- Nine out of ten women say they feel unable to talk to managers at work.
- One in five take time off to deal with menopausal symptoms, one in 50 are on long-term sick leave.

Male coaches and menopause

Anecdotally we would guess that this topic is not on the radar of many male coaches unless they have partners who have shared their own challenges of midlife and the menopause.

The reason we raise it here is that sometimes a presenting issue could be connected to the menopause and the client has not considered this as an option. We might help clients with their wellbeing and work-life balance without considering that these areas could just be the symptoms of the underlying issue of menopause.

Male coaches may assume that every woman would be aware if this was affecting her. This might not be true as clients report being taken by surprise when the symptoms appear even though they were approaching perimenopause age. Education of girls and women before menopause is still limited in many countries around the world. It also could be a sign of denial about the ageing process (another loss). Becoming more informed on this topic would be useful for any man, personally and professionally although many men can be wary about bringing up such a sensitive topic. (Devlin, 2019)

It might also be worth saying that younger female coaches might also miss this as a possibility of their clients' woes. A trip to the doctor is not the only option and a coachee may want to look at alternatives to hormone replacement therapy that involve practical lifestyle choices such as improving diet, exercise (like yoga), rest and recreation, and alternative therapies – which are topics within the remit of most coaches.

In the popular media, there has been some discussion about the existence of 'male menopause' and whether it exists or not as a recognisable medical condition, male clients may still be wrestling with impotence, loss of libido, loss of fertility and other loss issues connected to ageing. (Although of course some of these issues can occur during earlier stages in life.)

All the above is also relevant for supervisors who may find that the topic of menopause looms large as part of a restorative conversation in supervision.

Retirement and ageing

Like job loss, retirement can provoke a variety of reactions in people entering retirement and those around them. "You just retired, what are you complaining about?" (Laura, 2017). There may be anticipatory grief in the run up to the retirement date itself, with coaches handling a client's feeling of anxiety, sadness, loss of safety or security, and identity. This could be the case when a retirement is not planned (due to sudden ill health) or when it has been planned for many years.

Alternatively, some clients may be feeling positive about the next stage of their lives and want to use the coaching to plan and take actions on new hobbies, voluntary work and activities.

Retirees can often mourn:

- Loss of financial security.
- Loss of identity and sense of purpose (associated with status and a job title).
- Loss of a daily routine.
- Loss of social interactions and networks (leading to loss of mental stimulus and physical activity).

Mental and physical symptoms relating to negative perceptions of retirement can be:

- Fear.
- Sadness.
- Impaired memory.
- Insomnia.
- Fatigue.
- Weight loss/gain.

This is a remarkably similar list to the general symptoms of bereavement due to a death. Psychologically in retirees we may see anger, apprehension, anxiety, despondency, emptiness, or numbness.

This list is not often highlighted in the company's handbook of retirement, although over half of all UK organisations provide support for retirees and are now starting to offer personal coaching and workshops that focus on what to expect and how to ameliorate possible problems. Nevertheless, in other organisations it is not acknowledged as a grief event.

The brief presentation over a buffet lunch and the awarding of a gold clock was often the signifier for employees to 'shuffle off' quietly in the expectation of a fantasy life dreamed by others. Men particularly can suffer a "post-retirement void". Males may perceive job loss as social failure, but females can often move their attention from work to home (Noh et al., 2019).

Rather like in the immediate aftermath of a death when the frantic activity has died down and a griever's support network melts away, a retiree may be left with a feeling of being cut adrift without anything to tether them and because retirement is seen as a positive event by others, many retirees feel loathe to express their real feelings about their loss leading to a longer period of grief that can develop into depression. Retirees can swing between feeling upbeat about plans for the future and then back again to focussing on what they have lost. A coach can help by facilitating a reframe of the losses alongside the new aspects. This balanced view might be a real challenge with coachees who are preparing for retirement rather than fully retired and these are the clients we are more likely to see given they are still in work. We may see clients maybe taking an overly positive or overly negative view of impending retirement.

Retirement then links to another loss theme: ageing.

Retirement happens at a time of life for most people that signifies the ending of a lifetime in work or career. Indeed, some may have been in the same profession all their working life for 40 years or more. With more time to reflect on one's life, a retiree can sink into noticing the bigger existential questions that connect to getting old and their own death anxiety. (Osborne, 2012). "The elderly also experiences loss and grief as they begin to have a diminished ability in activities of daily living. This then can cause the elderly to lose a sense of purpose." (Zoler, 2006)

And of course, the older we get the more bereavement from death that we suffer which can have cumulative effect. Younger people may assume the older age group would be accustomed to grief and that the roller coaster may become more like a wave. Again, everyone can have a unique perspective on this.

Abortion

For some, abortion could also be considered a loss. It could be the loss of the promised future that feels tainted, or the loss of innocence and the fact that life delivered such a big decision, and for others it is also the loss of the identity (becoming a mother) that they may not want, at least at that time. As we see later in our case study, "Guilt Revisits from the Past" (See "Supervising through Bereavement" in Part II), a woman can decide to have a termination and be sure it is the right decision, but still feel grief and loss due to the varying situations in which the decision is made.

As human beings we are entitled to have our own opinion towards any subject in general, and abortion in particular. This is not the moment to say who is right or who is wrong (if this subject can be defined in such simple terms). What is important to highlight here is what if the opinion of the coach is completely opposite and different from the personal decision the client has taken?

> ### Maggie's supervisor case study: Personal intruding the professional
>
> I recall vividly when coach Mariana brought to supervision a case where her client was 7 weeks pregnant after a one-night stand and decided to terminate that pregnancy. Mariana's values are against abortion and as her client brought the topic to one of their sessions, she decided to carry on that conversation there and then, even though she was mindful her opinion was different.
>
> In supervision, Mariana was questioning her own style during that coaching session and how strict she may have come across in her interventions and how she could have checked on the spot whether her personal was intruding her professional self. We talked about one of voice, gestures, micro-expressions she could have had and types of questions, more incisive in one aspect than others. We mentioned the coach starting to have a hidden agenda and not being fully present. And we explored how else she could have dealt with this topic.
>
> The interesting thing with supervision is that most times, if the coach doesn't have an anticipatory and exploratory mindset before things happen, chances are that all the learning comes after things have already occurred and supervisor and coach then look into things in retro-spectively. There might be some damage control to do afterwards and definitely some learnings to reap that will inform the coach's approach next time it happens. This is another reason why it is so important to have regular supervision as the supervision session is the space to explore and inform the type of professional one is and one wants to be and to work on, much more than to only work on what just has happened.
>
> We also discussed the parallel process that somehow had taken place, of the client taking the decision (so quickly in Mariana's opinion) to have an abortion and Mariana taking the decision to go ahead with the session even though something was not quite right for her.
>
> We need to be mindful, that for coaching to work well, both coach and client need to be in a resourceful state.

So far, we have explored a variety of losses that can befall our clients. In the next chapter, we focus on ourselves as coaches and what happens when the bereavement is ours.

References

BBC, BBC Stories, 2018. *How Does Grief Change Over Time?.* [video] Available at: https://www.facebook.com/watch/?v=2168915343327846 [Accessed 18 August 2021].

Berinato, S., 2020. That Discomfort You're Feeling Is Grief. *Harvard Business Review*, [online] Available at: https://hbr.org/2020/03/that-discomfort-youre-feeling-is-grief [Accessed 6 April 2020].

Brach, T., n.d. Resources – RAIN: Recognize, Allow, Investigate, Nurture. [online] Tara Brach. Available at: https://www.tarabrach.com/rain/ [Accessed 16 September 2020].

Buckley, A. and Buckley, C., 2006. *A Guide to Coaching and Mental Health.* 1st ed. London: Routledge, p. 23.

Csikszentmihalyi, M., 2002. *Flow: The Psychology of Happiness.* 2nd ed. London: Rider, p. 75.

Devlin, R., 2019. *Men… Let's Talk Menopause.* 1st ed. Practical Inspiration Publishing.

Gallwey, T., 2000. *The Inner Game of Work.* 1st ed. New York: Random House.

Holmes, T. and Rahe, R., 1967. The social readjustment rating scale. *Journal of Psychosomatic Research*, 11(2), pp. 213–218.

James, J. and Friedman, R., 2009. *The Grief Recovery Handbook, 20th Anniversary Expanded Edition: The Action Program for Moving Beyond Death, Divorce, and Other Losses including Health, Career, and Faith.* New York, NY: Harper Collins.

Jones, M., Eichenwald, T. and Hall, N., 2007. *Menopause For Dummies.* 1st ed. Chichester, West Sussex: For Dummies.

Kessler, D., 2019. *Finding Meaning: The Sixth Stage of Grief.* London: Rider.

Knight, I., 2019. A survivor's guide to empty-next syndrome. *The Sunday Times*, (17 November 2019), p. 5.

Kübler-Ross, E., 2009. *On Death and Dying.* 40th ed. London: Routledge.

Laura, R., 2017. *Understanding Grief And Mourning The Loss Of Your Work Life In Retirement.* [online] Forbes. Available at: https://www.forbes.com/sites/robertlaura/2017/08/27/understanding-grief-and-mourning-the-loss-of-your-work-life-in-retirement/ [Accessed 22 June 2021].

Mazumdar, T., 2021. *Miscarriage rates overRates Over 40% higherHigher in black women, study suggestsBlack Women, Study Suggests.* [online] BBC News. Available at: https://www.bbc.co.uk/news/health-56889861 [Accessed 28 April 2021].

Menopausesupport, n.d. *FACTS – menopausesupport.co.uk.* [online] Menopause-support.co.uk. Available at: https://menopausesupport.co.uk/?page_id=60 [Accessed 18 August 2021].

Newson, L., 2021. *Preparing for the Perimenopause and Menopause.* Milton Keynes: Penguin Random House.

Noh, J., Kwon, Y., Lee, L., Oh, I. and Kim, J., 2019. Gender differences in the impact of retirement on depressive symptoms among middle-aged and older adults: A propensity score matching approach. *PLOS ONE*, 14(3), p. e0212607.

Osborne, J., 2012. Psychological effects of the transition to retirement. *Canadian Journal of Counselling and Psychotherapy*, 46(1), pp. 45–58.

Smith, S., 2019. Maybe He's Grieving: Understanding the Unexpected Way Men Grieve. [Blog] *Lakefront Psychology*, Available at: https://lakefrontpsychology.com/2019/08/23/maybe-hes-grieving-understanding-the-unexpected-ways-men-grieve/ [Accessed 18 August 2021].

Starr, M., 2018. *New Research Shows Most Human Pregnancies End in Miscarriage*. [online] ScienceAlert. Available at: https://www.sciencealert.com/meta-analysis-finds-majority-of-human-pregnancies-end-in-miscarriage-biorxiv [Accessed 18 August 2021].

Travis, J. and Ryan, R., 2004. *The Wellness Workbook*. 3rd ed. Berkeley, Calif.: Celestial Arts, p. xvii.

Torjesen, I., 2015. Half of the UK population can expect a diagnosis of cancer. *BMJ*, 350(Feb 03 14), pp. h614–h614.

Van der Kolk, B., 2015. *The Body Keeps the Score*. 1st ed. London: Penguin Books.

Vaughan Smith, J., 2019. *Coaching and Trauma*. 1st ed. [s.l.]: London: Open University Press.

Vinerman, L., 2017. By the numbers: Antidepressant use on the rise. *American Psychological Association*, [online] 48(10), p. 120. Available at: https://www.apa.org/monitor/2017/11/numbers [Accessed 8 June 2021].

Whitmore, J., 2004. *Coaching for Performance: Growing People, Performance, and Purpose*. 3rd ed. London: Nicholas Brealey.

Worldometer, n.d. Abortion Statistics – *Worldometer*. [online] Worldometers.info. Available at: https://www.worldometers.info/abortions/ [Accessed 15 December 2020].

Zoler, M., 2006. Elderly face grief and loss differently than do others. *Caring for the Ages*, 7(11), p. 14.

Chapter 3

The Bereaved Coach

Coaches are human beings too, human beings with feelings and emotions who interrelate with others and who also have their own stories and narratives. Coaches also grieve and go through bereavement. It is normal, it is expected, it is good that it is so, for them to have experienced what might be some of the feelings, emotions and behaviours their clients might go through when dealing with loss and to acknowledge it when working with them.

Nevertheless, it is paramount the coach exhibits a high level of ethics when it comes to work when they, themselves are bereaved. Point 4.2 of the Global Code of Ethics for Coaching (Appendix 3) about the ability to perform states that "Members will be fit and healthy enough to practice. If they are not or are unsure if they are able to practice safely for health reasons, they will seek professional guidance or support." That is why when we are bereaved or not fit for practice we ought to pause and reflect, get supervision if needs be and understand what you need as a human being before acting as a professional being.

The coach is a resource to the client (you are your best tool) and when bereaved it might be that the resource is not as full or as enlightened as it could be or should be, in order to provide the best service and the best possible coaching for that person in that moment in their lives.

It is important to respect life itself, its cycles, regardless of whose lives we are talking about. As professionals, our duty is to provide the best service we possibly can to our clients. We need to ensure that there is a significant investment into continuous development and continuous learning as coaches. It will refresh skills, enhance competencies and it may increase knowledge on a new tool or model, that can be used during coaching sessions or in between coaching sessions.

As well as the skill enhancement that might take place from time to time, there is a continuous process that doesn't have an end – a coach's self-care.

DOI: 10.4324/9781003087502-5

In the next section, we will explore what it means and what exactly the coach can do to tend to himself or herself taking into consideration their own personal circumstances and ultimately, the service they provide.

Coach case study: The bereaved coach

When my best friend died unexpectedly at a young age I was devastated. We had been best friends since we were four years old and aside from my husband, he was, without doubt, the love of my life.

During the time of this experience, I had three coaching clients all at different stages of their contract.

On hearing the news my emotions went into a tailspin – ranging from shock, anger, sadness, and inconsolable grief. In addition to dealing with the loss I was supporting his partner to arrange his funeral and clear his apartment – it was an odd time.

During the time of the funeral, flat clearance, etc. it was clear that I was going to be kept very busy and distracted. What I also very quickly realised was that I needed to give myself the space and time to grieve.

As part of my training, I was always advised that as a coach you must be 'well' in order to coach effectively. It was therefore an easy decision to contact my clients, explain the situation and let them know that I would not be coaching for a month and would review the position thereafter.

I gave all my clients the option to move to another coach and I had a couple of coaches on standby. I was fortunate that all my clients were both understanding and wanted to wait for me.

What I learned about grief and loss was that you need to experience it and give yourself the time to 'grieve well'. I do think it is possible to grieve well, this for me was achieved by surrendering myself to it and listening to my body. If I wanted to laugh, I laughed, if I wanted to have a primal scream, then I took myself off and did that! Having an active role in his funeral and taking care of his possessions was also a final act of 'kindness' that I could give him – in truth the kindness proved to be to myself as having him 'around' brings me great comfort.

If I was to pass on any advice to a fellow coach I would say listen to your body and surrender to it then to remember your training. You can only coach if you're 'healthy' yourself. By giving myself a break and permission to grieve it took the pressure off me. I think clients appreciate you being 'human' and recognising that you need time to heal. Now that I have experienced this horrific event, I hope to be able to safely use the learning with any future clients who experience loss. I went through my own Kübler-Ross Curve and feel I now have a deeper understanding and appreciation of the emotions

> a person may experience and be able to hold them safely whilst they explore their path.
>
> **Catriona Hudson**
> Director Heroes and Stardust
> www.heroesandstardust.com.uk

Self-care for coaches

Self-care is twofold. The coach who is bereaved and therefore needs to face that and deal with the bereavement, and the continuous self-care for the professional.

When the coach is going through bereavement, it is paramount that they pause coaching. Even if they are feeling well and believe they can handle any topic the client might bring. Pausing (or even, stopping completely) is not a sign of weakness. On the contrary, it is a sign of excellence and mastery. As in nature there is a time for everything: for blossoming, for growth, and also for resting before regrowth. Face this pause as a time for fallow, when one can reflect if needs be, can take stock to understand the impact of that loss. Regardless of size or importance, something has changed and has intruded into their professional being and the way they see and feel the world. It is a moment to reconvene and to analyse, to breathe deeply not only physically but also emotionally, to understand what parts of our emotions need some fresh and cool air

For how long should a bereaved coach pause/stop coaching? There is no right answer. As mentioned before bereavement is a unique process and there is no-one-size-fits- all. For some it might take a few weeks, for others several months and for some others a couple of years. **What is relevant in this situation is that the coach is mindful of the process he is going through, understanding what is going on, not with a judgemental lens, but rather with a compassionate approach, observing all that is emerging for them and how that might impact the way they coach.**

If the bereaved coach notices their poor concentration when others are speaking, it might be a hint that the time is not ripe yet to move back into action and restart coaching. If thoughts easily wander, paying attention is difficult and becomes more sympathetic than empathetic, these are all cues to continue the halting process in your coaching practice.

Another important tip is to notice the level of challenge one inflicts on the client. If the challenge is too little or on the contrary too

> *fierce and strong, it also may suggest to the coach that it might be hard to balance support and challenge, and perhaps the coach has returned to work too soon.*

As a bereaved coach, how can you be conscious of that when grieving? We would speculate that the bereaved coach who believes it is time to get back to coaching, is obviously thinking about it, so he will be in that thinking and reflecting process so can easily enter a step of validation and confirmation.

> *Coaches can validate this by requesting feedback from the ones surrounding them with regards to this balance of support versus challenge, about their attention deficit, or level of sympathy versus empathy.*

Additionally, he can confirm with a coaching supervisor, who will be able to witness, to mirror back, and to reflect to the bereaved coach what they are experiencing when talking and working with them.

This confirmation is important, as it reinforces the coach's self-confidence and ethics. However, a deep bereavement journey might end up irrefutably in depression, which we touched on earlier. According to psychologist Ana Caetano (2020), depression is an illness that kills many in the world and one needs to pay attention to the early signs, such as tiredness, lethargy, lack of enjoyment on tasks that used to provide joy before. She believes the coach (and subsequently the supervisor) can help in the primary prevention of depression by assisting others to promote their talents, increase their self-awareness and set goals for what they want to achieve. Nonetheless, if the signs of depression are already there, the coach may need more appropriate support to treat this as a mental illness. A supervisor with her supervisee may need to strongly recommend the coach to stop coaching for some time, until this phase of their lives is terminated or at least under control.

Notice that searching for a more appropriate level of support when it comes to dealing with depression is also a form of self-care. Refer to the previous chapter for when 'normal' grieving may tip into depression.

Another important point is the necessary continuous self-care any professional needs to go through. We are not machines nor robots and we need to ensure we are on top of our game. Clearly, that includes physical pauses and rests throughout our day and the necessary vacation/holiday period, when our primary agenda is ours and our main preoccupation is to be occupied with our preoccupations and ourselves and what is ours alone (family, growth, body, mind, soul, etc.).

However, self-care is much more than physical breaks, mindfulness and breathing exercises. Self-care encompasses caring emotionally for ourselves.

Understanding how we have dealt with things that came our way, listening to our internal voice and reflecting on our own stuff. If we don't do that, it is akin to all our arteries becoming clogged up with fat (albeit undesired things, resentments, etc.) that basically interfere in the normal process of flow. We get impacted, close our eyes to the world, our shoulders sink, we don't even notice an important breakthrough for the client, so start easing up on challenging others and not help them see different perspectives and we solidify in a certain view and do not apply the necessary level of curiosity to spark a transformation in others. The coaching dynamic may become mechanical, dull, not transformative and we may start "coaching the problem and not the person" (Reynolds, 2020).

We see self-caring as a process of emptying our own vessel, so it is ready to receive whatever the client needs to take away for their own, so both coach and client, can focus on a transformative relationship rather than a transactional one.

This emotional self-care can take many forms:

- **Getting a supervisor, to enhance coaching mastery**
  The supervisor can help the coach understand what best self-care she needs at that moment in time. Through questioning, witnessing, reflecting, the exploration will lead to an identification of actions that can be implemented and/or feelings that can be further explored in order to get the coach back to a resourceful state where she is an inspiration for herself as well as for her clients.
- **Employing a coach, counsellor, or psychologist to help deal with any dark sides**
  Other professionals can assist the coach in any emotional triggers that were activating when coaching others. The triggers might turn into obstacles in becoming the best professional that person can be for that client. Here, two things are relevant to consider. First, pausing at least for a while the specific coaching relationship, and second, get adequate support for the coach to analyse and understand what happened that influenced the dynamic with his client.
- **Cultivating knowledge by reading thought-provoking books, or participating in breakthrough debates**
  For some coaches increasing their knowledge on certain topics, learning from experts provides comfort. Whilst the essence of coaching resides in the not knowing and being comfortable in it, some people become more open to it from a place where they evaluate themselves through how much knowledge they have about a topic. Therefore, cultivating this knowledge is, in their view, a way of self-caring for themselves. In these cases, integrating focus groups, debating circles on breakthrough ideas, innovation, and any topic relevant for them will provide them with a feeling of accomplishment and self-care.

- **Sharing own feelings and fears with someone who they trust**
  Getting empathy from someone we trust is another way of self-caring. It gives us a sense of being understood or an opportunity to unload, to restore and a refreshing way of self-caring.
- **Doing something enjoyable, such as a hobby**
  Doing an activity that we really like gives us the feeling we are doing something only for us, giving back to us as our own reward, compensating in a sense. This activity might be physical exercise, but it can also be a hobby, cultivating mindfulness, a feeling of being useful or creating something. In these terms, many people revert to an old hobby, or start something new to develop their artistry side, enrolling in painting classes, dancing classes, sewing, pottery, creative writing, to name a few. One of Julia's coachees returned to water-colour painting that had been abandoned many years ago in the busyness of life.
- **Practising a sport not for obligation but for inspiration**
  We all know that if we want to change our emotional state, the shortest route is to change our physical state. Hence, the advice to stand up and go for a walk to the cafe before replying to that tough email, or drink a sip of water, before intervening in a hot discussion, or deep breathing before answering a hard question. All of these are somehow linked to our physical body and alter, even if in only a minor way, its state. Practising sports will definitely lead to a different emotional state (we pick this up in the lens of neuroscience later), since it releases certain hormones such as endorphins and serotonin in our bodies, that guide us to a sensation of accomplishment and into feeling happier.

  Nevertheless, we would like to raise your awareness on doing sports from a place of inspiration instead of obligation. By this we mean that if you force yourself to exercise, for instance, then it is less likely to have such a positive effect. An obligation to exercise will not contribute to your self-care and instead will add on more pressure and frustration if you do not follow the plan. The inspiration will take you to a state where you will find even more resources, more wholeness to unload pressure and reload with positive feelings that later you can share with your clients and the people around you. Finding a sport that provides inspiration is key, because you will then be in a place that can action it or not, depending on what you really need in that moment in your life. For many it is cycling, or hiking in the quietness of the mountains, for others it is the adrenaline that surf provides, and for some it is the calmness that yoga or walking by the river gives them.
- **Travelling to different places to embrace different ways of living and experiencing life**
  Travel is the ultimate way to experience the various colours of the palette of our world. There is always an untapped potential of discovery. In this

world, there are plenty of different places and ways of living that can open our eyes and lead us to reflect upon our own lifestyles and to take decisions on how to achieve inner balance, whatever that might be. Hence, if you can access travelling, even in your own country or district, consider it as a part of self-care.

- **Meditating, having some time to allow your mind to just wonder without attachment to any thought**
Meditation is only just becoming widespread in some countries. This free tool, available to everyone and everywhere, has not yet been taken up widely and therefore its potential has not yet been released and tapped into. Letting the mind wander without attachment develops self-care on several fronts; it relaxes the mind, it teaches the art of detachment, and it also balances inner energy and develops attention. However, it doesn't suit everyone, and we take this up later in Part II.

- **Stress management techniques**
According to Professor George Everly and Dr Jeffery Lating (2017), from John Hopkins University in the USA, a good way of self-caring comes from stress management and breathing techniques. The stress management techniques include relaxation exercises, interpersonal support, faith, and a positive attitude. As we discussed earlier, faith is a very personal dimension appreciated by many people, who share their stories of how believing in something beyond has provided them with different viewpoints of what is happening to them and can certainly help them put the situation into perspective.

Self-caring is a commitment to oneself, to excellence, regardless of profession. Step into it and you won't go back again. In Part II, "Supervising through Bereavement", we will look at self-care in more detail as an integral part of restorative supervision.

Maggie's Personal Story:
I remember vividly that day when I got the news that the father of my four-year-old daughter had passed away. Before I knew this, I set off for a coaching session at 9 a.m. that day with the CEO of the local branch of a major multinational company. As always, I arrived a few minutes before and was received by his secretary and as I was talking to her, I was strangely assaulted by a coughing fit. It was so severe that it did not go away even with a sip of water or medication. The client was late, and the cough persisted to the point that I decided I was in no condition to have that coaching session. I left coughing, my face so red from all the efforts of trying to control the cough and the cough itself. This had never happened to me before, and it was a nice spring day, no allergies, no flu, nothing. It was strange and what was stranger was that as I drove back home, the cough suddenly disappeared.

As I entered my home, switched on my computer and started my working day back in the office I received the phone call that changed my life forever. The news fell on me like a dark cloud – the father of my four-year-old daughter had passed away at age 48 from an epilepsy seizure during the night.

I went straight into the denial stage of the Kübler-Ross Curve. I recall saying on the phone numerous times, "It is not possible. This cannot be true. You are lying."

And then all my life roles vanished apart from one; being a mum. I put my life on-hold and focussed on my daughter. I consciously took the decision to stop my coaching practice for 3–4 months and focus on the wellbeing of my baby (they will always be our babies, regardless of their age!) and concentrated on the logistical and admin stuff, such as his will, the things my daughter inherited, bank accounts, pictures, etc.

Delivering this tragic news was the toughest thing I have ever done in my life even though I had read a lot about breaking this type of news to children and how to do it.

Putting my coaching practice on stand-by helped me focus on my priority at that moment and gave me comfort that I was doing the best for my clients too, as I was guarding them from my own stuff, and preventing it from interfering in my professional context.

Financially, it was tough for those few months, but it felt right not to work when my mind was wandering about so many little details related to this death, when my attention span was a wreck and when my face resembled worries, sadness, and alienation.

This pause in work also gave me time to self-care, to rebuild my focus and to understand other perspectives and angles to life. I didn't rush this experience and frankly it later gave me common ground with many of my clients.

This is my recommendation (Maggie) *to my supervisees or anyone who asks my personal and professional opinion: Pause. Take time to go through the situation. Be there for the ones who need you. Be there for your inner self. Notice what is emerging for you and give voice to that. Protect your clients from your fragility and for your eagerness in returning to normal. Don't force things. And in time, you will find your way forward.*

Julia's Personal Story:
My father died in June 2018 (my first close family death). He had been ill for many years and died in the hospice where my sister worked (an added stressor as well as a comfort for us as a family.) I was unsure about how I would feel when he eventually died, but I suspected (and subsequently this

turned out to be correct) that I would not be "classically" bereaved when he died. For me there was no weeping or wailing and to outsiders this may have seemed harsh. Our relationship with our parents can sometimes be complex and I think I mourned the loss of a relationship I would have liked but never had. I was not angry and blaming as my father was a good man, just not the father I would have liked. Initially I decided to clear my diary for a couple of weeks because as executor of my father's estate I knew I would be extremely busy dealing with funeral directors, lawyers as well supporting my mother. It quickly became apparent that actually I was not fit for work, not just from a time limitation perspective but because my memory appeared to have deserted me, and I descended into the recognisable brain fog that others described. This was so unexpected given that I didn't count myself as 'bereaved'. I ended up taking a month off work and as it was the summer my return to work was gentler and more phased afterwards, as I went into the quiet month of August. When telling people the news of my father's death I was fascinated by people's responses. The people who do not know what to say and those that make assumptions about your feelings based on how they would feel; even a close friend who seemed puzzled that I didn't seem upset. Death is still such a taboo subject, so I took to LinkedIn to find out what other coaches and supervisors thought. This uncovered a rich seam and an obvious lack of research into this topic as a coaching issue.

When I look back at how I came to be co-authoring this book, it strikes me that the journey started 20 years ago at the age of 38, when I had my first terrifying experience of fully connecting with the idea and emotion of being dead one day. This started a journey of reading many books on death to "find the solution" to my existential angst. When I finally stumbled across the idea of writing a book on bereavement, grief, and loss (after my father's death and meeting Maggie João) I discovered I had a head start on the research. My dedication at the front of this book is to my father who unwittingly sent me on this path and perhaps paradoxically, is a fitting legacy of our relationship.

My advice (Julia) to *coaches and supervisors from my perspective is that bereavement truly does show itself in numerous ways, so enquire, be curious, see it from their viewpoint and not your own.*

Serious illness: The ill coach

The American physician, John Travis, first presented the illness-wellness continuum in 1972. And as you can see from Figure 6, it ranges from illness to fitness. It is relevant to highlight that the comfort zone was named by Travis as "the neutral state", where there is no sign of harmful symptoms;

Fitness

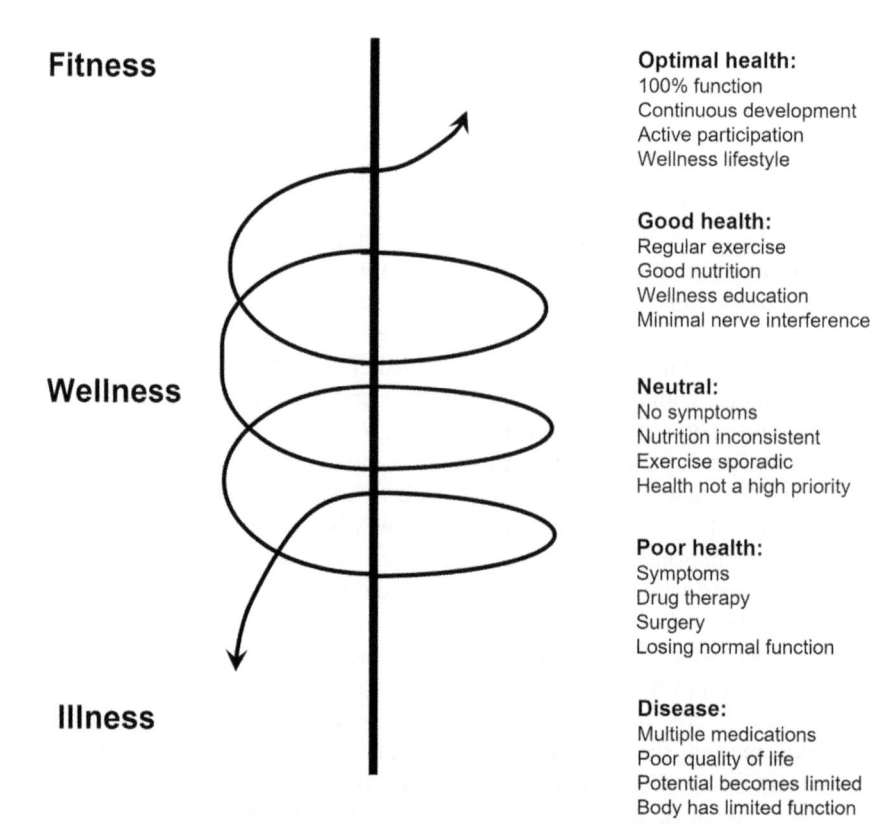

Wellness

Illness

Optimal health:
100% function
Continuous development
Active participation
Wellness lifestyle

Good health:
Regular exercise
Good nutrition
Wellness education
Minimal nerve interference

Neutral:
No symptoms
Nutrition inconsistent
Exercise sporadic
Health not a high priority

Poor health:
Symptoms
Drug therapy
Surgery
Losing normal function

Disease:
Multiple medications
Poor quality of life
Potential becomes limited
Body has limited function

Figure 6 The illness-wellness continuum.

however, as an example, when our eating style is inconsistent and we do physical exercise irregularly, it leads to a stage of false wellness. This represents that classical image of the iceberg, in which so many (important) things are hidden under the surface.

Figure 6, adapted from Travis's work (2004), shows a spiral in constant movement between illness, wellness, and fitness.

Everyone can get sick and, worse, can get seriously ill. Some of these diseases are the results of the lifestyle we have had for many years, consciously or unconsciously. Some of us are more conscious of this, and this is not a judgmental warning as it's a challenge for us authors too. What is relevant is to know in detail what coaches can do to prepare themselves in case of a sudden disease or illness that prevents them from continuing their coaching activity. There are a few things they need to pay attention to when it comes to their coaching practice.

These procedures depend on the stage the coach is at in relation to their health and the disease they are facing. If the coach is required to be away from the practice for a certain period, it is only expected that they inform their clients of this absence. Some coaches disclose the reason for it, some others prefer not to show that level of vulnerability. At this stage, we are not going to explore what is preventing you from becoming vulnerable in front of your clients. This would be a very interesting point to bring to supervision, and we acknowledge that everyone is different, every coaching contract and coaching relationship is different and that you need to understand what is important for that relationship in that moment of absence, and also be ready to reflect what has triggered you to disclose or not disclose.

When you are moving from the poor health stage into the disease stage on the continuum, there could be different considerations. One of these is to ensure that in the case of more severe circumstances with your health, all your clients need to be contacted and informed. If you are too ill to do this personally, have a list of all client contacts, so that the person you entrusted this task with can easily get in touch and explain what is going on and the reason for your silence. We understand that this may be construed as a data protection breach. However, if the coach covers this in the contract, and it is agreed with the client, it is no longer considered a breach. Please note that you must also make clear to a client and sponsor/ other stakeholders that you have this provision in place so that they are aware (and have agreed by signing your coaching contract specifically on this point) that another person may have sight of commercially and/or personally confidential information in your notes/records when they come to handle/dispose of them.

If you Google "death of therapist" or something similar there are many services being promoted that cover this situation. Basically, what they provide is the creation of a professional will for the coach. The term "Will" is a misnomer in this context. Not so much of what one will get from the death of the professional, but rather what one will need to provide in case of the death of the professional. So, in this "Will", you identify a person who you trust with these tasks, which might be to contact and inform your clients, or publish your death in a relevant journal/newspaper or inform the charter or the professional body to which you have been associated with. Some service providers (for a small fee) will also destroy coaching notes, close your website, and remove you from social media too. Some insurance companies will require client notes to be retained for up to seven years after the death of a coach in case of a complaint, so clients and sponsors also need to be aware of this too in the contract. This may involve changing any privacy notices you may have on your website and in materials.

Many of these services reinforce the ethics behind this point. The Global Code of Ethics created by the Global Coaching Alliance includes point 2.28 "Members are required to have a provision for the transfer of current clients and their records in the event of the termination of practice" alluding to the coach's death.

If you have never thought about this, then now is a good time. Who would you entrust this task? Our family could be easily swamped after our demise. Would you want to add to their suffering by requiring them to deal with your coaching practice? It might be wise to entrust this task to someone who is not part of your family and belongs to your circle of peers and colleagues. Have a think about it and choose whoever makes more sense regarding your circumstances. A professional executor service for only £30/$50 may be the practical choice and peace of mind. In Part II we discuss "clinical wills" for coaches and supervisors.

Coach case study: Will I ever be able to coach again?

Apart from the initial shock and concern about the future, one of the major impacts I felt after my heart attack was the immediate response of those close to me, my loved ones, my friends, my associates, fellow coaches, and my clients. My wife and family were wonderful, and I learned how positive it feels to have people rooting for you when you need them most. The fears at the beginning felt real enough and focussed on questions which did not have answers such as "How ill am I?" "What will the future be like?" "How much future have I got?" Being able to continue working and specifically coaching was a secondary issue then.

The realisation that so many people cared and were concerned was both moving and very supportive, helping me to deal with my fears and worries. It made my initial and subsequent recovery easier to think about and sustain. As time passed, it also enabled me to review my coaching practice and what it might mean for myself and my clients. This was aside from my immediate concerns such as "What do I tell them? "How will they be able to maintain their progress?" and "How will my illness affect them". All my clients were supportive and understanding and after discussing it, some of them began work with my fellow coaches who were people I knew well and trusted. This reinforced for me the importance of having great relationships with skilled and reliable fellow professionals. Several were happy to wait for a period while I considered when I might be able to work with them again. I cannot thank my clients or my fellow coaches enough! I was also grateful to have a very wise and supportive supervisor who helped me think through and navigate the choppy waters of returning to work. Who would choose to coach others without supervision themselves!?

In thinking about my return to working with clients I had to fundamentally consider the impact on myself and my clients of what had happened to me. I felt ready to return, indeed was anxious to return, after around three months and I became very much more aware of the impact of many of the things we learn as coaches but "take as read" in the way we work. These included being empathetic, compassionate and being ready to share my own vulnerability. I had always thought myself to have these attributes as a coach but now I found myself taking a much closer look at their meaning and I resolved to ensure my illness became an opportunity for me to become an even better coach.

The illness reinforced for me, just how important to the success of a coaching relationship is the ability to maintain that crucial balance between empathy, tolerance, understanding and compassion whilst remaining objective and challenging the client in a way that is appropriate for them. This may seem obvious, but we take our ability to do this for granted at our peril.

As coaches, it is not an unusual experience to find ourselves wondering what the longer-term impact of our working together has had on our clients and hoping the positive things they have taken away will stick. I have had the benefit of being able to write this looking back with hindsight and have learned, that despite the passage of time, even small shifts in perspective, moments of clarity and revealing our own vulnerability and humanity when appropriate, can leave our clients with many good things to sustain them long after we have ended our coaching relationship.

Roger Williams
Coach
New Focus Consulting Ltd

The dance between coach and client through bereavement

The dance that takes place between coach and client through the client's bereavement journey is a dance that provides for both parties; not only the client but also the coach because he becomes more whole and resourceful by helping others in this journey. As metaphor is a useful tool for many coaches, we explore the symbolism of the dance here. Coach John Leary Joyce (2011) often uses this analogy on his speaking engagements for the EMCC. He describes the analogy between coaching and tango and how it reveals similarities with the relationship between coach and coachee.

However, we would like to bring another angle, a different angle, perhaps a fresher one.

We are going to refer to an image (Figure 7) first introduced to Maggie by Brazilian coach Luciane Schütte (2018), which is of a trapezist, hereby illustrated by Cristina Salvador. Anything can be used for this image: a death, a departure, a transition being it a divorce, or a professional move planned or unplanned, parenthood, in fact any change.

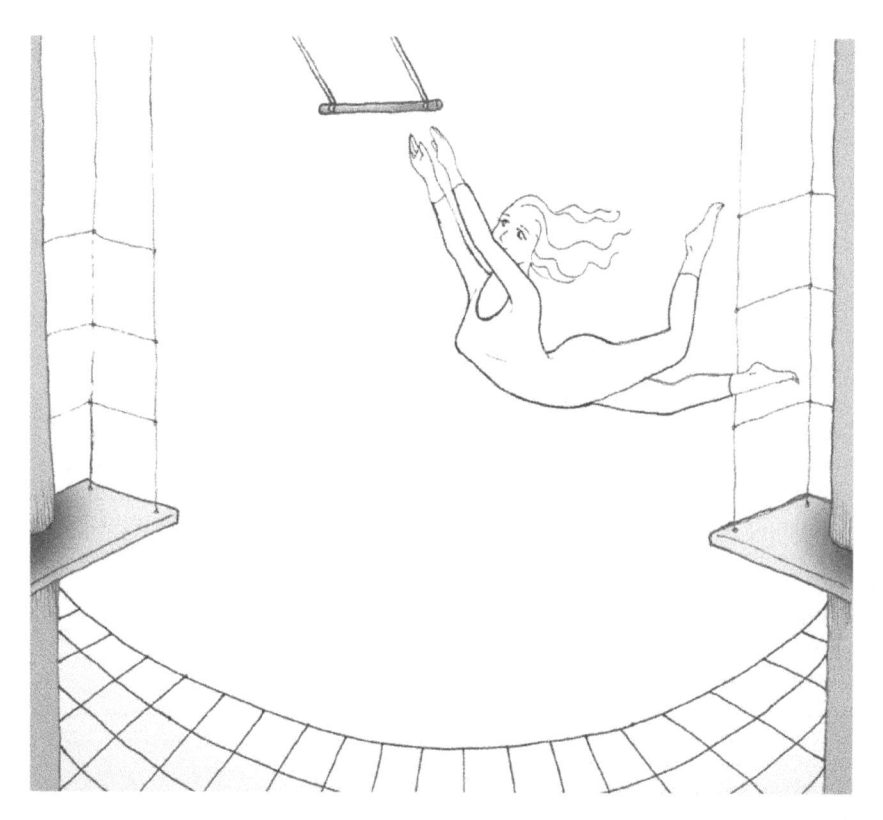

Figure 7 Illustration of a trapeze artist by Cristina Salvador (www.cristinasalvador.carbonmade.com).

This illustration represents change. And can be a useful visual image when conversing with clients. We describe it here as a way of describing it to your client.

Imagine yourself on a trapeze, so high you cannot identify the faces of the people down below, some will be applauding you, cheering you on, or some may secretly hope you fall. Pretty much as happens in any situation that involves change. Now, imagine you, the trapezist, are voluntarily willing to take that jump (rather like when change is prompted by you and not others). However, there are situations when the jump was not initiated voluntarily by the trapezist, but rather something or some event, or someone pushed her to take that leap. This is analogous to when we are not going into the change willingly. This can be the case for death, some separation and divorce, redundancy, illness, etc.

Let's continue exploring. The trapezist, you, starts to jump, regardless of it being a voluntary jump or not. You are in the air, alone, just you. You haven't yet got a hold of the trapeze. Before you get a hold of the trapeze there is just you, nothing else, in the air, no other resources than the internal ones. In these split seconds, when everything seems overwhelming, there is no rewind button nor a fast forward one, they are there and sometimes the pain can be unbearable.

And this is exactly where many clients are when they come to coaching.

How to use the trapeze metaphor

So, how we work with them then can take many forms. One can work on what each part of the image represents for the client. For instance, the safety net below, the pillars on the left and on the right, the trapeze itself.

We can also highlight that the trapezist does not have a parachute, so she doesn't have any other resources but her internal ones such as focus, resilience, inner dialogue, positive talk, mindset, past experiences, objectives, dreams, planning, care, love, agility (learning and emotional), the various multiple intelligences (Gardner, 1983), physical strength, willpower, faith, etc. And then we explore what these resources can do in that specific split second, who does the client become if she had a handful of these resources, how would they impact the rest of that leap, what becomes possible?

The rest of the image is focussed on facilitating the client to hold on to that trapeze and arrive safely at the pillar of the left-hand side and once there to turn back and appreciate the journey that just took place and reflect back what happened exactly, what shift occurred in the client that made that journey possible.

This type of flying dance has different paces and rhythms and that is fine. It also has various factors depending on the coach and on the client and the relationship they created between themselves and for themselves.

The trapezist's leap can also allude to a leap of faith in so many circumstances or a flight that so many of us dream of one day accomplishing. Working with this analogy, since it is so visual and rich, can help the client move forward in their bereavement journey in a safe manner and can be a gift for both the client and the coach.

Another exercise one can do with this image is to colour it in. Ask the client to colour it and then to explore the colour choice and the feelings the coloured image brings up in them.

There are many subliminal elements in the illustration, such as the fact the trapezist is smiling when taking on this endeavour, or that there is no one else in the image, showing that this process is very personal. The fact that the trapezist is feminine, can also highlight that in many languages the word change, or death is feminine. This leap can also be taken as death itself taking a leap and moving to a new stage of understanding.

As mentioned before, this illustration can be explored in many different ways depending on what makes sense for you and your client and the context she is going through.

In our next section, we focus on the dance between client, coach and sponsor and the way that endings of all kinds (and the way they are handled by organisations) can make all the difference to an employee's capacity to navigate grief and loss healthily.

References

Caetano, A., 2020. *Como Identificar Sinais de Depressão?* Speech at the 4th Coaching Conference GPC-APG, 17 September 2020, Lisbon.

Everly, G. and Lating, J., 2017. *The Johns Hopkins Guide to Psychological First Aid.* Baltimore: NJ: John's Hopkins University Press.

Gardner, H., 1983. *Frames of Mind.* New York, USA: Basic Books.

Leary Joyce, J., 2011. *Tango Coaching: Leadership and Followership.* Speech at the EMCC Conference, 17–19 November 2011, Paris.

Reynolds, M., 2020. *Coach the Person, Not the Problem.* Oakland: Berrett-Koehler.

Schütte, L., 2018. *O Voo do Trapezista – Atravessando Crises de Mãos Dadas.* 1st ed. Brasília: Brazil.

Travis, J. and Ryan, R., 2004. *The Wellness Workbook.* 3rd ed. Berkeley, Calif.: Celestial Arts, p. xvii.

Chapter 4

The Organisational Machine

Something else we have to consider, particularly when working with corporate clients is the confidence both client and coach may have about potential support from the organisation. Even life coaches who have been contracted privately for coaching may still have to facilitate a discussion with clients about what they will do about their coaching work.

Sometimes the mechanistic nature of how organisations work is in complete contrast to what is required by an employee who is grieving.

It would be wonderful to say that most organisations get this right but unfortunately there are more examples of poor practice than good. Often this is unintentional and is a function of trying to take a logical black and white approach to a topic that can be like nailing jelly to a wall. If everyone grieves differently and to a different timescale then this can throw up all sorts of issues for organisations, human resources teams, and the line manager of the bereaved.

What does grief in the workplace look like?

Let's start with the most frequent bereavement – when an employee has suffered the death of a loved one. In the top one hundred of the Stress Scale or Social Readjustment Rating Scale (SRRS) Holmes and Rahe (1967), the death of a spouse or life partner, in particular, is a significant stressor that can lead to physical, emotional and/or mental ill health. Many of us carry an unspoken hierarchy of acceptable loss which recognise some bereavements as worse than others. For instance, the death of an elderly parent may be viewed as inevitable whereas the death of a child feels more shocking and distressing as it seems to go against the natural order of life, not only for the parents but for everyone observing. David Kessler (2019) says that no loss is greater than another, "If the love is real then the loss is real" even if that is "only" a pet.

Where do organisations go wrong?

There are numerous ways in which organisations can mishandle the grief and loss of the employees. Here are some of the most common ones.

- **Providing the incorrect type of support**
  Many models of bereavement are based on knowledge from a clinical setting and also from service settings where service users are coming forward and accessing bereavement support voluntarily. Unfortunately, we know that many people do not seek support for a variety of reasons. This doesn't necessarily mean an employee does or doesn't need specialised bereavement support. Informal support (which a coach could provide) may be enough. Business Psychologist Leanne Flux (2020a) says the majority "may gain from informal support where they can express their emotions and where they perceive their grief is responded to in a non-judgemental and understanding way". Her research found that employees who had a manager who acknowledged and responded to their loss as being supportive compared to those who felt they were being ignored, fared better.

  This sounds appalling. How could a manager ignore an employee's bereavement? But as we have seen elsewhere, managers are human too and might be bringing all their own historical baggage and uncertainty into play.

- **Lack of consideration for long-term support**
  How to deal with a bereaved employee is not on the curriculum of many leadership development programmes; nevertheless, it is something that anyone working in organisations must get to grips with, due to changing demographics. Because of the Covid-19 pandemic demographics in society, In some organisations there are three or four generations working alongside each other. Coupled with the fact that many employees are now working and living longer, there is an increasing chance that managing a greater diversity of age range and health conditions will become more common within the workplace. At some point, all managers will probably be required to have a conversation with an employee about a death. The huge death toll during the Covid-19 pandemic if extrapolated to include on average 8–10 family and friends of each dead person, suggests that coaches and supervisors are extremely likely to come across clients who were affected by loss during the pandemic. This will apply to managers too. And as we have already pointed out, loss during the pandemic could have been from loss of livelihood, identity, health (the ramifications of long Covid are unknowable so far), divorce, educational opportunities, etc. Perhaps as coaches we need to include in the future, as a standard part of our contracting and biographical enquiry, the question "What impact did the Covid-19 pandemic have on you?" (João and Menaul, 2021). Rather like we do when we talk to the older generation about the Second World War.

- **Lack of clarity around time allowed off work**
  Employees who have experienced a bereavement are often expected and compelled to return to work sooner than is healthy. Employees are more

likely to go on to take sick leave then return too soon (grief can suppress the immune system leading to other physical symptoms) and if they are in work there is a danger of presenteeism. Anecdotally we hear that many employees use annual leave after a bereavement if there is little formal support from their employer, or if they feel uncomfortable naming their leave as sick leave.

Employees who already have a demanding job in normal times may be overwhelmed by a bereavement that tips the balance and leads to burnout. Safety is also an important feature, and this would also depend on the role of the employee. Emotional and physical fatigue (possibly through lack of sleep) could be catastrophic in jobs that require use of machinery or the responsibility for the care of another. The employer, therefore, has a legal duty (Flux, 2020b) to conduct a health and safety assessment.

- **Lack of HR guidance**

Policies and procedures are important as guidance and give a framework for handling bereavement but most research has discovered that the line manager sets the tone by how they respond far more than what the HR policy says.

A good place to start for any organisation is to make sure they are doing what they 'must' do first (i.e. within the law of their country) and things they 'should/could' do that are deemed to be good practice. An excellent resource for managers and coaches in the UK are the guidelines on bereavement by the Advisory, Conciliation and Arbitration Service (ACAS) (2021) which is clear on the 'musts' and 'shoulds', soft skills, and has some excellent case studies. Research of the American market shows that many have used this ACAS document, including Stanford University's own guidelines for its staff. However, most of the USA's outlook tends to be focussed on avoiding litigation. If you are reading this book and you are a HR practitioner or an internal coach who is a manager too, then becoming familiar with this document will give you a greater sense of confidence on navigating the sensitivities around this topic.

- **Misidentifying performance issues**

At the start of this book, we highlighted the classic symptoms of grief such as loss of appetite, disturbed sleep, fatigue, lack of concentration, memory loss, poor decision making, distraction, relationship problems. "Grief brain" from loss may not receive as much prominence as "Baby Brain" during pregnancy, but it is just as real. Flux (2020b) notes that the average time taken off work is between three days and 24 weeks. This begs the question of how often do employers make the connection between long-term sickness and a previous loss event?

> **Maggie's coaching case-study: Misaligned expectations**
>
> Lurdes came to me because she had returned to work after her surgery to remove her breast cancer and she wanted to explore her new identity and to smooth some things around going back to work.
>
> Very soon it became clear to Lurdes that her line manager and her peers behaved awkwardly and did not know what to say. Besides the wording on the messages, which they had all sent but were not adequate in her mind, she felt expectations were not aligned between everyone involved. Some peers treated her as a little child, taking on more of her work so she would not get tired doing it, whilst others didn't even know she was supposed to return that week.
>
> Lurdes felt "misplaced" and we worked on what she would have liked to have happened and what to ask for. As many companies are starting to work on official policies for internal support for their people returning back from illness and surgeries, many of the survivors also feel obliged to educate them and to support the company in figuring out what that support could look like. Organisations would do well to listen to employees like Lurdes.

Actions for line managers

There are a number of things managers can do alongside official policies. These are:

- Acknowledge what has happened and express empathy for your employee's loss (as a minimum).
- Recognise and verbalise your acceptance that it is understandable and OK to be not OK during this difficult time without making the employee fear for their job.
- Refrain from launching into a theoretical lecture on what they can expect from bereavement, especially if that has been a personal experience for the manager too.
- Give clear guidance on work expectations (nearly all the research highlights that the 'whatever you need' approach doesn't help. It's rather like the old chestnut, "my door is always open", and then managers wonder why people still don't walk through the open door). Sometimes the bereaved are in no fit state to ask for what they need, even if they knew.
- Take charge of informing their work colleagues so the employee doesn't have to keep having emotionally wrought conversations on a loop.
- Give some work over to other colleagues temporarily so that the employee is not under pressure to complete work while technically on

bereavement leave. Most colleagues are glad to help as a way of channelling their own need to show support to a grieving co-worker.
- Interpret policies flexibly. Unlike parental leave, taking time off in blocks may not be useful. Employees may require taking leave as and when needed during the 'bad days'.

Many of these tips are for a manager helping an employee to handle a bereavement that has usually happened outside the workplace. There can be an additional level of complexity when tragedy strikes internally.

In this example, the coach then has to help their coachee, as a manager, deal with a maelstrom of emotions such as fear, shame, anxiety, anger, guilt, and regret; either their own and/or emotions being projected onto them by others. Not only will they need a coach to hold the space expertly for the processing of current feelings, but this type of event can also easily trigger issues of unresolved grief and loss in the coachee/manager. This is then added to what the coachee might see as a more pressing need to sort out the conflict created in the team and from the family. If the culture of the organisation is fear-based, then views become polarised as right or wrong as people 'take sides'. When we are threatened it creates anxiety that can lead to defence (which can come out as an attack, i.e. retaliate first).

As coaches we may be able to facilitate some of these best practice measures alongside line managers depending on our contract with the sponsors.

Considerations for coaches and supervisors

If an unexpected loss occurs during the duration of the coaching programme what can coaches and supervisors do?

Here are some questions to explore:

- What was my original contract here and with whom? How might the contract need to change (permanently or temporarily)?
  This might depend on how involved a sponsor had been in the original set up of the coaching. If you have privately contracted with your client and no one else is involved then it could be a straight forward discussion between you and your client about what support they need right now from you or others (including the conversation about the appropriateness of counselling), the benefits and pitfalls of continuing with the coaching programme at this present time, and how long a delay they may need. This would also be the case for internal coaches.
- You may need to think about what your own wishes are regarding the extension of a contract and how willing you are to put the contract on hold and for what time. For example, your client may want to press pause on the coaching with no sense of how long they will need. How do you feel if they come back to you to finish off their contracted

coaching in three, or even six months' time? A year? Longer? As an external coach, this would also be dependent on whether the client had paid for their coaching in advance and therefore if you are still holding their 'credit in the bank'. If they have not paid in advance and they never return, how would that feel for you? These are questions to explore in supervision about your loss of income and also unfinished business with your client. Sometimes it is difficult to know when to re-approach a client after loss for fear of intruding too soon and appearing insensitive.

- If you can agree up front that you will gently check in with them after a set period with no obligation on their part to restart the coaching if they are not ready, then at least you have a future steer.
- In some rare situations, you may not have the opportunity to talk to your client particularly if the grief and loss event was sudden ill health for them or their family or a death in particular tragic circumstances, for example, suicide or murder. In which case, it is possible that the only discussion you have initially about the contract and the coaching is with the sponsor and not the client. Julia had a scenario where a client died suddenly, and she only received the news via the account manager of the coaching consultancy whose contract she was working on at the time as an associate coach.

Always take the death of a coachee to supervision no matter how well you think you are dealing with it, as it is such an unusual situation and if nothing else it can lead to rich learning for the coach about endings.

What should a coach do if the contract is three-way or multi-party contracting?

In this case, much of the above is still appropriate, especially talking to your client first about their wants and needs at this time and how you can support that without leaping in to rescue them. However, you do have a responsibility to the sponsor if they are paying you or have already paid. As coaches we see ourselves in service to the coachee first. We would have a conversation with them and encourage them to talk to their employer themselves. Then depending on what came out of this conversation, either the possibility of pausing the coaching or changing the original contracting, then that could happen later between coach and employer. As we have seen, employers don't always approach bereavement well and as a coach (with permission from your coachee) you may have to be the 'voice of reason'.

For some coachees the loss may have brought such radical changes to their lives that the coaching may no longer be necessary, say if the client leaves the organisation, or other objectives come to the fore due to the wider ramifications of life changes, for example, taking on greater carer responsibilities at home which require a change of work role and/or flexible/reduced working hours.

These changes may not be obvious initially so a coach would do well to confirm a pause of coaching with the sponsor with an open invitation to re-contact as and when the employee is ready in whatever format required.

Take care that those 'credits in the bank' with the organisation are not approached in a hard-headed way by the sponsor or you may find yourself being asked to provide coaching for someone else instead. Again, every situation is different and if the coachee is obviously not going to return to work then this could be a pragmatic solution. Showing understanding, empathy and flexibility while maintaining an ethical, authoritative stance as coach is the watchword.

This case study, however, describes a similar situation where the organisation can be tone-deaf to the sensitivities of moving coaches to other clients while the original person is on sick leave.

Coaching supervisor case study: When a coach dies

As a supervisor, I had been working with several supervisees (coaches) as part of a contract, providing supervision to support coaches working with middle and senior leaders within education. My reflections are twofold.

Chen had been diagnosed with terminal cancer and due to her failing health, had withdrawn from her role as a coach.

Klara had developed a close working relationship with Chen over a couple of years and had been talking to her socially and considered her a friend.

Impact on Klara

As part of our supervision relationship, myself and Klara had shared our knowledge and feelings about Chen's diagnosis in several of our supervision sessions. We both recognised that we shared knowing and having a relationship with Chen (mine professional and Klara's as a peer coach and a friend). Understanding this connection and sharing our feelings about Chen's illness and how it was impacting on us, as individuals and as supervisor and supervisee, deepened our rapport and sense of trust.

When Chen died, it had a significant impact on Klara and on me. Our first session after the death, was solemn and much of the time was spent in a restorative space.

Impact on Supervisor and supervision space

I was conscious that Chen's death resonated with me because both my mother and my aunt had died from the same cancer diagnosis as her. I had talked to Chen about this in one of our final sessions and she had shared that she knew she would die from the disease. Her death was quite impactful for me and did bring back some of the memories which were associated with the deaths of my family members. I brought these reflections to my own supervisor and explored the parallel processing and how to apply the seven eyed lens model to help to manage the 'leakage' of emotions (mine and Klara's) within the supervision sessions.

Impact on coaching and supervision system

Through the conversations with Klara, we both recognised that the ripple effects of this death were being felt within the cohort of coaches, of which Chen and Klara were coach members. Klara knew that the coaching organisation was aware of the death, and she had asked them if they felt that as an organisation, they should 'recognise' the event and reach out to the coaching cohort. The response from the organisation was that, as independent associates, the organisation felt no responsibility for the cohort or coaching system. The only thing they actioned was to move all of Chen's coaching clients to other coaches, in effect feeling they had discharged their sole responsibility irrespective of how coachees may feel about starting afresh with another coach, who were perhaps shocked and saddened at the death of their coach with whom they had only just started to build trust and rapport.

As the supervisor, I disagreed with this approach, and I challenged the organisation to reconsider this decision. I raised this challenge with my supervisor, as my sense was that this decision was both wrong and short sighted. Despite two more conversations with the coaching leads in the organisation, the decision remained unchanged.

Chris Birbeck
Coach and Coaching Supervisor

- **What are the inherent dangers here in the overlap between client, coach, and sponsor?**
  As a coach there may be a delicate balance between allowing your client to orchestrate their own access to support but at the same time gently pointing out the responsibilities of the line manager, especially if you have

previously been in conversation with managers as part of a three-way process. The difficulty occurs for coaches when they become too involved. The challenge is not to be emotional if you see your client being treated badly by a line manager who doesn't know how to respond in the best way. There is no easy answer, and we would say explore it with your supervisor as each scenario is unique and even though you have a duty of care to your client there is still a fine line to tread. We have had coachees who were already working on relationship issues with their manager as coaching, which can make objectivity for the coach fraught with judgmental emotion towards a line manager who appears not to be doing 'the right thing'. We know then that we can feel a real pull to rescue clients, see them as a victim and firmly place the manager in the persecutor corner. If you are an internal coach, it may be easier to suspend the coaching as well as being able to have different conversations internally with line managers due to proximity and previous dealings (on the other hand, you could be inclined to get more involved than you should because of your prior organisational knowledge).

- **What support is available to my client within the organisation and how much should I help them to access it?**
CIPD research (McCartney, 2021) found that only 54% of employees were aware that their employer had a policy or any support in place for bereavement. So, if they don't know, they may not ask. It could certainly be your role as coach (or supervisor) to ask this question to raise awareness of the possibility. Ensure that you are placing the responsibility with them no matter how much your heart may be aching for them. Simply asking the question "Who in your organisation is likely to know about bereavement policy and that you would be happy talking to?" will allow them to think through who to approach and where to look. You as coach are unlikely to have access to an internal resource anyway, which makes this boundary easier.

- **What support is available to my client outside the organisation and how much should I help them to access it?**
External support may feel a tricker area to navigate particularly if you are feeling that the coachee/supervisee is showing helplessness, and not accessing suggested resources[6] such as websites, books, advice lines, etc. If you are able to provide signposts for your clients to external bereavement support, legal advice, books, websites, and recommended therapists, then that is in service to your client. What you can't do is make them take that advice. However, if there is a serious and more urgent duty of care issue arising with your client then you may have to take a more action-focussed approach. An example would be clients

---

6 A list of resources can be found at the back of this book.

who are having suicidal thoughts which we tackle later in Part II. This requires a different level of intervention and decision-making by the coach. If you do not fear for the safety of your client (or others around them) no matter how sad and emotionally upset they are, then you do have to treat them as adults. It can be easy to drop into parent mode, with your client positioned as a child to be helped.

If you are continuing to meet your client, it is acceptable to check in again to ascertain whether they have accessed any of the resources, but it is still down to them. The timing may not be right just now, and the resources may only mean something for them later. Our advice would be to note everything down in your client notes and records to maintain good ethical practice and assuage any potential risk should something untoward happen.

We have on many occasions discussed with clients the option of accessing therapy for a variety of reasons and we have talked about how they may find a counsellor and where to go; some do this, and some don't. If the continuation of the coaching is not dependent on them accessing therapy, then we still leave the final decision of counselling to them with the full knowledge discussed between us, on whether this will impact ultimate outcomes of the coaching.

- **Should I keep in touch with my client on bereavement leave?**

As we stated previously, if you have the opportunity to talk to your client before bereavement leave then raise how you could communicate with them. They may not be able to think this through themselves if grieving, so you may have to step into your role as a coach with your knowledge of bereavement (you are reading this book!). Take the lead in contacting them perhaps by email initially if that feels less intrusive, instead of your communications entering too much of a personal space via text or messaging services.

If you don't have the chance to speak before they go on bereavement leave and you hear of their loss second-hand, then a message of condolence is appropriate plus a gentle promise that you will check in with them after a period of time. Its length may depend on what type of loss they have suffered and any personal background you may know about them. A good example would be religious affiliations and implications for the timescales of rituals and funerals, (for some religions, the funerals are arranged very quickly after death) or the circumstances of the loss (post-mortems, autopsies, inquests, and other legal processes) as these can extend grief and loss and potentially the bereavement period.

- **What is the coach's role for return-to-work support, ongoing, and beyond?**

Phased returns are useful for some employees but not all, especially if physical and mental exhaustion is still an issue. A coachee may have many things to make decisions about that are different at work after their bereavement, for example, a client who is taking official guardianship of a young niece or nephew after the death of the child's parents. For some this becomes the key role of coaching. Returning to work might be dreadful from several different perspectives. These are moments of some emotional confusion, and it is helpful to explore with the client; what might be some strategies to make this return more "X" for them, (they define X) depending on what their needs are. Helping a client to a 'new normal' may require some of the tools that you would usually find in any coach's toolbox. Suggested coping strategies to help bereaved clients step back into work mode are:

- Focus on self-care by using a self-care wheel (Figure 11) Part II adapted from Ross and Wonfor (2019) to work with clients so they are attempting to get some wellbeing fundamentals in place, like a good sleep routine, exercise, and nutrition. This can be especially useful to facilitate if a client was not particularly good at these areas before the loss occurred.
- Encourage taking time off – clients may still be tempted to do some level of work at home if working from home has become normalised. Obviously, this will not aid their recovery and fears that their employer will expect this should be explored against the reality. From a brain perspective, the amygdala (the emotional storehouse of the brain) may be working overtime and perceive threat from all different directions because of the grief. However, for some clients, taking time off may be the worst thing to do, as a form of distraction may be what they need. Nevertheless, there is a difference between being busy and underperforming, so tackling a major project may not be appropriate for them at this time.
- Explore the availability of support groups – you may want to provide names of therapists, websites, books, etc. that specialise in loss. Again – unless you believe your client to be at risk – treat them as adults and allow them to take responsibility for following up help when the time is right for them.
- Challenge negative thought patterns and help to reframe using all the usual tools and techniques that a coach would use for other topics. This really does depend on the timeline of the loss. Although there is no set time in which someone should be 'ready to move on', it is patently clear that encouraging clients to reframe a loss that has only just happened will not be appropriate, ethical, or successful and could even cause more damage. However, as part of a return-to-work strategy, this might be a welcome practical action that an employee is looking for from a coach.

Coach case study: How to support someone when time is limited

Gemma worked for an international company and was on a Leadership Development Programme that included three one-hour phone sessions. During a face-to-face chemistry meeting we clarified her coaching goals and I also asked, "is there anything else that would be useful for me to know?". She replied that there wasn't.

The initial coaching focussed on how Gemma could adapt her leadership approach to address the business challenges she was facing. Halfway through the second session, she added that she had recently buried her sister and was now caring for her young niece. She explained that she was facing a court case to fight for custody and understandably, this was an added layer of stress to the issues she faced at work.

I felt extremely sad for her and responded in the best way I could 'in the moment' by showing empathy and asking how she was coping and asking about what other support she might need. She seemed to be coping well by talking to close friends, however, did not want to burden her family with her own worries. This approach was useful given we only had 30 minutes, but I felt concerned about how best to support Gemma in our final session. I was mindful that we only had one hour left and I am not a bereavement counsellor. I was also worried about the different layers of loss she was facing – the loss of her sister, the potential loss of custody, and the potential loss of her family unit if she gained custody. I wanted to prepare for the final coaching session to provide the best possible experience for Gemma.

Supervision in this situation was invaluable. One key thing I took away was to draw on my own knowledge and skills from an HR background to explore the support she was receiving from her organisation. Furthermore, to use my authority and inform Gemma that from my experience there are HR policies in place to support people. As a coach, we often feel that our role is to listen, reflect back and ask questions. I was reminded by my supervisor that as coaches it is sometimes useful to draw on our experience and knowledge.

A second key learning was to share my feelings in an open way, rather than trying to manage (or 'hide' these) with the mistaken belief that I was being professional. I recognised that Gemma had held back from telling me about her personal situation (which could have been for a variety of reasons) and was pleased that she had confided in me. It was useful to be prompted by my supervisor that being open about our feelings as a coach often leads to a deeper level of coaching.

> In our final session I told Gemma that I felt sad about her situation and had been thinking about her. She responded positively and was also more open about the impact of her personal situation at work and home. This led to increased self-awareness that she might need additional support. Sharing my experience was also beneficial and left Gemma with additional options of how she could seek help from the business.
>
> **Anne Stojic**
> Chartered Psychologist and Coach
> www.goodworksense.co.uk

Loss in the system: Grief loss, leavings, endings, and exits

So far, we have discussed bereavement in the workplace due to a death but as we discussed earlier clients may show up grieving other losses (consciously or unconsciously) and that grief may seem out of proportion or may emanate from a long time ago.

Many coaches are handling grief issues frequently without naming them as such. The Covid-19 pandemic exacerbated the loss felt for some clients especially around loss of livelihood, enforced retirement, and estrangement from usual environments and colleagues. Some of these issues were already there but clients had developed effective strategies to disguise them. From childhood we have often devised 'survival strategies' to protect ourselves when feeling unsafe. Later we will pick up the connection between the three selves of the trauma self, the survival self, and the healthy self that might come to the fore during times of loss, and how to deal with this in coaching and supervision.

Therefore, it could well be that our bereavement role is to help people grieve an ending they hadn't recognised, in order to move onto something new.

There are layers of loss that can occur during a pandemic. The model of supervision and mode seven, in particular, are classically the wider context. (Hawkins and Shohet, 2000).

In mode seven we often see the concentric circles emanating out from a person's work environment to encompass the global picture and its relationship to coachee, supervisee and all interconnections.

For many during the Covid-19 pandemic, the layers were more akin to the family relationship perspective of mode seven, originally by Hawkins and Shohet (2000). So instead of corporate culture, environment, stakeholders, we may see more at the centre about a client's family, friends, work colleagues, and the ripples backwards and forwards depending on the type of organisation and sector they were working in during their loss.

Helping your client to process unresolved endings

Another important aspect of helping the client navigate through bereavement is to help them identify the new identity they have inherited with that specific loss. Human beings cling to narratives as they feel like 'home', and as time goes by many do not know how to reinvent themselves and be redefined with another story. Owning the story that comes to an end is important for the client to be able to proceed.

William Bridges (2004) talks about five distinct stages to an ending that make a nice addition to the Kübler-Ross Curve (Kübler-Ross, 2009) and can feel more applicable when coaching in a work context.

Using the Bridges's model of endings, transition and new beginnings can be a revealing turning point for the client. Bridges points out that endings can also be seen as new beginnings and in between there is a transition phase (rather like our trapeze metaphor). He defines transition as being the internal psychological process of adapting to change. As we have already mentioned before it can happen slowly or quickly. It depends on many factors, such as the personality, the surroundings, the support network, the intensity of the relationship, the situation/person that we lost/died.

The five stages to an ending are:

1   Disengagement
2   Dismantling
3   Disidentification
4   Disenchantment
5   Disorientation

1   Disengagement
Throughout history, there have been themes of disengagement as a life ritual, for example, initiation ceremonies where people are separated from their families. In the modern world, we can be willingly or unwillingly disengaged from activities, relationships, settings, and roles that have been important to us, such as redundancy. During the Covid-19 pandemic, several of these things were taken away from us. However, many people reported finding many positive things about lockdown as if it had been a gift in disguise.

Often, we hear of this 'gift', from people made redundant or surviving cancer. They certainly would not have volunteered for either and when they are in the midst of it, then it doesn't feel like a gift... that may come later. This can often be seen in divorce where one person may make the decision to leave which then allows the other to confront what was obvious all along; that the relationship was not working. It takes an opportunity to disengage before you can see what was right in front of you. You also have to get to that mind shift yourself – no one can tell you.

If something is still working on the surface, it is difficult to imagine any viable alternative until you are forced to by circumstance.

2   Dismantling

"Disengagement" can only go so far in creating an ending. Pieces of an old way of life have to be taken apart piece by piece in "Dismantling".

The Kübler Ross Grief Curve talks a lot about the emotional dismantling we do when bereaved, but we also need to do it cognitively as well. So, in the same way that the bereaved adjust to labels such as 'widow' or 'orphan' – if going through a divorce clients may have to get used to saying; 'I' and not 'we', or after a merger at work using the new system and the new company name.

Bridges uses a lovely metaphor of remodelling a house. We have to destroy the old bits of the house and then there is a stage when it isn't the old one, but it isn't the new one either! (The phrase we used in the Covid-19 pandemic, 'the new normal' speaks to that). And as builders always tell you, it takes more time and money to remodel something rather than building from scratch.

3   Disidentification

This is about your identity, often as a person or a role in the workplace. As we discussed earlier, when you ask people, "Who are you?", their self-concept is often wrapped up in labels such as 'wife', 'mother', 'accountant', 'daughter', etc. The psychologist, Al Seibert (2005) in *Resilience Advantage* says this makes people vulnerable during change: who are you once your children have flown the nest? Who are you if you lose your job… or even your spouse? People sometimes resist by changing their appearance or their name as a way of gaining new identity. The old identity stands in the way of transition, says Bridges.

4   Disenchantment

To look at the stage of "Disenchantment" we need to think about 'enchantment'. We can become enchanted or stuck with our perception/image or story about how things are and how they are meant to be, for example, people of a certain pay grade should have certain offices or areas or better chairs. Often this is a perception that is rarely challenged – "Who says they should?" – and can leave people adrift without rules or certainties. Changing the story requires letting go of unwritten rules.

However, our lives are littered with disenchantments about things that we 'believed in'—lovers, friends, new careers—that turned out to be not what we thought or wanted. We forget that to develop and grow in life it's not just about adding to previous wisdom; sometimes there has to be loss first.

Disenchantment is a good sign that we are moving towards transition, which is a process, whereas change happens in an instant. It is a sign to reflect and go below the surface and if you are not able to do this, then no learning will occur; you will become disillusioned instead and maybe doomed to repeat the same mistakes with a new partner, new friend, new job.

5 Disorientation

When we feel disorientated, we may feel we don't know which way is up or down. It is recognisable to most of us when we feel lost, confused – discombobulated in modern parlance. To quote Bridges (2004): "One of the first and most serious casualties of Disorientation is likely to be our sense of (and plans for) the future."

A coachee once spoke about how disillusioned she became after going through a job evaluation process that did not remove any pay but placed her further down the hierarchy after 30 years in the company. She went from being a high-performing, motivated employee to someone who had no interest in previous goals and plans, and was slowly slipping into a form of depression, to the consternation of her managers.

We may try to frame this stage in a positive way, 'it's character building', but it's not meant to feel comfortable. This discomfort is meant to be meaningful but not enjoyable. It is a time of emptiness. In a historical context, it is like being sent out into the wilderness away from the tribe as part of a ritual. It feels foggy, unclear, a dead or non-world, 'not normal'. This creates a fear of the emptiness that Disorientation can engender.

If we rush this change, we risk going back to something that wasn't working or had outlived its purpose.

It is extremely hard for all of us to float around in this sea of nothingness without fighting the urge to get out. It has been said many people who drown would have survived if they had not fought or thrashed about in the situation but floated on their backs. The problem is how to override the natural reaction of our threat response to, "Do something ... anything"?

Ultimately, the reason we resist endings is that this time of nothingness and uncertainty also reminds us of our fears and fantasises about abandonment and death.

Coach case study: Moving on too soon

Niall worked as a Global Vice President for an International Blue-Chip Organisation; he was recruited as a Fast Stream graduate with potential and had been hugely successful. Having held several high-profile positions, Niall decided he would take advantage of early retirement, he also had personal responsibilities and dependants, so was excited about the opportunity to step back and start a training and development consultancy, aiming to work flexibly two to three days a week.

After 15 years on a Fast Stream trajectory, Niall left. As an extrovert plus having held a powerful and influential position, surrounded by team colleagues and peers who admired Niall's capability, suddenly life was very different. Having enjoyed all opportunities to travel internationally now Niall's world had shrunk and demands on him and his time from the family also came as quite a surprise.

Initially Niall wanted to have me as his coach to work with him as he started up his own business. He was very curious, and at the same time appeared disinterested – I sensed this was because for the first time in a while he felt vulnerable and wasn't the expert in the room. He also became quite defensive when I described some of the challenges relating to starting a coaching business and started to look irritated – glancing at his watch. I reflected this back to him, and his comments were that he didn't believe it could be that difficult and as he had such a good reputation and network, he doubted he would experience any of the complexities I had shared with him. Niall said he didn't need my help after all and thanked me for my time.

After about six months Niall made contact out of the blue, and early retirement was not quite as expected. Niall's attempt at starting his own business had floundered. Niall started to open up about how as an extrovert he found the time alone, and the lack of connection with others excruciatingly difficult. He had not considered retirement would be like this, he said he expected to step into a coaching business and be in demand.

Instead of seeking support, Niall had applied for another job, very similar to the one he previously held but he was unhappy.

Eventually, Niall and I discussed what was really happening, and how the transition into retirement and the situation he found himself in had been extremely difficult and had not measured up to Niall's hopes and dreams. Niall started to appreciate he was actually quite depressed and having an identity crisis, this was compounded by the fact he believed that his network had failed him, and his boss was a bully. Perhaps some of this was true for Niall, however, his expectations were unrealistic too.

Niall and I continued to coach together, he became more realistic and discovered new opportunities in a voluntary capacity which met his needs for validation and appreciation. When Niall reached this point, he ended the coaching relationship very suddenly, as now all was well again.

Occasionally I see Niall, he is very distant and there is still that vulnerability, however he has never had an "ending meeting" and the experience of retiring and losing his identity, I sense, was a period of his life Niall would rather put behind him. Perhaps bereavement support rather than business planning was what Niall really needed.

A Performance Coach and Supervisor

In Part I, our focus has been on coaching through bereavement for client and coach. In Part II, we switch our gaze to supervision, whether it be a coach having supervision around grief and loss or a supervisor who supervises others in this context.

References

ACAS. 2021. *Managing Bereavement in the Workplace – A Good Practice Guide.* [online] Available at: https://www.acas.org.uk/time-off-for-bereavement [Accessed 23 February 2021].

Bridges, W., 2004. *Managing Transitions Making Most Of Change.* 2nd ed. Boston: Da Capo Press.

Flux, L., 2020a. *Grief in the Workplace.* [online] Linkedin.com. Available at: https://www.linkedin.com/pulse/grief-workplace-leanne-flux-bsc-hons-msc-mbpss/ [Accessed 3 September 2021].

Flux, L., 2020b. *Grief and Workplace Support.* [online] Linkedin.com. Available at: https://www.linkedin.com/pulse/grief-workplace-support-leanne-flux-bsc-hons-msc-/ [Accessed 10 February 2021].

Hawkins, P. and Shohet, R., 2000. *Supervision in the Helping professions.* Maidenhead: Open University Press.

Holmes, T. and Rahe, R., 1967. The social readjustment rating scale. *Journal of Psychosomatic Research*, 11(2), pp. 213–218.

João, M. and Menaul, J., 2021. *Coaching Through a Covid-19 Pandemic.* [webinar series] [online] Association for Coaching, March/April 2021.

Kessler, D., 2019, *Finding Meaning: The Sixth Stage of Grief.* London: Rider.

Kübler-Ross, E., 2009. *On Death and Dying.* 40th ed. London: Routledge.

McCartney, C., 2021. *A guide to compassionate bereavement support.* [ebook] CIPD. Available at: https://www.cipd.co.uk/knowledge/culture/well-being/bereavement-support#grefafter [Accessed 7 April 2021].

Ross, M. and Wonfor D., 2019. *Self Care in Coaching Supervision.* [Webinar]. [Online]. Association of Coaching Supervisors, Available from: https://www.associationofcoachingsupervisors.com/community/aocs-april-2019-webinar-self-care-in-coaching-supervision

Seibert, A., 2005. *The Resiliency Advantage: Master Change, Thrive Under Pressure and Bounce Back from Setbacks.* Oakland, CA, USA: Berrett-Koehler Publishers Inc.

Part II

Supervising through Bereavement

If you have read this far as a coach, you may view this next section of the book as not for you. We would urge you to read on. This section is not just for supervisors. It is for coaches too and not just coaches who are in regular supervision and feel supported by their supervisors. This section of the book also provides coaches with (what we hope are) new and interesting models, theories, and approaches that are applicable to many aspects of coaching and not just those pertaining to grief and loss. They also provide psycho-education for coachees.

So please read on!

Chapter 5

Extending the Learning Edge

What is coaching supervision?

According to Cochrane and Newton (2011) coaching supervision is a learning relationship where both "coach and coach supervisor are in a place of continuing enquiry into the 'who' the coach is and the way in which that manifests into the 'how'". Both authors reflect that people grow best when they feel safe, safe enough to be challenged and to be curious about the way they are, the way they show up and act. What better place is there than in a coaching supervision session, where the coach can explore his own attitudes and approaches and can challenge himself and be challenged by someone he values and admires?

Hawkins and Smith (2006) defined supervision as "the process by which a coach, with the help of a supervisor, can attend to understanding better both the client system and themselves as part of the client-coach system, and by doing so transform their work and develop their craft". After which Hawkins (2011) emphasised the relevance the relationship between supervisor and coach has, and how it leads to transformation.

With both these definitions we are clear that it is fundamental that the relationship between both supervisor and coach is open and candid so that growth and transformation might take place. However, the growth and transformation are not just for the coach. The beauty resides in the fact that both coach and coach supervisor will benefit from the challenge, growth and transformation mentioned; this is where reciprocity[7] comes into play.

Supervision is a process that started in the therapeutic environment, where therapists have their own supervisors to clarify ideas, ensure quality of practice and receive mentoring on their development in the profession. At the beginning, when coaching supervision was not yet so developed, many

---

7 Reciprocity – According to Verywellmind "Reciprocity is a process of exchanging things with other people, in order to gain a mutual benefit. The norm of reciprocity, sometimes referred to as the rule of reciprocity, is a social norm where if someone does something for you, you then feel obligated to return the favour".

DOI: 10.4324/9781003087502-8

coaches were receiving supervision from trained supervisors in psychotherapy or counselling. Hawkins (2011) states that the first coaching supervision training took place in 2003 and the first research into coaching supervision came only in 2006. It distinguished this type of supervision as coaching supervision, to differentiate from other professions' supervision. The seven eyed model (Figure 8) was adapted for use from therapy to become the leading model in coaching supervision.

Many supervisors use this implicitly or explicitly in their supervisory work. This is a way of looking at case work from multiple perspectives while allowing a focus not just on the client but the client's system, the coach, the relationship between coach and client, the coach-supervisor interaction, and any parallel processes rippling through the entire system.

Coaching supervision is key for both individual and team or group coaching, especially in topics that are linked with mental health and also the coach's own development and competencies enhancement.

Most recently, supervision of supervision became the focus of research conducted by Dr Michel Moral and Eve Turner (Moral and Turner, 2019). The findings of their research showed that supervision of supervision is becoming established across the globe and the key benefits are twofold. First, the in-depth reflection and second, a different perspective on development. According to the majority of respondents in this survey, they acknowledge that the relationship in supervision of supervision is more adult, more

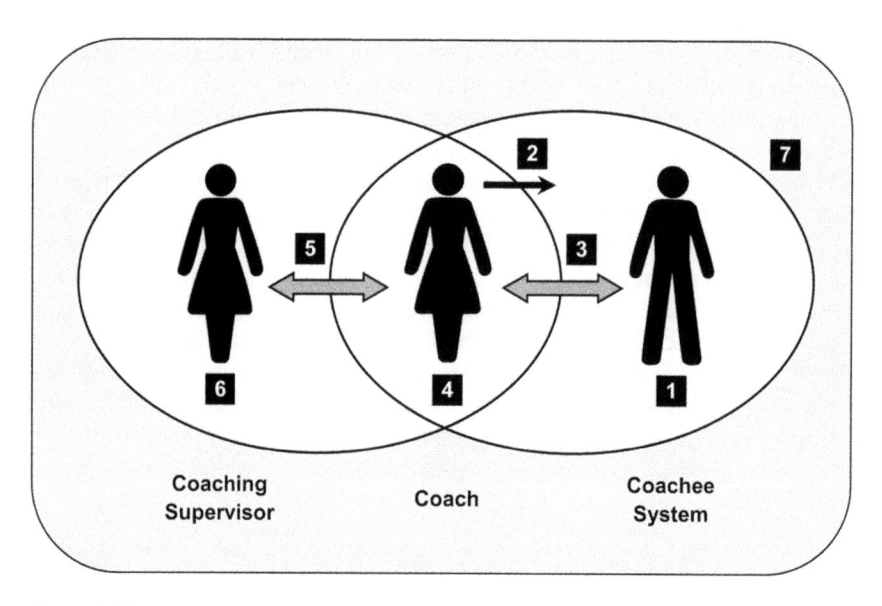

Figure 8 The seven eyed model adapted from Munro-Turner (2021).

in-depth and more generative, focussing greatly on ethics and assuaging risk, on answers into the VUCA world, and finally on systemic representations.

Regardless of what level of supervision you are taking, it is paramount that you get supervision. Some coaches prefer group supervision to individual supervision, as they manage to get answers to their issues whilst learning from the case studies that others bring and additionally increasing their own network. Obviously, group supervision will not explore in as much depth compared to individual supervision, where the coach is much more exposed and might learn much more about themselves compared to the more superficial result one might get from a group setting.

As coach supervisors, we do value and promote group supervision sessions, even though they might be considered a quick fix, a rapid solution for the coach's issue. Metaphorically speaking, it is the entrance porch of a house, where you meet and greet and where you adjust yourself before going into the house and explore the topics (the rooms) in more detail. Some houses (some issues) we want to get closer, go in, explore, question, challenge, and leave stronger, more knowledgeable. For some other houses, it is enough to stay out in the porch and understand what could be inside or focus more on the links to the external parts, like the garden, the garage, etc. which might reflect relationships with sponsors, organisations, bodies, and others.

So, what happens in a coaching supervision session? And what happens in a coaching supervision session where bereavement is the topic?

Cochrane and Newton (2011) mention that supervision has three functions: management, support, and development, which are the vertices of what they call the supervision triangle (see Figure 9). This terminology is in line with Proctor (2000) who refers to supervision has having three main pillars: normative, restorative, and formative. Whilst in the normative element, one focusses on the quality control and resolution management of any issues brought, the restorative lays much more emphasis on encouraging emotional experiencing and support, and finally the formative is based on the development of competencies and capabilities for the long term.

For supervision to really work it needs to create a balance between all these three pillars, very much like a three-legged stool. If by any chance one of the legs is damaged, there is a likelihood that the stool collapses or is less useful, meaning the coaching supervision relationship might continue even though one of its objectives is not being served.

If the coach supervisor is too focussed on the normative or the management element, she might become too rigid and not allow space for the supervisee to grow as the space might be filled with black or white approaches to the issues brought and be based on a working environment such as "I know, you don't know". This might occur with topics linked

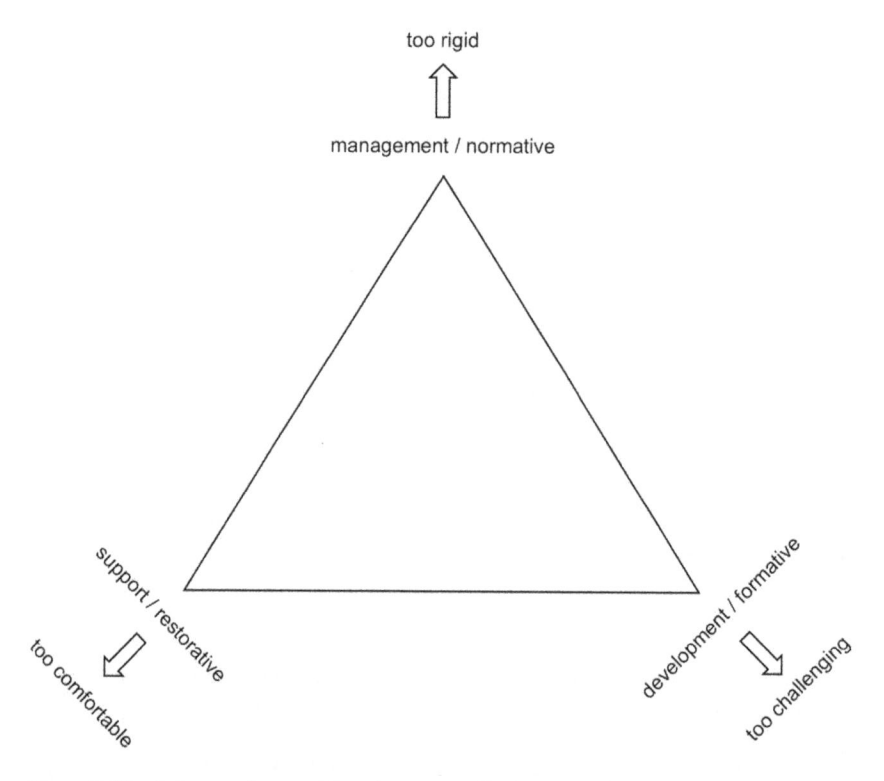

Figure 9 The balance of supervision functions. Cochrane and Newton (2011).

with ethics dilemmas brought by the supervisee. Supervisors with a D and C DISC[8] profile might tend to dwell in this function.

If the coach supervisor is too supportive and focusses too much or too long on the restorative function, then the supervision might become too comfortable. This might be the case for issues linked with bereavement and not being fit for practise due to personal illness of the coach or even their family members. The supervision becomes too cosy, the challenge is too little, and the encouragement is high. Supervisors with an I or S DISC profile might have the tendency to stay in this function.

If the coach supervisor is too focussed on the formative part, this means that she relies on the developmental function and therefore the supervision might become too challenging and in fact might become too much for a

---

8 DISC is a behavioural self-assessment tool which centres on four personality traits: D for dominance, I for Influence, S for Steadiness and C for Conscientiousness or Compliance, creating the four DISC styles. (www.en.wikipedia.org)

coach who comes to supervision to get some help in tackling his issues within the coaching relationship. Supervisors with a strong D profile might also dwell on this function.

> *According to* Cochrane and Newton (2011) *the answer resides in combining the functions by combining the ends of each axis in the supervision triangle. Therefore, we can combine management and support which leads to the compliance of standards, ensuring safety and safeguarding ethics. We can also combine education (development) and management leading to promoting growth within the system and a learning context, which are the basis for collaboration. And finally, we can combine support and education which leads to co-creation where the learning relationship provides awareness of parallel processes and opportunities for reciprocity.*[9]

Many different topics may be brought in to coaching supervision from ethical dilemmas to reinforcement of approaches, competency development, and exploration of triggers and how to reach the best coach version for a specific client. When it comes to coaching through bereavement it is common that the topics brought in are related to two dimensions: the client's dimension and the coach's dimension.

Within the client's dimension, one can identify themes that are very much linked with more tools or exercises to help the client navigate through bereavement of loss in general or death in particular; sometimes even confirmation of the type of questions used or methods applied (refer to "The Bereaved Coaching Client" section of this book).

However, it is within the coach's dimension that supervision can tap into the enormous potential of the coach, as it explores triggers, hidden themes, and patterns, and will enable the coach to understand what is conditioning her approach. Some of these triggers, already mentioned in this book, allude to memories brought by a certain expression or gesture the client used, or might bring back feelings that were not yet fully dealt with. It is in this moment, that it makes sense to revisit the idea of the coach being, or not, fit for practise. And if the answer is "not really" that is okay, because it allows the coach to choose to protect herself and the profession from doing anything that is not adequate or conforming (such as telling, instructing, or break down in the session) and get appropriate support.

It is relevant to highlight that supervision also works on two levels:

---

9 Parallel process is a phenomenon noted between coach and supervisor, whereby the coach recreates, or parallels, the client's problems by way of relating to the supervisor. By opening ourselves as supervisors to the experience of others, we might start to have that experience ourselves. (Cochrane and Newton, 2011).

'back there and then', and 'the here and now'. The continuing development of the conscious competence of the coach who is the supervisee, is what makes supervision so enlightening, as it uncovers themes that might have been hidden in the back 'there and then' and somehow show up in 'the here and now'. The safe space provided in this learning relationship and the supervisor's attitude in naming and being curious with what is happening in the 'here and now', help the supervisee see more clearly what has been hindering, blocking, or simply conditioning the best version of the coach within themselves.

"We don't take cases to supervision. We are the cases."
–John Patton

For those who are coaching supervisors, the expression "personal intruding the professional" might be familiar. It is important that we as coaches and coaching supervisors are aware that our 'hot buttons', ways of being, thinking, and acting intrude in our professional side. The dosage is key: if too much it might be unhelpful, but also if the supervisor does not show her human side it might create a sterile unbalanced relationship that avoids learning altogether. As in everything, the answer lies in the balance between things.

Helping the coach with client bereavement – ethical best practice

One of our main concerns as coaches is to feel that we are helping the client with whatever topic they bring and do no harm. When it comes to helping the client navigate through the enormous change a bereavement throws at us, there are a few aspects to be aware of.

One of them is how far do we as coaches go in a coaching session when grief comes up? As already discussed, some aspects of our work combine many competencies that a therapist would also use in a therapy session. However, the focus is different and we as professionals need to understand where the focus lies and where do we draw the line and refer to someone who has more expertise.

The Global Code of Ethics for Coaching is very clear on the guidelines it sets on the ability to perform. Point 4.1 — "Members will operate within the limit of their professional competence. Members should refer the client to a more experienced or suitably qualified practicing member where appropriate" —clearly states that coaches need to be very conscious of when they are out of their depth and are to refer to other colleagues who have more experience and qualifications on that specific field.

What we have learnt is that when the client is in an apathetic, lethargic state, or even when they are embedded in deep sadness, then it is better to refer to therapy. We will see this by the appearance the person has —but mainly the voice tonality — the energy the person lacks, and what they share about themselves and the situation they are going through. When the client is sad, and still focusses on today and tomorrow and you can entice a conversation about activities to do with carrying on living and looking ahead, then this indicates that coaching is appropriate to them.

> *On the contrary, if the client does not make eye contact, doesn't smile, doesn't answer the majority of the questions we pose, or answers, "I don't know", "I can't even think about it", or "it doesn't matter anymore", and doesn't reply to any mild challenge we pose them, all these indicate that the person might be in need of therapy.*

According to coach and supervisor Marie Faire, even though coaching might not be the best approach in some cases, if we have the client in front of us there and then, we are not going to shut the door and refer them to another practice in that moment. The worst the coach could do is to turn their back on someone who is in need. If the coach does not know what to do in that moment, then just listen, pay attention, and reflect back, maybe even without an objective for the session per se, just holding that space, not shutting it down. And then as the session draws to a close it is important that we then discuss the possibility of a therapist with the client. Ethically speaking, it is as bad to do coaching when what it is required is another sort of help, as it is to shut the door, and not hold the space and listen to someone who really needs to be listened to.

It is in this transition phase that coaches can have a tremendous positive impact on bereaved clients, as they help the client identifying the emotions they are going through and create and/or accept the new beginning that is unfolding ahead for them.

The support and challenge the coach can provide also include the exploration of the new identity and the new narrative the client wants to build for themself. As this is explored, more triggers might be fired off and the coaching partnership will then be ready to tackle them one at a time, to understand what its impact is in the new beginning and what the future might look like.

When the client rejects the idea of the new identity and the narrative created continues to be in the past then this is also a hint that therapy might be the best solution for the time being.

> *Another type of support the coach can contribute is the normalising of the grief coming through the loss one had. It is normal to feel bereaved, grieved, mourning. Normalising reconfirms to the client that they are not exaggerating nor being inadequate by feeling those emotions. However, do pay attention here, as there is also a line that might be crossed. It is normal to some extent.*

As we have stated, everyone grieves differently and feels differently. Whilst there is no one recipe for these situations, one intuitively also understands when the intensity of the feelings is not adequate and surplus to the scope of the coaching session. Coaching is also being okay with the unknown. When you do not feel okay, this is already a hint that something is ringing an alarm bell. The best advice we can offer you at this moment is to involve your supervisor, or in the case you do not have one, get one and explain the situation and what it is doing for you. Together with someone who has more experience and sees the situation from outside and in a systemic way, you will find the best solution for that case – which might be to continue to coach the client, or simply to refer them to another therapist/colleague.

One other concern that coaches have is about paying even more attention to being empathic, as sympathy is a whole new temptation when the client is looking so fragile in front of us, especially when we have been through the same type of loss like losing a loved one. In these situations, being self-aware is paramount, namely, understanding that our triggers are going to fire off and what is our normal response to them. Let us provide a concrete example: a client who is a mother and has recently lost her son and the coach who is also a mother who has gone through the same loss. Coaching this situation might trigger something and take her back to that moment of loss; re-feeling everything again might be very vivid and if this coach also has a nurturing preference, then they might accept the temptation to dwell in sympathy for too long. On the opposite side, if the coach prefers structure, it might be that she does not allow time for the client to understand and explore the emotions and the feelings they are going through.

To resolve this situation, it is clear the pace in a coaching session is the one that belongs to the partnership, not the coach. The coach who listens and partners with the client to define when the best moment is to move forward will be serving the client.

The best ethical practices require the coach to apply empathy and compassion, not sympathy. As we earlier suggested: be a heart with ears! For all the cases, the best practice is to provide the psychological safety, because with it the client can just be, share the load with us, with the world, empty their own vessel and make room for new perspectives, new feelings, new beginnings.

Re-contracting also is considered best practice. If the circumstances have changed then even a different type of coach might be better – be it more supportive or on the contrary not taking everything at face value and seeking to challenge the bereaved client.

As you read this last line, the word "challenge" may feel alarming. You might be thinking, "I don't want to add more stress to the life of my supervisee", "I don't want to be the one who throws the client into another sad situation". Firstly, it is important that the coach understands that when we have someone feeling sad and fragile in front of us, the balance could change and what might be normal to explore before, now becomes more intense. Pay attention to what is going on for you too, as this might take you away from the partnership and centre in yourself and your ego. If that is the case, refocus, take a deep breath, name what you are going through: "I don't want to add more to your plate …". Do not hide from your coaching role and downsize the challenge the client needs to listen to, needs to be confronted with, needs to be put in front of him or her. Timing becomes even more important, as this might signal the (un)conscious intention of remaining in sorrow and creating excuses to stay in a less functional dynamic, compared to the one the client deserves or even requires, to reach their objective or to navigate through the change that bereavement brought to them.

So, do not let sympathy or your own fears of adding more to their plate, take over your presence and powerful questioning skills. After all, it is a coaching session.

Another relevant point that raises concerns for coaches is to share or not to share their own stories, narratives, and examples. Whilst some may feel this is not coaching, as extensively mentioned in the literature and in Part II of this book, only the coach can make a judgement call in that specific moment as to what to share or not to share at all. Obviously, the session remains the client's, but if the coach highjacks that session and starts to share the way she has grieved and what happened to her and advises the dos and don'ts of navigating through loss in general, clearly this is wrong and should not happen, and it is a clear violation of the Code of Ethics.

Nevertheless, there are moments when the coach can share a sentence, a moment with the client, with the intention to provide reassurance, confirmation that life works in mysterious ways, and that loss knocks on everyone's door. Our judgement call in the here and now is to create a bridge to create common ground with the client that will strengthen even more the relationship. As in everything it is also a matter of 'dose' – even the 'antidotes' have a certain percentage of 'poison'. So, be mindful of what is the most appropriate dose of you sharing your own story. If the client looks aloof, or on the contrary, too interested in what you did next and how that made you feel, those are signals that it is time to stop. They might be looking for a recipe and a step-by-step approach on how to live their own bereavement.

Sometimes, it is okay to share a moment or two, for the sake of providing a different perspective and new way of going through something that seems similar. But not from a place "do it as I did it", "I know it better", or "I have been there, where you are now".

> *All of these unbalance the learning partnership that the coaching relationship has created and the bond between you two might be negatively impacted by it.*

Essentially, we need to dance in the moment to the 'music' the system is playing, which might not be the one the client brought in the first place, which has evolved to into something else, serving him and informing the partnership of what needs to move forward.

There are some useful real-life perspectives in Appendix 2 from our research that might aid some reflection on the ethics of this.

Academic Jonathan Passmore and coach and supervisor Eve Turner (Turner and Passmore, 2019) have developed an ethical decision-making framework that acts as a practical tool for coaches and supervisors, helping them to navigate through ethical dilemmas and to raise their ethical awareness to the next level. The framework is based on the acronym APPEAR, with each of the words representing a step of the process.

Both authors of this model advocate that the practices related to ethical dilemmas vary from professional to professional, therefore their aim when developing the APPEAR model was providing coaches and supervisors with an easy way to reflect on ethics and to take more ethically informed decisions. This model can be applied in coaching supervision and also in supervision of supervision.

The model integrates six stages:

- **Awareness** – In this stage, several aspects of awareness are explored between the professional and their supervisor, which can go from self-awareness: exploring topics such as own values, belief system, and cultural identities, to awareness of what is going on in the system, what other peers are doing, what is accepted, and non-accepted by the community of practice, by the law, or the organisational norms.
- **Practice** – This is the stage where coaches put into practice what they have explored with their supervisors, engaging with their clients in a way that reflects the awareness that has been awaken at the previous stage.
- **Possibilities** – At this point, the purpose is to generate alternative courses of action the coach or supervisor could take. Sometimes it can start with a simple brainstorming based on "I could do A or B", and as the conversation with the peer or supervisor evolves, more options are explored contributing to a more informed picture.
- **Extending the field** – In this stage, the aim is to start extending the thinking of the coach or supervisor by considering a wider frame and by exploring the entire system where the ethical dilemma is occurring. A call to the indemnity insurance provider could be an example.
- **Acting on reflections** – This stage is based on the creation of an action plan, namely steps, timings, and whose support is required to implement the course of action.

- **Reflecting on learning** – There are two types of learning reflections: the one that is related to the process and the various stakeholders involved, which will inform what they have learnt as coaches, and the type of reflections that focus on the issue and themselves which will inform what they have learnt about themselves in the process. The fact that these reflections act upon these two dimensions – professional and personal – will generate new insight and contribute to a masterful journey.

According to the authors, even though there are no guarantees to a successful outcome in all circumstances related to a given ethical situation, what the model grants is an increase in the professional's sensitivity and awareness in their practice by considering a variety of factors that goes way beyond checking the code of ethics. For Turner and Passmore (2019) the importance of having a more reflective approach to resolution of ethical dilemmas is crucial.

It is interesting that for some, ethics is a topic that comes when something wrong happens and therefore, they need to act upon something that has already occurred and needs some damage control or collateral damage analysis. Whilst for other practitioners, ethics is something you reflect upon in a conditional state: how would it be if …, what if this would happen to me …, anticipating future uncomfortable situations, running your own practice in a way as to avoid these situations and/or to resolve them even before they arise.

To which one of these clusters do you belong?

Helping the coach with bereavement – their own pain, grief and loss

The role of coach supervisor is a privilege. The working alliance between coach and supervisor has many similarities between coach and client but in some ways, it is quite different. For many supervisors, their relationship with supervisees is based on many hours, months, and sometimes years of working together on topics that can range from "What went wrong with this client at the last session" all the way to "Who am I as a coach and person and how do I want to live my life and develop my career in line with my values."

To get the best from supervision, the relationship must cultivate trust and generate a safe environment in which the courage to be vulnerable becomes the norm. This is hugely beneficial for both coach, supervisor and ultimately the client (who they are both in service to). However, this can be a double-edged sword. The closer the relationship between coach and supervisor, the more compassion one can feel towards the suffering of another. When a supervisee brings a deeply personal loss issue (either generated from something happening to them, or via a client issue) then the challenge for the supervisor is to work compassionately with their supervisee while maintaining a frame for their work together. The bottom line is that this is not therapy for the coach, and a supervisor has a duty of care to the supervisee and coachee if relevant. However, sometimes a coach will need their supervision session to have a largely supportive or restorative focus.

Some considerations when grief and loss enter the supervision room:

- The immediate response of the supervisor with a bereaved coach.
- Identifying when a coach needs therapy.
- Discussing a retriggered loss response.
- Resilience building in coaching supervision.
- Polishing the personal and professional mirror.

How might a supervisor work with a coach experiencing a sense of loss?

The immediate response

A good example here would be a coach requiring an 'emergency' supervision session because one of their elderly parents has been diagnosed with a serious illness. This can create anticipatory grief and a question mark over whether the coach feels fit for practice in the short term. Sometimes this is only temporary after the initial shock has subsided, with the coach requiring space to formulate a practical plan of action to postpone client work for only a few days. Being able to verbalise what to write in an email, or what to say in a phone call to a coachee, can be helpful to work through with a supervisor. However, this type of scenario also stirs up other emotions for the coach on what to share with clients during the emotionally heightened initial stages of such a diagnosis. Later, what might a coach do – particularly as life and coaching work resumes and goes on alongside the inevitable challenges of supporting a parent in a long process to recovery, or at worst a terminal diagnosis?

Here is a real example of a coach bringing personal loss to supervision and are extracts from a supervisor's notes.

> AB arrived on the session to tell me that her mum is terminally ill and may have only months to live. This explains why she had moved back to her hometown which she had not shared with me before. She wondered how much to say in our supervision, so we had a discussion on how she is resourcing herself to be fit enough to do client work and to be vigilant of anything within the work that may chime with her situation. She said she would probably take a month off when it happens. I did initially think she was underplaying the relevance to her coaching work but by the end there was an appreciation of keeping herself from harm. Later we got into some case work, and I wondered if I feared to challenge her in places because of her news.

The next supervision session was ten months later:

> AB spent the first 15 minutes talking about her mum who died six months ago. She reported feeling OK and had wondered if it would hit her later although she did say that she probably did her grieving at the time of the diagnosis. AB looked fresher and unburdened. She had spoken to a psychotherapist colleague about issues with client work and whether to tell them or not about her bereavement. AB decided to alter the message depending on the client. She had not had any problems yet except one client who talked about her own mum's death for about 10 minutes and AB felt a slight wobble but was alright. She has a referral for a counsellor but may leave it a while as she has only recently come out of a counselling relationship. Will check in again next time.

Coaches can be fearful of how much they want to remain private about this type of situation and how much may be helpful to share with a client. After all, we are all human and showing some of this 'courageous vulnerability' in a managed and professional way can be useful for clients to witness. It is an opportunity to role-model a way of being that is not often allowable and can be frowned upon in a corporate context. Some coaches have reported that it felt more honest to flag up possible interference to clients, so if anything triggered for them in a coaching session it would be easier to discuss with clients. Other coaches have said that a sensitive sharing has sometimes elicited new information from their clients about their own experience of grief and loss which has then created significant shifts of insight in the overall coaching. Clients may unconsciously need permission in this way, to disclose more taboo subjects. This does contain a health warning, though, for supervisors. Every scenario is different, and supervisors must facilitate their supervisee in working out what is best for them right now and then perhaps later. A distressed and ill coach is not going to be a good or safe coach. A coach who appears to be close to doing harm to self or burning out by soldiering on, while showing obvious signs of not coping, is not safe or ethical. Coaches and supervisors may have to be more prescriptive and directive than they may like to be if they see this happening. On these rare occasions, a supervisor may have to clearly state: "I'm deeply concerned about your wellbeing and that of your clients. I strongly suggest you do not carry on working currently. How can I support you to find a way of taking some time off from your practice even if only temporarily?"

Additionally, the supervisor would do well to take this to their own supervision to check that they are not taking too much responsibility for their supervisees by being parental or engaging in rescuing behaviours.

Paying attention to the following will help a supervisor to gauge what may be required as duty of care to supervisees and ultimately the coaching clients. Many of the indicators we noted for coaching clients will be the same for supervisees at a personal level. The difference is when it may impact on their work as a coach.

Being recently bereaved as a coach can hinder a coaching relationship due to:

- Assumptions – based on our early experiences about what behaviour is expected around grief and loss.
- Unconscious bias – attitudes, experiences, cultural norms, expectations that are unique to an individual.
- Projection – pushing grief away and placing the anxiety elsewhere.
- Risk of not being fully present. The interference of trying to put our own feelings into a box.
- Not fit to practice, for example "grief brain" – memory loss, fuzzy thinking.
- Retriggering of previous trauma/loss issues (see Part II, trauma'). "The Lens of Trauma".

However, being bereaved as a coach can be in service to the client because of:

- Being comfortable with vulnerability and more intense emotions– for example shame, guilt.
- Ability to explore deeper and/or some other aspects.
- Building a different type of empathy.
- Being a role model for compassion and self-compassion.
- Bereavement occurring some time ago and therefore less emotional.

What to pay attention to as a supervisor with a bereaved coach:

- Making a health and wellbeing question a standard part of contracting with all supervisees to initiate an invitation to consider physical and mental health awareness for coaching competency.
- Re-contracting for the coaching work – check whether this can be done even temporarily to allow a breathing space for the coach.
- Referral to other coach/counsellor – if the coach has a long-term problem, then other support may be necessary.
- Ethical Sensitivity: is the coach fit to practise right now? Possibly later with this client? Perhaps never at all? Can the coach ever work with this client or does someone else need to take on the work?
- Consider as a supervisor one's own self-care and possible triggers as parallels with the supervisee and coachee. It is vital to engage with supervision of supervision.

Coach case study: Grieving and the restorative relief of supervision

My partner's father became seriously ill and had an extended stay in hospital, during which plans were made so he could be discharged, but he died whilst still in hospital. As we lived 180 miles away, both myself and my partner had to find ways to manage work, alongside visiting and keeping in touch with family during this time and following my partner's father's death.

I realised that I needed to look after myself, to help me support my partner, my partner's family and to be present for my partner's father, as well as ensure I was still at my best for my coachees. I was also aware it was important for me to acknowledge how I was feeling about my partner's father's health and the grief I experienced on his death.

I continued to work over the months that my partner's father was in hospital and after this death. I felt I needed a focus that provided me with the sense that I was making a difference for others and working with my coaching clients was part of this.

To maintain good coaching practice throughout this period, I found these five areas particularly helpful:

1. Supervision was critical so I was more conscious of what I may inadvertently or unconsciously bring into my coaching practice.
2. Coaching helped me acknowledge how I was feeling and recognising that looking after myself wasn't selfish but essential.
3. Techniques that helped me focus on the present and the positive things that happened each day. Mindful breathing became an essential part of my preparation before each coaching session to help me find the right frame of mind.
4. Managing my commitments in a way that enabled me to feel I could drop everything if I needed to whilst still working in a professional manner.
5. Re-evaluating my personal time to focus on activities that better held my attention and reduced the amount of time I was spending dwelling on my sense of helplessness with our situation.

However, I wasn't clearly aware of the toll it was taking on me, when my partner's father first went into hospital and our continuing visits during this time. I was so focussed on everyone else; I wasn't fully paying attention to myself.

I was careful to maintain good coaching practice with my existing clients and prepared for these sessions with care. However, it took me much longer to realise that much of my other work was slipping,

> I was struggling to focus, and I was avoiding some of the more challenging pieces of work I had previously committed to. My learning about loss was that during this time each of us processed and managed our grief in different ways. As a family experiencing grief and loss, it both brought us together and also created tension and friction amongst us.
>
> Untangling the complexity of thoughts and emotions in supervision at this time had a profound and positive effect on balancing work, coping with prolonged uncertainty and grief and maintaining well-being. Acknowledging that it's okay to not feel okay and having the space to express that, made all the difference.
>
> **Siân Taylor**
> Leadership and Executive Coach
> www.siantaylorcoaching.co.uk

Resilience building through supervision

Resilience is the ability to bounce back following challenges that have stretched us beyond our comfort zone. It is the ability to recover quickly. Being able to learn effectively is the key to resilience so that the ability to try and fail, and then learn from those experiences is crucial. We are all born with a certain amount of resilience but then it's a question of how we build this up through our lives.

As coaches we often work with clients on this topic but how good are coaches at building their own resilience? As described earlier, supervision has a restorative or supportive aspect too which can often be overlooked. It is an opportunity to receive support; both practical and emotional in the sense of sharing issues and when appropriate reassurance, to avoid coach burn out and/or mental health issues, that is do no harm to self.

Our experience of supervision is that a coach's self-care is not always explicitly focussed upon until desperately required, either due to a personal event such as the family one described earlier or a more work-focussed issue that a coach is struggling to deal with because fatigue is interfering with their ethical decision-making process. It is hard to do a good coaching job when you are tired.

> Julia had a supervisee struggling to engage with a client. On exploration it emerged that the coach was working at an organisation on a retainer package which almost made him a de facto internal coach. Some days he was completing four or five ninety-minute coaching sessions in a day on consecutive days. The perceived lack of

engagement with his clients was unsurprising at the end of a working day after writing coaching notes and grabbing lunch on the run. By holding up the mirror to the coach it became obvious to him that he had created this situation himself by agreeing to the contract in this way and that he was not doing a particularly good job because of tiredness and memory issues. He often forgot the name of his last coachee and what they looked like. He was in danger of completely burning out and not exactly a good role model for his busy clients. As we like to say, "Take care of your wellness or you will be forced to take care of your illness."

There are two key ways to become more resilient:

1 Building resilience through renewal and wellbeing.
2 Building character through adversity.

1 Building resilience through renewal and wellbeing

Luckily, most coaches avoid extreme burnout situations nevertheless a useful way to bring this topic explicitly into the supervision room is to focus on renewal and wellbeing. This is about paying attention to their work-life balance and ensuring their bank balance of nourishing activities (those that feed mind, body and soul) regularly outweigh any depleting activities (those that drain energy and enthusiasm). Many coaches do some of these things well but sometimes not systematically or regularly. The crucial thing is that these things need to be worked on and built up before they are needed. As the old saying goes, "It's best to fix your roof when the sun is shining".

A good model for supervisors to use with their supervisees is to explicitly introduce the self-care wheel below. Figure 10 "Coaching Excellence", puts the requirement for self-care into context so that a coach sees it an essential part of their coaching practice and in no way just a 'nice to have'.

Figure 11 "The self-care wheel for coaches" then takes the discussion to the next level by stimulating reflections on which areas may need more focus and support like sleep, inspirational people, or surroundings to rejuvenate, and give spiritual succour.

To make ourselves springy and bouncy we need to be proactive about taking care of ourselves and show ourselves some compassion. As they imply on aeroplanes during the safety demonstrations, "if you don't put your own oxygen mask on first; you can't help anyone else with theirs".

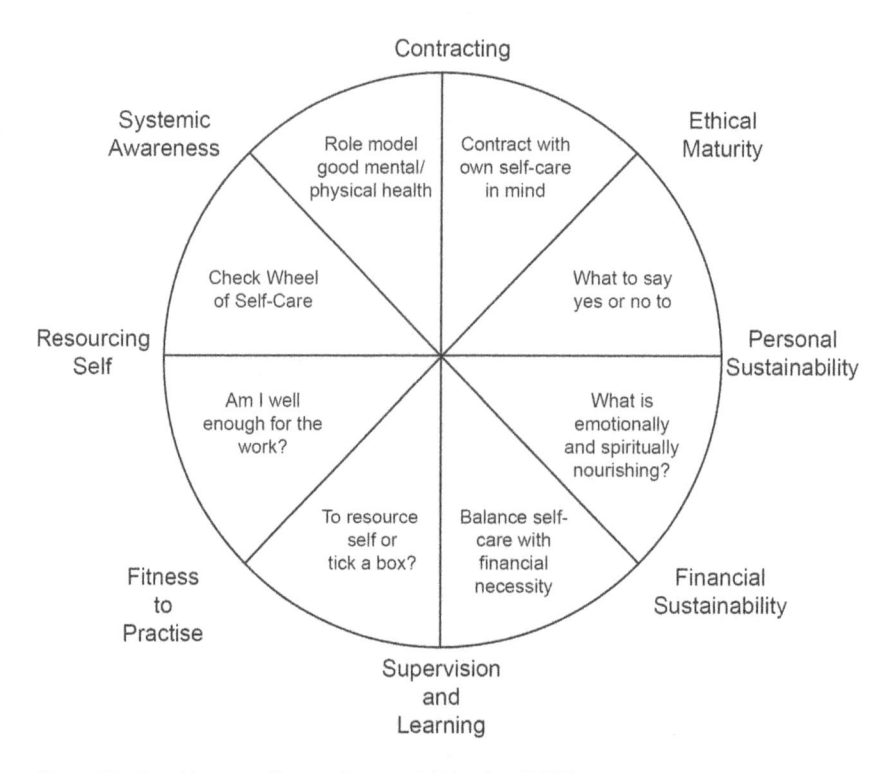

Figure 10 Coaching excellence. Ross and Wonfor (2019).

2 Building character through adversity

Coaching and supervision can help us develop the core inner "selfs" that Seibert (2005) describes. They are self-confidence, self-esteem, and self-concept. As we saw earlier many of these are behaviours driven from childhood experiences; however, self-concept develops as we get older or sometimes problems occur for people if their self-concept is tied up in external things such as a job role. When this is taken away by retirement or redundancy then these type of people can crumble because their idea of themselves is not built on a solid core of their own emotional self-worth.

One of the other ways that coaching can help to build resilience is to examine our thinking styles and look at how sometimes the way we think and view the world affects our resilience because of our response to adverse events.

This can be summed up by:

EVENT + RESPONSE = OUTCOME

The same two people can experience the same event, for example redundancy, bereavement, but how they respond will impact on the eventual

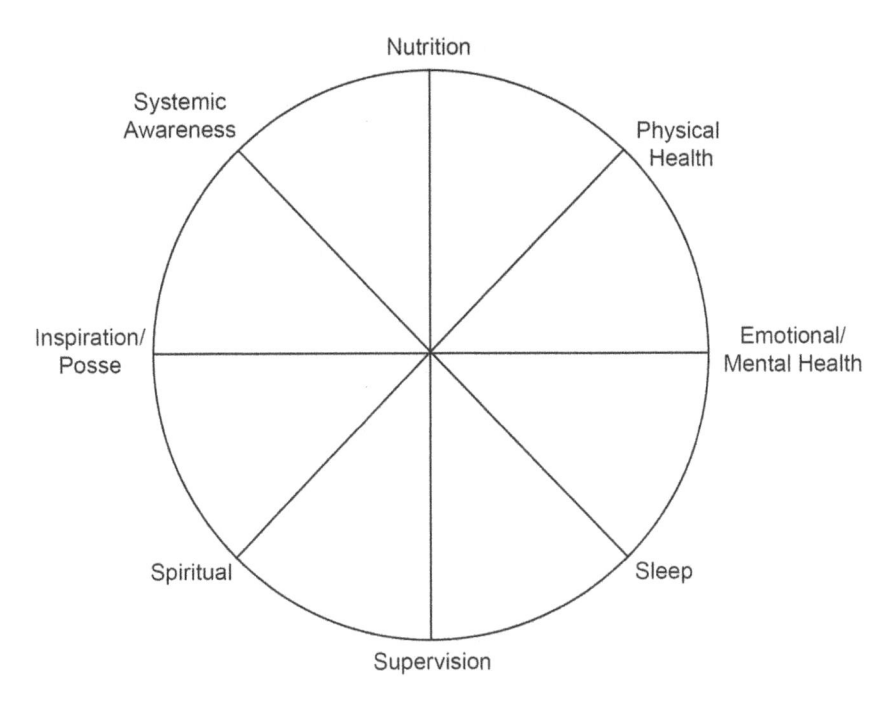

Figure 11 The self-care wheel for coaches Ross and Wonfor (2019).

Wheel segments (clockwise from top): Nutrition, Physical Health, Emotional/Mental Health, Sleep, Supervision, Spiritual, Inspiration/Posse, Systemic Awareness.

outcome. This may be due to external factors in their lives; however, all things being equal, it is usually down to a more positive thinking style leading to greater resilience. Thinking time allows us to widen the gap between an event and our response to it (Kline, 2002).

Giving ourselves more thinking time will help to:

- Increase our awareness of habitual patterns that take us into habitual thoughts and feelings.
- Unpick and unpack some of our values and beliefs and the consequences of holding them.
- Become more flexible in our thinking – less single-tracked, so we can generate more solutions to life's problems.
- See things we can control or influence in some way as being distinct from things we cannot control and therefore should not waste valuable resources on (resources being our energy and thinking time).

These are all legitimate topic areas in supervision, especially with maturing coaches as they start to move from Level 1 and 2 perspectives (self- and client-centred) through to Level 4 (process in context-centred) (Hawkins and Smith, 2006), which we discuss later in Part II.

Resilient coaches are therefore more able to handle bereavement, grief, and loss issues compassionately and competently without overidentifying with their client and/or rushing to rescue, or even withdrawing in fear.

When a coach might need therapy

As we discussed earlier it is not a coach's responsibility or within their skill set to diagnose, and this is similar for supervisors. However, supervisors by their training and experience may have more knowledge or even a gut feel that this intervention is appropriate. As with coachees, the emphasis is on a dialogue between supervisor and supervisee to discuss a way forward. Where it is different in supervision is that the supervisor has duty of care for both the supervisee and their coaching client. This may lead to certain situations where the supervisor must be more directive from an ethical standpoint and strongly urge a coach to stop coaching and seek other help.

As we discussed earlier it would be rare for a coach to dismiss their supervisor's recommendation but if they did, a gentle reminder of the section of the ethical code that refers to being fit for practice is essential.

This would be alongside a discussion on what could happen and what would be the risk to health and reputation of the coach (as well as duty of care and competence toward coachee). The same rules that we abide by as coaches around breaking confidentiality and officially 'reporting' a client, would be the same for supervisees (if in the extremely rare occurrence that a coach disregarded something serious that did harm to self or other, or broke the law).

Retriggered loss response

Some of the above focusses on a supervisor's duty towards their supervisee in the immediate aftermath of a bereavement but what might a supervisor do with a supervisee who has an emotional reaction to something from the coaching system that connects to an old loss?

The following case study is an example of how it may manifest in supervision and would be applicable to most scenarios brought to supervision.

Julia's supervision case study: Guilt revisits from the past

Francesca warned me by email before her supervision session that she was bringing something quite personal and emotional for her. We had worked together for ten years so I was curious about what this could be but felt honoured that she was going to share it with me.

She started off tentatively telling me about her client, Janine, who she had been coaching on and off for about two years. I remember we had talked about Janine before on a work-related topic; however, Francesca had never shared before that Janine had been going through fertility treatment for many years and that it had always been a background theme as Janine went through the turmoil of numerous IVF cycles. This time however Janine arrived at her session to declare that she and her husband had decided to stop treatment because of the financial and emotional burden it was taking on them both. Janine was still trying to come to terms with the fact that this most surely meant that at age 45 she would never have a baby. Up until this point Francesca had been supportive and encouraging with Janine and they had built a solid relationship together. However, Janine's decision had "completely floored" Francesca and she was unsure how she could continue her work. Initially I was puzzled by the strength of Francesca's emotions which seemed out of proportion and I initially wondered whether their relationship had started to develop into a friendship and unhealthy dependency.

First, I asked what the feelings were and then if there was fear but that didn't seem to be productive. As soon as I asked, "Is there shame?", then Francesca began to sob and out poured her own story. Francesca shared with me that twenty-five years ago she had had a termination at eight weeks pregnant. At the time she felt it was the right decision because she had only known her partner for a few months and had just started a new job. The story of visiting the clinic and being accosted by anti-abortion protesters in the car park had added to the trauma for her and as the years wore on, she began to regret her decision and actions. She later had a son but lived with the sadness that she may have made a mistake back then. She was equally adamant that she still supported a woman's right to choose. However, she was feeling racked with guilt about the termination as she compared this to Janine who could not have any children. Francesca felt she could "no longer look her in the eye" and show empathy without feeling a fraud. Francesca had discussed this with counsellors at various points in her life and had felt she had found a place of peace and acceptance she could live with until Janine's news.

We explored the guilt and what that meant for her relationship with Janine. She knew she would never be able to share her own story, but would she be able to support Janine whilst keeping appropriate emotional boundaries for herself? Francesca was a big fan of the Thinking Environment principles by Nancy Kline, so I suggested we set a 'boundaried time' within the session where I would be her thinking partner, not get in her way by interrupting with questions or reflections but would be fully present so she could verbalise anything she wanted to. We agreed twenty-five minutes and when finished she was to say, "I'm done". Francesca initially verbalised more of her story from the past which quickly morphed into feelings of sadness, anger, self-compassion, and wistful regret. Tears flowed again. After twenty minutes, there was a long silence where we just sat together, and she appeared to run out of steam. I then asked, "What more do you want to think, feel and say about this?" This time she talked more about Janine and how she might be feeling and the compassion she felt towards her client at this difficult time and that her own experiences were irrelevant. What was more important was how she could be in service to Janine now.

Given their long working relationship she felt comfortable that she would be able to support Janine to make some emotional and practical decisions about her life and work now Janine was charting a different course for the rest of her life and career without a family. At the end, Francesca said something that struck me emotionally too, "Actually Julia, maybe I was meant to work with Janine on this and perhaps this is a way of finding meaning for myself and that some good will come out of the loss of my own child all those years ago, in service to Janine."

Polishing the personal and professional mirror

This phrase beautifully sums up the central plank of supervision. Supervision is a place to reflect on our professional capabilities and how they might grow as well as our personal growth. We believe that CPD (Continuing Professional Development) should also mean 'Continuing Personal Development', and by continuing to polish the view reflecting back at us we are able to gain a clearer picture of ourselves and our work. Becoming a master coach is a journey not a destination and supervision is a major vehicle on that journey. Hawkins and Smith (2006) and Hay (2007) describe a way of reflecting on the stages of that journey and how to move up the gears with regular reflective practice.

To be able to handle grief and loss issues as confidently as is humanly possible (an important caveat because each situation will be unique), then both coaches and supervisors would benefit from greater psychological awareness in their work. Supervisors by the very nature of their supervisor training and greater experience as coaches tend to have a stronger edifice from which to build. As discussed earlier, the seven eyed model is the foundation on which most supervisors develop their craft plus additional approaches, models and theories that blend over time. Carroll and Shaw (2013) describe this as a "philosophy of supervision", and supervision as a way of being (with insight and wisdom, albeit coming from a place of not knowing much at all).

Earlier we talked about the coach's journey in supervision and the measure of maturing competence. As well as using supervision to build resilience through the restorative function, the educative or formative function of supervision serves to develop coaches from what Peter Hawkins (2011) describes as "novice to journeyman to master craftsman".

Looking at the four stages of development through supervision, a question for coaches to hold in partnership with their supervisor is what or where is the next development edge?

Moving through the stages is not a tick box exercise but more an opportunity to provide space to dialogue (Hay, 2007).

The four levels are:

Level 1 – Self-centred
Level 2 – Client-centred
Level 3 – Process-centred
Level 4 – Process in context- centred

Level 1 and 2– Self-centred and Client-centred: has the coach moved past these two stages now on a regular basis or is there a tendency to drop back to conscious competence on occasion?

Level 1 - Self-centred:

- They still feel dependent for reassurance on their supervisor.
- They regularly feel anxious, insecure about their role as coach.
- They feel highly motivated but often not notice 'obvious' things until highlighted by the supervisor.
- Still feel apprehension about being evaluated or assessed by a supervisor.
- Do not like or expect to focus on themselves in supervision.
- Spend most time focussing on specific aspects of coach and client's history, current situation or their personality style in supervision.
- Regularly feel impatient and fearful about never being able to move on from stuckness.
- See themself leaping too soon to premature judgement of coach/client and self, for example flight into health or demonisation of client/coach.
- Looking for a lot of support from supervisor on most sessions.
- Often forget about own restoration and nurturing needs to avoid burnout until reminded by supervisor.

Level 2 – Client-centred:

- Sometimes fluctuating wildly between feeling overwhelmed and dependent on supervisor to being overconfident, for example "Yes, I can do this!" to "I'm a rubbish coach".
- Starting to notice more complexity around the client, the coach, and their story rather than seeing a single issue.

- Realising now on an emotional level that becoming a coach is long and arduous (plus slightly embarrassed about how little they knew after coach training) and that this journey does not have an end.
- Have occasionally felt disillusioned by supervision and secretly held their supervisor responsible for failing them by not being good enough.
- Noticing the supervisor starting to back off and be less structured and be more collaborative by providing emotional support for feelings oscillating between excitement and disappointment.

Level 3 – Process-centred:

- There is increased awareness of sessions where they share things with their supervisors in a collegial way that they may be interested in as an equal coach, for example, sharing stories and examples alongside professional and personal confronting.
- Most of the time they are now able to flex approach to coachees to meet individual and specific needs.
- Almost immediately they notice the wider context within the coach and client system including stakeholders and have developed helicopter skills to rise above it and look down for a bigger picture (mode 7), and can help the coachee see this.
- Able to be fully present with a coachee but also to widen out to the coach's relationship with clients (mode 3), coach/client's personal history/life patterns, coach/client's external life circumstances, coach/client's life stage, social context, ethnic background and all the parallels.
- Have now incorporated many more models, theories and other learning into their original coach training and use it frequently with coachees.

Questions to help move coaches onto and through Level 3:

- How do they regularly reflect-in action as opposed to reflect on action (as they coach or within supervision itself)?
- With coachees how comfortable are they in asking questions about their backgrounds outside of work and how do we all role model this here in supervision and in coaching?
- How much is this a regular feature of their work and with whom?
- How much do they share own self-experience with coachees?
- What do they consider cross-culturally in their work?
- How do we avoid the trap of operating within the dominant cultural paradigm (coach and supervisor)?
- How might we use supervision to consider thinking outside our existing cultural frames of reference?
- How much do they offer back to the supervisor as an equal sharing partner?

- In what ways do their styles differ (between coach and supervisor) and what impact has this had on interactions?
- In what ways are their styles similar (between coach and supervisor) and what impact has this had on interactions?
- How open have they been to being challenged professionally?
- How open have they been to being challenged personally?
- What is a parallel with what they do in supervision and therefore with their coaching clients?

Level 4: Process in context-centred:

- Now integrating all of Level 3 into the specific context in which they work. See themself as a Coach Practitioner at Master level, that is, showing personal autonomy, insightful awareness, personal security, stable motivation, awareness about confronting own personal and professional problems. Now operating from a philosophy of "Who you are is how you coach" most of the time.
- Let go of acquiring more knowledge for its own sake and not trying to find 'answers' in the 'next big thing' in the coaching profession. Their work balances authority, presence and impact in equal measure to create confident coaching relationships.
- Aware of the multiple layers in operation in between the client's system, the coach's system and supervision.
- Can feel themself shifting into a mode of integrating and deepening to a place of wisdom. Focus is often on 'being' rather than 'doing' with coachees, holding the space for clients, allowing what is needed to emerge.
- More conscious of boundaries and complexity.

Questions to help move into Level 4:

- What do they notice about the development of their own 'internal supervisor of their coaching' that monitors their work while doing it and evaluates realistically?
- What personal issues do they have that might affect their practise? What do they need to do to bring them into the light of day?
- What are their values and beliefs about themselves as a coach?
- What are their values about coachees?
- What do they get out of being a coach? What is their primary motivation for doing this work?
- Are they aware of their shadow side– for example, needs, lusts, power?
- What are they doing to increase ethical sensitivity? And therefore, the ethical sensitivity of coachees?

- How much do they look 'inwards' professionally and personally? How do they notice what is arising in everyday life in relations with others; that 'felt sense' that is present in the background of all relationships? How do they model this with coachees?
- How often/well do they get out of their head and connect more with 'knowing' via heart and gut?

This development framework is helpful for supervisors to use with coaches in order to develop long-term competences in dealing with a wider variety of coaching issues and particularly those with a psychological dimension such as grief and loss.

The death of a client

Finally, if we talk about helping a coach with their own grief and loss, we need to address what happens when the bereavement is about a current or previous coaching client. We have both had experience of a client death. Julia's experience was the suicide of a former supervisee and even though the work had finished a couple of years before, the shock was still palpable. Emotions and thoughts veer from those expected at the loss of a fellow colleague to fears around the responsibility regarding notes, record keeping and duty of care.

> **Maggie's coaching case study: The call**
>
> One day, Carla called me asking for Medical Coaching for her mother who had been diagnosed with a stage IV cancer. Carla felt her mother, Filomena, needed to talk to someone and organise some thoughts. I mentioned that coaching works if the person receiving it is willing. So, I booked a pre-session with her mother to understand if this could be some work we could do together. It turned out we could, and Filomena was very happy to talk to me about all that was happening in her life.
>
> We had three important sessions for Filomena, talking about the topics she brought up, all linked with what else she wanted to do and how to deal with her new identity and situation.
>
> A few hours before our fourth session Filomena texted saying she was not feeling so well and the medication she was now taking dried her throat and it was difficult for her to speak. We decided to postpone the call.
>
> A few days later, her daughter called. My heart pounded when I saw her name on my mobile screen. I immediately, thought Filomena had died. She hadn't. But Carla wanted to talk to me about the fact that her mother's situation had deteriorated very rapidly, and she was now in a hospice, under palliative care. Filomena could not speak

> anymore but could still hear well and Carla wanted my opinion about creating videos and photo sequences to play on her mother's room TV.
>
> I sensed the end of the line was coming and I felt an urge to write Filomena a short letter and put in my own words how I had appreciated our time together and wanted to say my goodbyes. So, three days later, I sent a text to Carla asking if it was ok for her to read to her mother a few words I had written on paper. The answer came a few minutes later by text, saying that Filomena had passed away two days before and the funeral had just finished.
>
> I never had the chance to say goodbye to Filomena nor to end our relationship. The closest I had to that was to read out loud the words I had put on paper to a cloudy sky. I was left with the feeling that in this type of coaching any session can actually be the last one. May Filomena rest in peace.

Unresolved endings

If bereavement, grief and loss are ultimately about endings then no book on this topic would be complete without discussing the theme of ending in detail. This theme can arise in supervision naturally and simply at first if, for example, a coach brings a dilemma about how to finish a coaching relationship. However, depending on the reflective abilities of the coach and their stage of development a supervisor might take the opportunity to broaden out "endings" to facilitate a deeper dive. This extends the learning edge of their supervisee towards a more systemic eclectic focus (Clutterbuck, 2020).

We often bring from childhood unresolved endings and losses and unmet needs, to belong (see attachment patterns later in Part II, "The Lens of Attachment".

Systemic constellations coach and facilitator, John Whittington in his blog (2020) talks about poorly managed and disrespectful endings in many organisations. Sometimes there can be some acknowledgement of the importance of the 'ending event' such as organisational provision of outplacement support for redundancy, retirement planning and coaching for other exits and transitions like role change or maternity leave.

Julia has been on the receiving end of losing jobs through rejection (another word for being fired), redundancy and end of a temporary contract.

> One redundancy affected me deeply and in retrospect I realise I was grief stricken and felt bereaved. This was even though the redundancy took six months to play out; plenty of time to prepare and accept. I remember people being puzzled at what they perceived as my overreaction and I heard regular comments of "don't worry you'll get

another job". This was usually followed by my swift and tearful reply of "But I don't want another job, I want this one!"

I recognise now that the role had been a turning point at an important time of my life. I had discovered my life's passion of people development, entered a warm and supportive team of co-workers who had the same values as me. The role was also a welcome distraction during another momentous ending as my first marriage began to unravel at the same time as the strain of new motherhood.

The irony was that when I first joined the organisation it took me a long time to trust my new manager and the team, because of my fear of belonging safely again after three previous jobs had ended badly, including two redundancies in only twelve months.

Coaching really came to the fore in the Covid-19 pandemic especially for the many thousands who lost their jobs. Many coaches have been doing sterling work in this area with career transition and/or outplacement coaching.

In coach supervision, a repeating theme is how many coachees are still carrying a negative legacy from previous job roles which manifest themselves in anxiety and fear about how they will move on in their careers.

In *Leavings, Endings and New Beginnings in Work* by John Whittington (2020) he reveals this toxic legacy that afflicts many employees. Leavings, endings, how and why people exit a company can often be handled badly by organisations (or completely ignored in some cases). "Career and organisational endings need to be attended to with as much care and focus as joining's – where there are often processes, rituals, information, dialogue and guidance." (Whittington, 2020)

As we saw in the earlier case study, "A peculiar transition", the death of manager can create huge ripples. The team were obviously still grieving in different ways and to different degrees whilst the organisation blithely ignored that there was anything they needed to consider about this situation with their new employee.

Not only is this disrespectful to the new leader it is also setting her up to fail as she tries to step into a system that still has lingering unfinished business swirling around this unresolved leaving. It doesn't have to be an exit as tragic as this example for it still to cause problems by not acknowledging what has gone before.

Coaches often see more day-to-day issues such as non-disclosure agreements (NDAs) as an example of companies trying to actively silence the past without fully realising the repercussions that can ripple for years. Not talking about the past does not resolve it at a psychological level; it leads to secrets and unresolved conflict.

During the Covid-19 pandemic, many of our rituals in the workplace were lost as people worked from home. Employees who could have expected a leaving party found that a few drinks in front of a Zoom screen did not really cement a sense of closure, and many found themselves cut adrift with just a brief goodbye email if they were lucky.

So as coaches, how often do we ask clients, who was in the role before them and where/why have they gone?

When we ask this question of coaches in supervision, we often spot a pattern in the career history of their client. One coach described a guarded, prickly client who was suspicious of any feedback the coach gave and interpreted open questions as a test. We quickly established that his last three jobs had all ended badly although he refused to 'unpack' what had happened because he just wanted to get on with focussing on his next career move. As we saw earlier with the five stages of transition, Bridges (2004) suggests that to have a new beginning we must start with an ending first. This client appeared to have a sequence of unfinished, painful non-endings.

Understandably, the coach was worried that his new venture would require him to actively seek feedback which she "was unsure he could handle". From his first job where he was bullied, via his next job where there was no management support, through to a recent redundancy, this coachee had inadvertently been pushed into a pattern of **not leaving well**, and then carrying this with him to the next job and then the next.

We also need to appreciate that our unresolved endings may also come from within us rather than the system that we take them into. Supervision is a great place to explore whenever a client may be bringing unresolved endings or losses from childhood and not realise that this is operating unconsciously below the surface and creating blockages to successful transition in the workplace.

Once trust has been earned in coaching, some biographical enquiry is useful to establish whether any of these 'ending patterns' are from 'there and then' and showing up in the 'here and now'. Too many coaches are scared to ask some basic questions that explore attachment patterns within family life for fear of straying into therapy. With clear contracting and an option to take deeper exploration elsewhere such as therapy, then shining a light on the past can be insightful for clients.

The "Lifelines" activity in Part III of this book, enables coachees to plot the negative and positive impacts of various moves and situations experienced in their working life, where they took a risk, how they made decisions, how they ended. So, remember to ask what came before.

References

Bridges, W., 2004. *Managing Transitions Making Most Of Change*. 2nd ed. Boston: Da Capo Press.
Carroll, M. and Shaw, E., 2013. *Ethical Maturity in the Helping Professions*. London: Jessica Kingsley.
Clutterbuck, D., 2020. An eclectic approach to coaching supervision. In: M. Lucas, ed., 101 *Supervision Techniques, Approaches, Enquires and Experiments*. Routledge.
Cochrane, H. and Newton, T., 2011. *Supervision for Coaches: A Guide to Thoughtful Work*. Routledge.
Hawkins, P., 2011. *Leadership Team Coaching*. London: Kogan Page.
Hawkins, P. and Smith, N., 2006. *Coaching, Mentoring and Organizational Consultancy: Supervision and Development*. Maidenhead: Open University Press.
Hay, J., 2007. *Reflective Practice and Supervision for Coaches*. 1st ed. Maidenhead: Open University Press.
Kline, N., 2002. *Time to Think*. London: Cassell Illustrated.
Munro-Turner, M., 2019. *The 7-Eyed Supervision Model*. [Blog] Mike the Mentor, Available at: https://www.mikethementor.co.uk/blog/the-7-eyed-supervision-model [Accessed 18 August 2021].
Moral, M. and Turner, E., 2019. Supervision of supervision for coaching and mentoring supervisors. In: Birch, J. and Welch, P. (eds.), *Coaching Supervision Advancing Practice, Changing Landscapes*. 1st ed. London: Routledge.
Proctor, B. 2000. *Group Supervision: A Guide to Creative Practice*. London: Sage.
Ross, M., and Wonfor D., 2019. *Self Care in Coaching Supervision* [Webinar]. Association of Coaching Supervisors. Available at: https://www.associationofcoachingsupervisors.com/community/aocs-april-2019-webinar-self-care-in-coaching-supervision
Seibert, A., 2005. *The Resiliency Advantage: Master Change, Thrive Under Pressure and Bounce Back from Setbacks*. Oakland, CA, USA: Berrett-Koehler Publishers Inc.
Turner, E. and Passmore, J., 2019. Mastering ethics. In: J. Passmore, B. Underhill and M. Goldsmith, eds., *Mastering Executive Coaching*. Abingdon: Routledge, p. 34.
Whittington, J., 2020 Leavings, endings and new beginnings. [Blog] *Life Love Leadership*, Available at: https://lifeloveleadership.com/leavings-endings-and-new-beginnings/ [Accessed 24 November 2020].

Chapter 6

The Changing Lens

Loss and grief through different lenses

As we have discussed, grief and loss can be viewed from varying perspectives.

We are therefore inviting practitioners who read this book to see the journey of working with bereavement as such, rather than a quest for a definitive answer. Both authors take different approaches with clients around grief and loss because of their backgrounds (including cultural influences), experiences (personal and professional) and personality.

The seven eyed model describes seeing several perspectives by means of changing lenses or outlooks on our views. This is analogous to visiting the optometrist to receive an eye test. We are presented with numerous different options of lens to ascertain what the world looks like through different strengths of lens, so we can find the right ones to aid us to see clearly. The following "Lenses" are intended to create new thinking and heighten reflective practice on grief and loss rather than a definitive approach. Also, the scope of this book restricts detailed examination of each of these major schools of thought in coaching and supervision, so we would encourage the reader to follow their interest and professional style via the reading list at the end of the chapter. We provide a brief overview of each "Lens" and then focus on the connection to bereavement, grief and loss.

- The Lens of the Drama Triangle
- The Lens of Attachment
- The Lens of Trauma
- The Lens of Neuroscience

The Lens of the Drama Triangle

The Drama Triangle (Karpman, 1968) is probably one of the most well-known models amongst coaches but how might it apply to bereavement, grief and loss?

Firstly, a brief overview of the Drama Triangle.

DOI: 10.4324/9781003087502-9

The Drama Triangle is a model of dysfunctional social interaction, created by psychotherapist Stephen Karpman in 1968. Karpman was a student of Eric Berne (who developed Transactional Analysis). Transactional Analysis (TA) was already well established in the 1950s by Berne as a response and development of family therapy after World War Two (Berne, 1967).

The importance of triangles was not new within psychotherapy, but Karpman came to see that the three-point triangle was significant. Two people left alone often have difficulty resolving conflict and will seek to include a third person to reduce tension. In therapy, this can often be the therapist, and in other circumstances it can be a coach, a facilitator, or a mediator. However, not all triangles are constructive, and the addition of a third person can be destructive in some situations.

Karpman conjectured that each point on the triangle represents a common and ineffective response to conflict, one more likely to prolong disharmony than to end it. Many people report playing out the drama (in the varying roles) inside their own minds as well as externally in dialogue with others. The Drama Triangle has been used intensively in psychotherapy but is now an addition to the psychological underpinnings of many coach training programmes.

The Drama Triangle has three roles (Figure 12) that rotate as we communicate (or transact). During an interaction, people ('players') can move positions on the triangle incredibly quickly.

The three roles are called:

- Persecutor
- Rescuer
- Victim

Each role has specific behaviours, beliefs, and perceptions associated with it. These are not roles that stay fixed, although most of us have a propensity to default to a favourite position when under some form of stress. We are all looking for some sort of 'pay-off' that can feel like a release of some sort as we try to defuse our own tension building up inside.

So, we can be all three roles at times, but not at the same time.

Here is a brief overview of each role:

> **Persecutor Role** – in the Persecutor position, we may feel threatened although our behaviour may show up as 'fight' rather than 'flight'. In this role we heap all the blame on the Victims. We can use guilt and shame to attack a Victim. As adults, you will see this in a variety of ways such as the use of ridicule, contempt, humiliation. Control and power are crucial in Persecutor mode.
>
> **Rescuer Role** – the Rescuer position can feel like a good place to be as it suggests caring and helping others. In Rescuer role, we are always working hard to 'help' other people, often through guilt (even when they

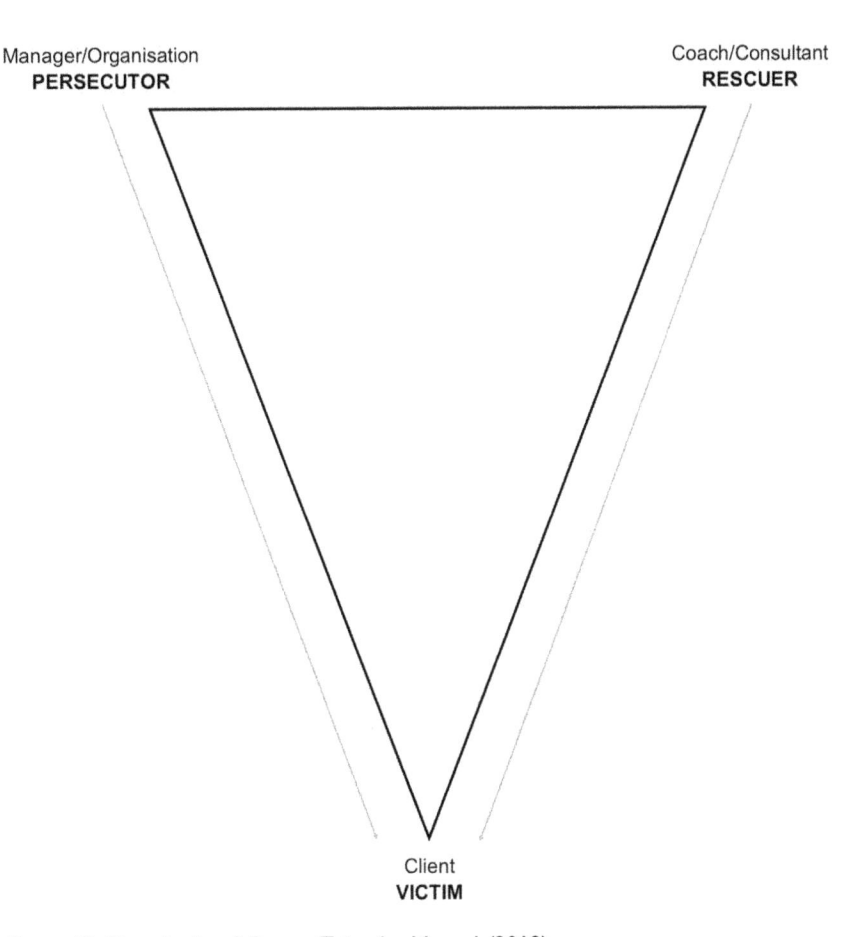

```
Manager/Organisation                                    Coach/Consultant
PERSECUTOR                                              RESCUER




                                 Client
                                 VICTIM
```

Figure 12 Organisational Drama Triangle. Menaul (2019).

haven't asked) and constantly applying short-term repairs to another's problems (usually a Victim), while neglecting our own needs. This means we end up hassled, tired, and suffering from some form of physical complaint, for example muscular pain brought on by stress, insomnia, poor eating patterns, etc. Vaughan Smith (2016) also skewers any warm fluffy feelings about being a helper with "Rescuing is a form of perpetration under the guise of kindness as it takes away the autonomy of the other and is a form of grandiosity".

Victim Role – as Victims we can be either:

a   **Pathetic Victim** – overwhelmed, helpless, and hopeless
b   **Angry Victim** – blaming, vengeful

As Victims we can deny responsibility for negative circumstances and deny possession of any power to change them.

As Victims we can also do less than half of the 'work' needed to sort out a difficult situation by pretending impotence and incompetence.

We often won't take a stand or stand up for ourselves assertively, have a tendency to act 'super-sensitive' and require kid-glove treatment. People around a Victim can feel like they are walking on eggshells waiting for the next drama to kick off.

Game playing in corporate life

In Chapter 4 "The Organisational Machine", we looked at the response of line managers and organisations to grief and loss, whether a traditional bereavement or another type of grief due to an ending. Sometimes a coach can get caught up in a drama triangle at this time due to the heightened emotional temperature of the situation. If the organisation does not appear to be sufficiently sympathetic to their employee's situation, then the organisation might be viewed as in the persecutor position by the coach and coachee. The grieving coachee may feel legitimately in the victim corner at this time after loss; however, the coach can then be drawn in as the third person in the conflict between organisation and employee. The coach may feel a real pull to rescue their client by doing too much for their client (increased communications, contacting others on their behalf, etc.) and becoming emotionally over-involved (worrying about their client **out of hours**). Empathy and compassion for the person suffering loss can become a disadvantage. There is a real danger of coach and coachee 'line manager bashing' together.

Loss and the Drama Triangle

Another way that the Drama Triangle shows up in people's lives at a time of loss is ironically when they are working hard to step off the Triangle. By using this model in coaching and supervision, we are empowering clients to understand it for the psychological game that it is. This is useful when clients are in a relationship conflict and want to find a way out from the seemingly intractable and circular problem with another person, for example, two peers at loggerheads with each other.

There is an element of mutually assured destruction about the Drama Triangle and if you try to leave the Triangle, those around you will try to (consciously or unconsciously) pull you back in to maintain the status quo. If you are in persecutor role and try to stop your controlling behaviours with victims, they may feel you don't care, so start to act up or lash out to make you re-join the dance and take control again, which lets them off the hook and they can go back to being helpless again. If you are in rescuer role and decide to start saying "no" more often, meet more of your own needs, and stop running after others, then the backlash could be that you are viewed as selfish, others then sulk, cry, stop speaking to you, anything that might entice you back into rescuing them again and giving them full attention. If in the victim role you decide to exert more independence and problem solve for yourself, then the persecutor and rescuer may view this as ungrateful behaviour and disrespectful, leading to more control and cries of "you can't do it without me!"

Higgins (2021) warns that by exiting the Drama Triangle, you risk losing relationships and possibly your entire social circle because of the enmeshed way that many people are interconnected. She likens it to an addiction and the loss of a previous life and/or identity that may have to be grieved over.

> "You'll need to mourn. Grieve the loss of who you thought you were if your identity was built up around your role. Grieve the loss of your relationship dynamics, which must all be forged anew, even if they're with the same people. It hurts."
>
> –Higgins, D. (2021) *Identifying the Drama Triangle*

Julia's coaching case study: Acting out grief via the Drama Triangle

Melissa was using coaching to improve her work-life balance. She worked long hours as a senior manager in the insurance industry. Unfortunately, during this time her mother was terminally ill in a hospice and Melissa was trying to take care of her elderly father alongside her brother as well as juggling her own family life which included four teenage children. When her mother died during the coaching programme, she took a few weeks off from work.

At her next coaching session, she looked exhausted and wanted to revisit her original plans of achieving a better balance between things that nurtured her and things that depleted her. She soon realised that her original plan now needed to change. Not only was she grieving the loss of her mother (although relieved her mother's suffering was over) and adjusting to the extra time this created, but she was finding it difficult to adjust to the changed dynamic between herself, her brother and her father. Her father in his grief had become much more vulnerable and needy. He now had an expectation that both would be there more often to support him.

Melissa was struggling. Even though she appreciated his great loss (her parents had been married for 60 years), she was finding that his blaming, helpless and powerless behaviour was making her feel frustrated and angry. Simple things that she knew he could do he would insist on phoning her about at work. She felt guilty if she didn't respond but when she couldn't because of work commitments, he would simply call on her brother instead and pretend that Melissa had not wanted to help. This meant on many occasions she fell into arguments at the weekends with her brother about who was giving more support. Melissa was beginning to feel that her father was playing them off against each other.

After exploring the theory of the Drama Triangle, we worked with an imaginary triangle on the coaching room floor. Melissa could see that here and now in the coaching room she was stepping into victim mode when feeling hopeless about her father (but also grieving her mother), "It's not fair, I'm hurting too". By responding to his every need she was feeling harried and fatigued and recognised that she was helping him too much through guilt until she became resentful. With her brother in the mix, she sometimes took on the role of blaming both him and her father by being aggressive and revengeful.

Standing outside the Triangle, she quietly said "We are all grieving. We have lost Mum in the centre and so we are all lost too". In coaching, she worked on her strategy to honour her own loss which involved making a photo album of her mother, as well as managing her emotions in the immediate moment they were triggered by her father. This involved the mantra "detach, detach" and seeing herself as if in as scientific experiment where she was the wise compassionate observer.

Looking at the alternatives to the Drama Triangle she could see that encouraging her father to accept his vulnerability and for her to verbally acknowledge that he was grieving, would then allow her to ask him questions about how he might problem solve something himself, rather than leaping to sort issues out for him. By discussing this approach with her brother, they agreed to communicate with each other at each stage rather than allow their father to divide and rule.

The Lens of Attachment

Attachment theory has been around since the 1990s and is a key underpinning principle in counselling regarding how we all relate to one another, that is, the emotional bond. Relationships are core to the work of coaches, so understanding this theory to appreciate ourselves and others is crucial (Bretherton, 1992).

In coaching supervision, it can lead to a rich discussion with supervisees in establishing "who they are is how they coach". For the more mature practitioner, it can take a basic biographical enquiry exercise and expand out into a depth of exploration that takes a coach from being purely client centred to one who sees the complexity of human interactions within and via a systemic lens.

The word attachment relates to, literally, our attachment to primary caregivers in childhood. Largely this is the mother, but also fathers and other significant attachment figures around us such as grandparents, teachers, friends, club leaders, and even our pets. The emotional bond that typically forms between infant and caregiver is how the helpless infant gets primary needs met.

How we are parented shapes our personalities and the way we relate to people in adulthood. It is the engine of subsequent social, emotional, and cognitive development.

Early experience of the infant stimulates growth of the brain and shapes emerging mental processes. It establishes in the infant's brain the neural pathways that will sculpt what are likely to be lifelong patterns of response to many things. Attachment affects personality development and the ability to form stable relationships throughout life.

Neuroscientists believe that attachment is such a primal need that there are networks of neurons in the brain dedicated to setting it in motion, and the process of forming lasting bonds is powered in part by the hormone oxytocin.

The genius of the attachment system is that it provides the infant's first coping system, the one that is a foundation for all the others; it sets up in the infant's mind a mental representation of the caregiver, one that is wholly portable and can be summoned up as a comforting mental presence in difficult moments.

Caring relationships in adulthood may elicit positive physiological responses ranging from modifying circadian rhythms to enhancing recovery from an illness.

There are two main attachment types although the literature sometimes gives different names for them, and most people are a mix of types (80% of people are a mix of secure/self-reliant):

1. Secure attachment – this arises when a primary caregiver has been emotionally available during a child's formative years and leads to safe/secure feelings.
2. Insecure attachment (three sub-types):
    a. Self-reliant (sometimes called anxious avoidant). This arises if primary caregiver has been remote/withdrawn.
    b. Anxious (sometimes called anxious ambivalent or sensitive). This arises if a primary caregiver has been unpredictable/inconsistent.
    c. Fearful (sometimes called anxious disorganised). This arises if a primary caregiver has been abusive (mentally/physically).

Secure attachment may show up in coaching and supervision as a client who has positive self-worth, good and independent relationships with the right amount of intimacy plus a healthy balance between negative and positive emotions.

Insecure attachment:

- A self-reliant style looks very positive and fiercely independent on the surface but can seek less intimacy by holding back, withdrawing when under pressure or disappointed. They work less well in groups and can seem remote or aloof at times.
- An anxious style is often seen in approval seekers who want to please others. They may have lower self-worth and blame themselves when relationships don't work out. They may need lots of support in coaching and supervision which can create the danger of dependence on coach or supervisor (especially if they have a similar attachment pattern). A coach and a client who are overly attached can easily convince themselves to carry on coaching when the contract ends because they can't bear to end (although the coach might rationalise this decision to their supervisor).
- A fearful style looks like the self-reliant type whereby they may move away from intimate relationships as a form of self-protection even though they really want the bond of good relationships. They may be unpredictable themselves and be clients who postpone or change times of sessions and generally disappear from the relationship. We have had numerous supervisees who contract for supervision, have one or two sessions then 'go off radar' for several months with no communication then suddenly return to supervision. Some do not return at all and so never do an ending in supervision. This begs the question about what the significance of endings for them is and why they are avoiding one.

All coaches would do well to do some in-depth work on their own attachment patterns with a supervisor. Like the Drama Triangle it can uncover habitual patterns of behaviour that need to be disrupted in order to achieve greater coaching mastery. As a coach (and supervisor) we may find ourselves responding to clients with our own style of attachment or normalising something we also see in ourselves. Our psychological development is ideally ahead of our clients. This does not mean we are perfect. We are all flawed human beings. Dysfunctional attachment issues may have disrupted our neurological wiring and hence our capacity for trust and safety (Vaughan Smith, 2020).

However, the more we examine ourselves, the more we can be in service to our clients. Coaches and supervisors are not therapists; however, attachment theory provides a framework for a discussion that gives credence to opening up new insights about what drives their behaviour and how to make better choices in the day-to-day relationships at work.

A supervisor can help by:

- Facilitating greater awareness around emotional intelligence competencies.
- Enabling greater self-disclosure and vulnerability to role model that which is needed in the coaching space.
- Having skills, systems and processes that radiate trust for a coach to model healthy self-dependence.
- Experimenting and encouraging coaches to explore the psychological underpinnings of their work.
- Managing transference from insecurely attached coachees and handling resistance by seeking to understand the resistance rather than trying to 'overcome it'.

Loss and attachment

If a coach reflects more on the patterns of relationship in their own family systems this can often lead onto themes of bereavement, grief and loss. By briefly examining what their relationship was with grandparents and parents this can unintentionally elicit values and beliefs particularly about bereavement and death. Asking how and when a grandparent died, for instance can produce an abundant seam of awareness for the coach. Questions such as:

- "How old were you when your grandparents/parent died?" – was a key attachment figure lost at an early age?
- "How old were they when they died?" – did their ancestor die at an early age and how did that impact others. (Many people report anxious feelings when they approach the same age as a parent who died and sadness when they outlive them and reflect on everything missed.)
- "What did they die of?" – this can elicit concerns about the hereditary nature of some illnesses.
- "How was death handled in your family?" – was death discussed generally? Did the client go to the funeral? If not, why not? What type of funeral was it?
- "What messages did you receive about bereavement and grief" – was grief not discussed? Were there rules about how the deceased were to be referred to afterwards? What expectations were there about the manner of grieving and how long to mourn?

Funerals can show up cultural differences that are useful to explore, but also attachment patterns that may go back a long way within a family system, but which ripple down through the ages. This is discussed in the "Lens of Trauma" later. It can highlight the death of a key attachment figure at a young age and the impact of that also impacts on sibling birth order (Blair, 2011), for example, a second child becomes the eldest after the death of an older sibling or a child is a replacement for a previous child who has died (and sometimes given the same name). It is not only death that can create this but also adoption, hospitalisation of primary caregiver, parental attention given over to other family members who are ill or disabled (effectively meaning the parent is 'lost' to a child).

Even going to boarding school at an early age is threatening to attachment. The age at which these events occurred can also be a rich vein of discovery particularly if it led to alternative attachment figures. Ingrid, a supervisee, described becoming closer to her maternal grandparents after her older sister died aged ten in a road accident, because she spent more time with them as her parents struggled to cope with the death of their daughter and eventually divorced.

Although parents are our primary attachment figures when we are very young (between birth and seven years), these do change as we get older. As well as death, other losses befall us as part of life and children can be affected by divorce especially if house or school moves are involved irrespective of how well the parents handle joint custody. Children will feel the loss of a life they once knew as well as the possible physical distance of a parent. With the prevalence of blended families in the twenty-first century, the fracturing of stepfamilies can often be a keenly felt loss.

In adolescence, we attach to friends, teachers and club leaders as we start to build relationships in the outside world. If these are successful, they lead to a more secure foundation of attachment. As time goes on romantic attachment and work relationships start to impact us (and possibly fill the gaps that were not filled when we were young). Broken romances at an early age can have a huge bearing on people's attachment patterns especially if the romantic partner was attached to as a replacement for something that was not given in the formative years.

Later we can be vulnerable to friendship disagreements or conflicts with peers at work because of our family patterns.

> A coachee of Julia's had been in major conflict with a work peer to the point that the peer had lodged a grievance against him. Attempts at mediation had failed and coaching was offered to both parties. Early in the coaching, it emerged that the coachee's mother had left the family home when the coachee was aged eight, taking his four-year-old sister with her. The coachee was left alone with his father who subsequently became alcoholic and abusive. Not only did the coachee lose his mother (unusual at that time, so some stigma attached too) but also the relationship with his sister. The coachee displayed many behaviours we would recognise as fearful caused by the relationship with either parent. He displayed low trust with many around him and the conflict at work

had been caused by his suspicious nature misreading a situation with his peer. In coaching it often felt that full contact was never met with him. He held back emotionally.

The Lens of Trauma

In recent years there has been a greater move towards trauma informed coaching. Rather like bereavement it has previously been seen as the preserve of therapy. However, as more research and evidence arise from neuroscience, we are starting to see where behaviours have stemmed from via the intersection between biology and psychology. Trauma is defined as "a neurophysiological emotional networked process". Taking a trauma informed approach to coaching (and supervision) is a large undertaking and requires far more advanced knowledge skills and attitudes than we have space for in this book. We would therefore encourage you to follow up references and do your own exploration as part of continuing professional development.

Here we will present some foundational elements of trauma and its specific relationship to coaching and then move on to link the connections with bereavement, grief and loss.

Trauma informed coaching

Trauma is a scary word for many and can be misunderstood. It is often associated with events such as wars, gangs, or mental health problems. Trauma is really an internalised reaction to an event.

Some prefer to use the word 'wound' instead of trauma as it feels more appropriate to speak of the wounds we all carry with us throughout life rather than trauma. Synonyms for trauma are pain, damage, ordeal, suffering, shock, upset, and disturbance. Trauma, however, does not have to be with a big 'T', Trauma with a small 't' can be very recognisable things in people such as grief, bereavement, illness, hospitalisation, bankruptcy, infertility, etc. It can however be formed in utero during pregnancy. We share the view of Julia Vaughan Smith (2016) "that the greatest percentage of all adult traumatology has roots in utero and the early years' experience". We now know that stress can be passed on through the umbilical cord from mother to child. Surgical interventions on mother or child can also have an impact as well as unwanted pregnancies or previous miscarriages.

Psyche trauma is therefore the result of these early experiences and connects with attachments issues we explored earlier. Unresolved trauma can therefore be passed down from grandparent to parent to child.

The most celebrated trauma model is that described by Professor Franz Ruppert (2015) and endorsed by many other writers and researchers within the field (Figures 13 and 14).

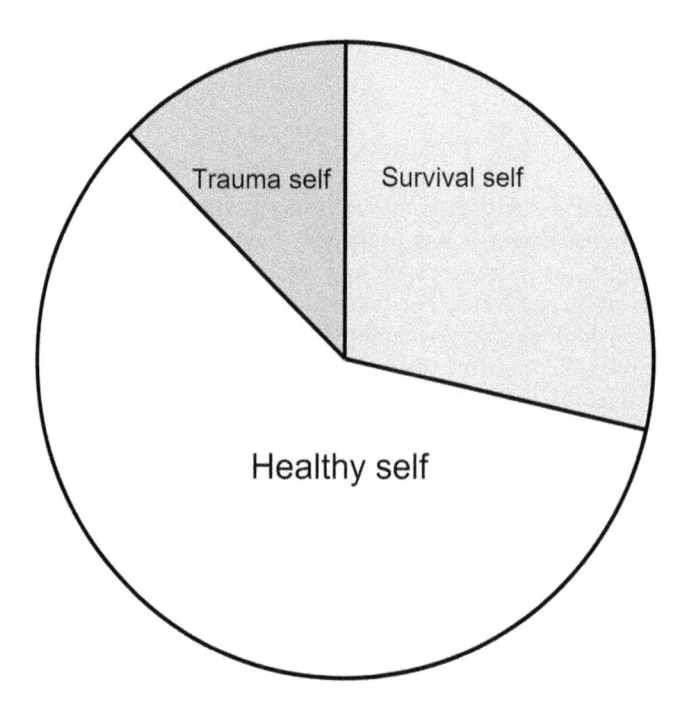

Figure 13 Healthy self, adapted from *Coaching and Trauma*, Vaughan Smith (2019).

He described a model for conceptualising trauma into the splitting of the psyche (an inner model of our minds) into three parts of the self:

1 Trauma self
2 Survival self
3 Healthy self

These "selves" are not of equal size in everyone. If we imagine it as a three-slice cake, then the slices can be different sizes depending on our experiences and responses. A relatively happy person is likely to have a large slice for their healthy self, a smaller one for survival self and an even smaller slither for trauma self. Someone who suffered more traumas would be the opposite. If something retriggers a previous trauma then this can lead to the survival self-becoming bigger in response.

Trauma self

This carries the emotional pain and is a fragmented memory (some of it not cognitively available to us because we did not have language then but resides

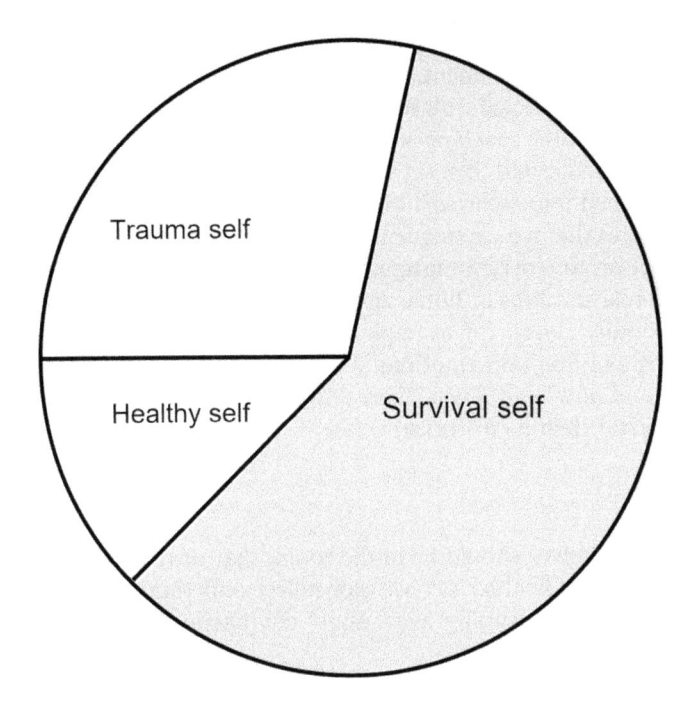

Figure 14 Survival self, adapted from *Coaching and Trauma*, Vaughan Smith (2019).

somatically in the body) which may emerge instead as physical ailments. With this memory we regress to the age we were when it happened. We know that a reaction to stress creates a flight, fight or freeze response. The fragmentation of memory comes about from a freeze and collapse response. It is physiologically a sensible way to protect ourselves from what we perceive to be danger (even if it isn't to an adult mind).

We have noticed especially in supervision that when supervisees talk about events from childhood they rationalise and excuse their own and other emotions and actions as if it was happening with an adult's mind. It is always worth remembering when psyche trauma is induced, it is at that age it happened and it remains that age. From an adult perspective, it could well be that there was really nothing to be frightened of when going into hospital aged five for a tonsillectomy, but as a child that may have seemed a terrifying existential threat to safety and absorbed bodily as such.

Survival self

This is more commonly known as defence mechanisms, which are an adaptation. They occur at the point of trauma in order to survive a perceived threat. This can lead to a loss of connection with our bodies. Survival defences can behaviourally look like clinginess, dependency, anxiety to please or the opposite like being fiercely independent, rejecting closeness and denying trauma. We know we have connected with someone's survival self in coaching when we get stuck or feel that the coaching is not going well. However, a client describing two abusive parents, and then saying, "it's fine, I've dealt with that now" should not be pushed into some sort of faux- counselling.

More 'normal' defences that we see frequently in coaching are controlling, distractions and addiction to work, wanting and not wanting change at the same time, entangled relationships at home and work, lack of awareness of own emotional and bodily states, for example, "I feel numb", or "I don't know what I'm feeling as I don't do emotions". We may see clients reacting to events in the 'here and now' as if it was 'there and then'. Counsellors have a saying "If it's hysterical then its historical".

Healthy self

In coaching, both healthy selves should be in the room; that of the coachee and the coach. When in our healthy self we can reflect and think and be unaffected by events. We are mentally alert, show compassion, empathy, learners' joy, love, and creativity.

Connecting trauma, coaching and loss

Carrying previous trauma can also make people vulnerable to other life events such as bereavement, grief, and loss.

As we discussed earlier about the interconnection between dysfunctional suffering and mental health, we are not here to diagnose, but to remain curious and normalise an interest in a person's early life as part of initial contracting and biographical enquiry.

Grief can easily retrigger a response of the survival self even if it is not directly related to the original trauma (even if we knew what that was). A person who has a fearful attachment pattern due to abusive or unloving parents may feel equally abandoned and lost at the death of a long-term spouse. All the pain and suffering is an emergence of the previous betrayal, hurt, terror, isolation and shame even if the spousal relationship was a contented one. Therefore, the echo of our trauma story is always interacting with the environment in which we find ourselves. This might emerge in several ways that are not obviously connected to the triggering event such as physical symptoms long dormant, addictions to drugs, exercise, dieting, gambling, or shopping. We may find our clients shut us out when previously they had been very open, or we may find ourselves working too hard for our clients to rescue them or prove how good we are.

One of the major impacts of loss is the way it shakes our identity; the "Who am I?" question. Part of our survival mechanism over many years may have been attributions given to us by others, for example, from our old bosses who saw us in a previous job or a family member who has just died. Clients may have been unaware that they were carrying these stories of themselves and that the image was not really them. They may have been carrying stories about others too. Many people come to see their deceased relatives in a different light, for better or worse, as time goes on after death and there is a reimagining of the relationship. Sometimes this possibility of a new narrative can be a devastating loss for people or conversely be extremely liberating: "Now my mother has gone I don't have to be who she wanted me to be".

The coach's survival self

Another point to consider is that there is always another psyche in the coaching room, also with three parts. As a coach, when we notice something isn't right with a client it's usually because there is an entanglement. A client's trauma self can be triggered in coaching, so their survival self becomes entangled with the survival self of the coach. We entangle our clients when we control, judge and engage in a drama triangle with them (whether that is rescuing, perpetrating or becoming the victim ourselves).

> Peter was a high achiever, driven from a young age to do well to please his parents, with an undisclosed fear of failure. As coach it was difficult to work with him as he was constantly pushing his high expectations onto the coach, who often felt not good enough. Their survival selves became entangled and stuck.

If as a coach you are working with a form of loss, then beware it may trigger your own loss issue if you have not explored them before and they capture you unawares. You will know this might be happening if:

- You are working harder than your client and you feel used by them.
- You feel pity and a need to rescue as a helper and not a coach.
- You feel strangely unmoved by your clients display of emotion, become bored, or irritated.

Noticing that this is happening (reflecting in action) as it happens gives an opportunity to step back without judgment and become an observer of your own processes with curiosity "How fascinating that I'm feeling really annoyed with my client who is crying about the loss of her job". You could allude to this in a softer way by saying "Something doesn't feel right. I'm feeling disengaged right now. How are you feeling?"

A good strategy would be to get more grounded (FOFBOC, or Feet on floor; bottom on chair), and practice mindfulness or to break state in some way, e.g. moving out of your chair, taking a coffee break, going out doors with your client.

A good technique after this is 321 reflective writing (see Part III) which gives the client chance to pour all their thoughts and feelings onto a page for a structured ten minutes and allows the coach to sit in silence and to gain more composure and compassion in the silence.

Supervisor case study: Death in a pandemic

Sabeen worked as an internal coach in a large organisation in the UK. She had worked there for six years and was in her early 30s and lived at home by herself. Her younger sister was a nurse on a Covid ward and lived with her parents and grandmother.

As part of her training to become a qualified coach, Sabeen was allocated supervision sessions.

In our first face-to-face supervision session, Sabeen was enjoying her coaching with four managers at work. She described her coaching sessions as being effective and rewarding and that she was enjoying her personal development through her coach qualification.

Our second session was several months later due to work commitments and the difficulties encountered in the pandemic. We met virtually and this time Sabeen was quite subdued not her previous bouncy personality. We discussed one of her coachees who had suffered from Covid and had been away from work for several months and just returned. Sabeen talked about how her coachee was finding it difficult at work as her health was still poor, but she did not want to let her team down.

As Sabeen continued, she began to cry quietly, and I was concerned to notice such a change in her personality from when we last met. I let her regain her composure slowly, just silently being there with her. She then began to tell me that her grandmother had only recently passed away due to Covid. Unbeknown to her sister who had not experienced any symptoms, she had brought it home from the hospital and her grandmother had caught it and unfortunately not recovered.

Sabeen then burst into tears again and told me she had not told anyone about this until then, having kept it from her friends and colleagues. She was particularly concerned that she was not able to be fully present in her coaching session with her coachee who had suffered Covid, and she realised that a parallel process was actively playing out in her mind.

I comforted her and spoke calmly whilst at the same time feeling tears come to my eyes. Sabeen did not know I had just recently lost a close friend due to Covid and my father a few months earlier. I recognised I also was experiencing a parallel process due to my loss. We sat together in silence experiencing our grief. When the time felt right, we then discussed what other resources Sabeen could pull upon to support her through this difficult time. We agreed that she would connect with the Wellbeing representative at work and arranged to meet again in 6 weeks' time.

I discussed this scenario with my supervisor and how best to manage my bereavement and grief when supervising coaches suffering their own grief. The ethical dilemmas not only in terms of the wellbeing of my supervisee but also the need to be aware of the wider system impact on the organisation. On reflection, I questioned my fitness to practise professionally during my own loss whilst recognising the need to pay attention to my own self-care and sourcing appropriate support.

During my next supervision session with Sabeen, I was delighted to find her in a more reflective space, and she described feeling more at peace. She explained that she had bottled up her feelings for so long without talking to anyone and I happened to be the conduit to her releasing her grief.

Carole Davidson
Executive Coach and Coach Supervisor
www.caroledavidsoncoaching.com

Is there something more serious with this client?

As we discussed earlier it is a judgment call about whether your client's grief at their loss is 'normal'. From a trauma perspective, we might not necessarily know something else has been triggered unless they tell us (even if we ask). The more intense those feelings appear the more likely they will move into their survival self and not be coachable at that moment. Express your concern for them and brainstorm strategies for additional help especially if they have accessed help before (you may want to ask how much that helped previously to remind them). This might not be just therapy but things like mindfulness, yoga, breathing, support from others.

However, if there is a fragility to the client that you are experiencing then listen out for more clues about their mental state. Many coaches are fearful of clients who have suicidal thoughts, and these may be more likely to be around during periods of loss than at other times.

Suicide risk of client

Suicide and thoughts associated with it are sometimes an extreme way for the survival self to deal with the pain from trauma. They want the pain of the situation to stop rather than being dead.

The key thing is not to be frightened if your client is saying things like "life is pointless, why go on?" One of the myths is that if you mention the word suicide it will cause someone to go off and do it. Coach Marie Faire, who writes our section below, puts it very pragmatically "Its unlikely someone thinks, wow suicide that's a good idea I think I'll google how to do it!". She says that suicidal thoughts are the iceberg under the surface with plans and actions only at the tip of the iceberg.

Suicidal thoughts are thought to be quite widespread across populations and that we are all on a spectrum of potential for this. What is important is our ability to self-regulate and have strategies for dealing with failure and success, our ability to reflect and the support we have around us.

However, there are some professional groups where statistically there are twice as many suicides, e.g. military and medical professionals, men aged 44–54. We often see high achievers in executive coaching because they have been successful with their strategies and climbed the career ladder. Like Peter who we discussed earlier, this may make them override early history and emotional vulnerability. Even a suspension at work can trigger a suicide, especially with those who may not have disclosed mental health issues before, and particularly in vocations where the job is a major part of someone's identity (Sheridan, 2019).

Also, as we see below, people bereaved by suicide can start questioning their own lives and have suicidal thoughts themselves. 9% of adults bereaved by suicide make their own attempt. In the UK in 2021, the NHS launched a dedicated support service for people who lose a friend or relative to suicide. A CIPD article (2021) said that for every death by suicide up to 135 people are affected. The key indictors to look out for, as well as verbalised thoughts, would be the degree of:

- Psychological pain.
- Stress.
- Agitation.
- Hopelessness.
- Self-hate.

If you hear something that sounds like suicidal thoughts, then take it seriously and enquire by checking you have heard correctly. Some coaches, through fear, may feel that it is not their role. However, if you are sitting in front of this person, then the client doesn't really care if your label says coach, counsellor, therapist, or any other definition if they are distressed.

Sometimes this might be their first time of giving voice to these thoughts. Be honest about your concern, as sometimes people do not mean it and quickly apologise for frightening the other person. If it is still worrying then facilitate a conversation about who else they have said this to – maybe a partner or a doctor– and what help they are receiving (Menaul, 2014). As a coach you do have skills in listening, asking questions, showing empathy and accessing resources. The research is clear that you can't make it worse by talking to them about it.

Try questions such as:

- What do you mean by..........?
- Would you like to say more about that?
- What has happened that has made you feel like that?
- Are you thinking that?
- Have you considered that you might..........?
- Are you concerned for your own safety?

As a coach you may have to be directive although you cannot force someone. You could offer to support your client while they call someone like a relative or the doctor.

Of course, in the extremely rare occasions where a person may be in imminent danger in that moment, for example, they call you to tell you they are going to harm themselves then your action is to call emergency services.

Bear in mind the act of suicide is no longer a crime in many countries and in the UK there is certainly no general duty to 'rescue'.

In the UK, the Samaritans is a well-known organisation for people in distress but probably what is not known is that as a coach you could phone them too to seek help and advice or even to process your own emotions in this type of circumstance. As ever, taking it to supervision is crucial.

Suicide bereavement

All of the things that are true about bereavement in general, are also true of bereavement following someone taking their own life. Marie Faire who writes the case study below has advice for coaches and supervisors about suicide bereavement.

If you are working with and supporting someone who has been bereaved because of suicide, here are some of the things that it is useful to consider:

- Supporter: This is tough to support – make sure the supporter is also supported through supervision.
- The bereavement process: This often takes longer than other deaths; it may take years.

- Unanswerable questions: Why did they do this? What could I have done? Listen and listen.
- Overwhelming emotions: As well as sadness and anger, frequently people experience fear, rejection, shame, or guilt (even when they are certain that there was nothing they could have done). As we noted above, it is not unusual for people bereaved by suicide to start questioning the worth of their own life and having suicidal thoughts themselves.
- Family reactions: Some families come together and support each other, others don't know how to speak of the unspeakable and isolate or worse still, blame each other.
- Isolation: Caused by real or feared stigma. The bereaved fear the question "How did they die?" They fear other people will not know how to react or may be inadvertently unkind.
- Post-traumatic stress: Often the bereaved are in shock. Frequently the death is unexpected and may be violent. They may suffer symptoms of PTSD – including real or imagined imagery of the death of the person involved.
- Denial: Lack of acceptance and denial that the person did take their own life may lead to the event being called 'an accident'. Typically, the consequence being unresolved emotional trauma for all concerned.
- In public: This may all take place in public – inquests, coroners, police, media may all be involved.
- Get help - See "Resources" section.

Supervisor's case study: The grief that dare not speak its name

My supervisee, Sarah had been asked to see Peter, a Director of an organisation where she is the "coach of choice". Peter, who was in his 40s, was financially successful, seemingly happy in his personal life and well respected at work. The Director of HR had noticed that he got upset at the recent retirement of one the longest-serving members of his team and had suggested that he book a session with Sarah. Sarah had met Peter previously, although she didn't know him well. The agreement was that she would meet with Peter and see if they could work together. There was no expectation that Sarah would report back to anyone and that if they wanted to have several sessions together, they should just "get on with it." – in the words of the HR Director.

Sarah met him virtually. He looked a little dishevelled, not as smart as she had seen him before. During the pleasantries, he wasn't particularly animated or chatty. He literally and metaphorically looked down.

She asked him directly if he was OK. He replied that he was OK (not convincingly) and said he was feeling a bit low as it was the anniversary of his father's death. Sarah said the usual empathetic things and enquired how long it was since he had lost his father. The answer shocked her – 27 years. He had died when Peter was just 15 years old.

Sarah is a compassionate and relational coach, and it did not surprise me that she stuck with him and gently (and bravely) explored further.

What was going on for him now 27 years on, she enquired? His father had died, at the same age Peter was now. He had been a good man and father. It was all so tragic.

"How did he die?"

Sarah told me, through tears, that she didn't know why she'd asked that question, she just did. Peter put his head in his hands and started to sob. His father had killed himself. This was the first time in 27 years that he had said those words out loud.

The story emerged that everyone had "conspired" to keep it quiet, to say he had a "dodgy heart"; letting people think it was a heart attack. As a family, they had soldiered on. He had taken the role on as the "man of the house". He never saw his mother cry, not even at the funeral, so he didn't either, until now. Peter was wondering and questioning what life was all about.

At the end of the session, he both apologised and thanked her, he said he would see her next session.

Sarah cried. She reflected. She worried and asked herself ... did I make it worse? Should I refer? Was Peter also having suicidal thoughts?

She then phoned me.

I assured Sarah that allowing someone to talk about their grief and suicidal thoughts will not make it worse. The research is uncontroversial and unequivocal. Asking him whether he was having such thoughts, would tell her the urgency and also indicate to whom she should refer. Talking prevents suicide.

As it turned out, telling Sarah his story was a turning point for Peter. Whilst he had been having suicidal thoughts, they were just thoughts. He got the bereavement counselling he needed, alongside support from Sarah. The "secret" was out, he said he felt he could "breathe" and get on with his life.

Marie Faire
AC Accredited Master Executive Coach and Coaching Supervisor and co-founder of the Beyond Partnership.
www.thebeyondpartnership.co.uk

Post-traumatic growth

It's worth making the final word in this section a positive one, which relates back to some of our earlier points about growth through grief. Calhoun et al. (2006) looked at what wisdom was garnered by people who have survived difficult experiences, especially through bereavement. They coined the term post-traumatic growth after seeing the positive changes made by grievers after a traumatic event. They listed areas of growth in 58%–83% of survivors such as:

- Increased personal strength.
- Increased compassion and connection with others.
- Increased gratitude for life.
- Finding a new mission in life or purpose.
- Engaging with existential questions.

The interesting point from a coaching perspective is that Calhoun et al. (2006) say the process of recovery comes from reflecting with an expert companion. They point out that this should be an expert at listening but not necessarily a professional "someone you can be open with, who's accepting, who isn't going to give you simple answers or platitudes or just give you advice – someone who is going to go on a journey with you". Could this be a coach?

They also make a connection with resilience in that people who have good resilience before an event can bounce back to how they were before but for some the tragedy upends their life so much, perhaps shattering core beliefs, that this is impossible to go back to – hence the growth aspect is more important for them. However, it does depend on what else people were struggling with before the bereavement and if this event was just a long line of other challenges, then being expected to grow may create more pressure and be an insult.

Finally, there are some ideas emerging about post-traumatic growth for systems, communities, and nations that have gained traction because of the Covid-19 pandemic. The journalist, Moya Sarner, (2021) postulates that the National Health Service in the UK, born in 1948 out of the ashes of the Second World War is such an example of post-traumatic systemic growth.

The Lens of Neuroscience

Here is another topic that requires more space than we have here. It is also a changing picture as scientific advances continue accelerating. We suggest specialised training and continuing professional development.

Here are some broad concepts and how bereavement, grief and loss impact and are impacted by the brain.

What is neuroscience?

It is the field of study encompassing the various scientific disciplines dealing with the structure, development, function, chemistry, pharmacology, and pathology of the nervous system. It involves the brain, spinal cord and network of sensory nerves (neurons) throughout the body. It looks like a new word but was coined in the 1960s.

The brain has 80 billion neurons and capability to connect to 10,000 other cells, so 80 billion multiplied by 10,000 shows the complexity of brain networks. It is an integrated system and has three key areas (Figure 15):

1. Brainstem – it keeps us alive, is completely unconscious and controls breathing, heart, and other vitals such as eating, sleeping (it's our old reptilian brain inherited from early life on Earth).
2. Limbic system – is the emotional centre and storehouse of memories (our prehistoric brains as early humans) emotions being an important source of motivational energy.
3. Cerebral Cortex – the logical, thinking sequential brain (our brain which evolved later over thousands of years).

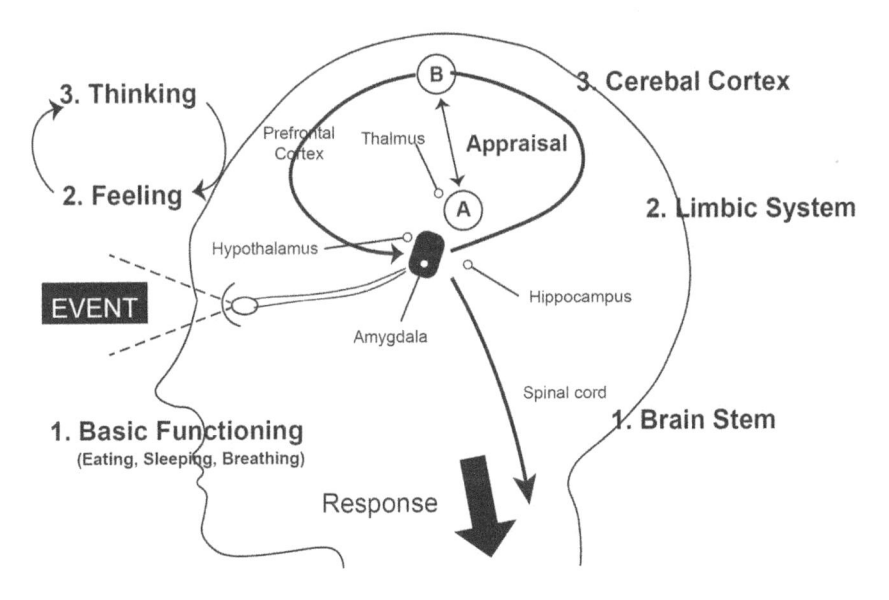

Figure 15 The human brain.

Psychiatrist and Nobel Prize Winner in 2000, Eric Kandel, described how the brain:

- is neuroplastic throughout adult life and not **set** from childhood; this was a big breakthrough in the 1980s and 1990s;
- can create itself through change via stimuli from the environment;
- is not just about creating new synaptic connections in the current neurons;
- can re-map itself. Through MRI scans we can see how brain change has occurred after some intervention either physically or even mentally (like coaching);
- is created by our minds rather than the other way round.

Neurotransmitters are released at the ends of neurons (nerve calls) and cross the synaptic gap to intersect with other neurons thus creating an electrical surge.

Millions of these firings are happening continuously in the brain to enable us to do anything and everything.

Neurons that fire together wire together which create superhighways and underpin our abilities to perform certain functions well or not.

There are many but the key neurotransmitters are:

- Oxytocin which is called the love or hug hormone and levels are raised when we feel good with someone. It is secreted by new mothers to bond with babies and people in love but is apparent in all warm, contented, and connected relationships.
- Serotonin has links to daylight, sleep and mood, plus feel-good factors for memory, and learning.
- Dopamine is famous for the 'runner's high' and can appear to be low in people with depression.
- Noradrenaline secreted by adrenal glands that can create fight or flight (or high performance and challenging energy).

Kandel proposed several key principles about neuroscience including:

1. Nature **and** Nurture is crucial (not either/or).
2. Experience transforms the brain.
3. Memories are imperfect.
4. Emotions underpin memory formation.
5. Relationships are the foundations of change.
6. Visualisation and doing are the same to a brain.
7. Our brains don't know what our minds are thinking.

Principle 1: Both genes and the environment interact in the brain to shape the individual. Both nature and nurture are equally capable of modifying brain structures. Neuroplasticity is the ability of the brain to change and develop new connections and continues at least to age 80 and beyond.

Genes govern everything and are involved in a complex dance with the environment. The vast majority of genes are expressed in the brain, and any normal or disordered behaviours are a result of genes operating together. Coaching can be seen as an environmental tool for shaping neural pathways.

Principle 2: Experience transforms the brain. New experiences and creating new neural pathways, can physically change the brain. The areas of our brain associated with emotions and memories such as the pre-frontal cortex, the amygdala, and the hippocampus, are not hardwired (they are 'plastic'). Circuits in our brain change in response to experiences, not just during development, but after injury, or during learning and memory formation and events such as bereavement.

Principle 3: Memory systems in the brain are interactive. Memories are not a perfect account of what happened; they can be constructed at the time of retrieval in accordance with the method used to retrieve it, for example, a question, photograph, or a particular scent can interact with a memory resulting in it being modified as it is recalled. We are our memory. If we constantly forgot everything each day, we would not know who we were. Our short-term or working memory is where we think through present thoughts and our long-term memory is where we store past events and learned meanings. The emotional upheaval of grief means that we may lose some of the capacity of our short-term memory, or grief can bring up old memories from long-term storage and we may be confronted by items that don't feel 'true'.

Principle 4: Cognitive and emotional processes work in partnership. There can be no knowledge without emotion. Emotions, feelings, and memories are interactive. We may try to be rational and make rational decisions in a computerlike way but often during periods of uncertainty such as loss we struggle to make decisions or make bad ones which may be particularly important at work.

Principle 5: Bonding and attachment provide the foundation of change. The therapeutic relationship between coach and client can have the capacity to help clients modify neural systems and enhance emotional regulation, so our role as coach in times of loss can be to create that bond.

Principle 6: Imagining activates and stimulates the same brain systems as does real perception. This principle is well-known in sporting arenas where athletes 'run the race in their head' as if it was real and the brain lights up in the same way as if it is real. This creates familiarity and confidence. The unconscious is where most of the work of the mind gets done; it's the source of intuition and dreams, and much information processing. The unconscious mind registers perception long before we are consciously aware of them. It can be a place of hidden fears, values and beliefs. Both coaching and counselling can bring some of these ideas to conscious awareness in order for us to explore and deal with them.

> *Using the visualisation techniques from the "Activities" in Chapter 7 can be a great aid for clients.*

Principle 7: The brain can process non-verbal and unconscious information and exert great influence on thought, feelings, and actions. It is possible to react to unconscious perceptions without consciously understanding the reaction as we discussed in the lens of trauma.

> *Information processed unconsciously in coaching interventions can still have an impact, consequently the importance of allowing time between coaching sessions for the unconscious mind to do some more work is crucial.*

Neuroscience and coaching

All coaches, irrespective of theoretical orientation 'coach the brain' and this can be seen as "a dance between metaphor and science" (Vaughan Smith, 2020).

> *Every memory is a set of interconnecting neurons so everything that stays with us forms a unique map. If we access these maps more often, they stay with us, so as coaches encouraging learning by practising actions repetitively could lead to permanent long-term change. Coachees being asked to journal can create this good quality of focus and keep brain circuits active for longer. On the other hand, as coaches, we need to pay attention to solutions and less to the problem otherwise the wrong thing gets hardwired.*

Very small changes in neurotransmitters (the brain's chemical messengers) can lead to big changes in behaviour due to the interconnectedness of the brain. Working out which small changes create big shifts in behaviour can be where coaching comes in.

Our brains can be said to be operating to the laws of quantum physics in that we can change them by conscious effort, for example, the questions one asks influence the results one sees. Shining the light on something new creates new neural connections.

Using our energy to pay attention to something will then hardwire something new and is therefore self-directed neuroplasticity although working memory is limited. We can only shine a spotlight on so many things at a time. In coaching, small steps are best. It takes a lot of energy to stay focussed and we are easily distracted. For the coach and coachee it can be akin to physical exertion.

The Polyvagal theory

This is an area of biology that has come to the fore in both counselling and coaching circles only in the last couple of years and is a helpful addition for coaches and clients with a limited science background as it makes sense of some of the thoughts feelings and behaviours arising especially during bereavement. Rather like trauma informed coaching and psycho education for clients, Polyvagal theory can be useful as education for certain clients to understand what is happening to them.

The theory was first proposed by Stephen Porges (2011) who called it the biology of safety and danger.

We know the brain responds more to threat than to reward and is an adaptation giving evolutionary advantage in the face of a threatening world. It does however cause problems in the twenty-first century when we are unlikely to run across a fierce animal that wants to eat us. Our autonomic nervous system is on guard scanning our environment constantly for threats, which explains why we often err towards negative thoughts before positive ones. The main highway of the nervous system is the vagus nerve which runs down the spine from the brain and forks off into other areas of the body including the gut. This feedback loop underpins the importance of taking note of what our bodies are telling us as they scan the environment. As we saw earlier, we are not necessarily consciously aware of this, and coaches will be familiar with those clients who seem to be cut off from their bodies when asked where they might be feeling a particular emotion.

The impact of the autonomic nervous system

There are two main branches of the autonomic nervous system that react to ensure our 'survival':

- The sympathetic nervous system.
- The parasympathetic nervous system.

The sympathetic branch is in the middle of the spinal cord and is the pathway for action; it senses danger and triggers adrenalin release. If you have ever had to slam on the breaks whilst driving and noticed how your legs shake afterwards, then that is the fast pathway down your spine into your legs that has just saved your life.

The parasympathetic branch has two subbranches and these are the pathways of the vagus nerve. This nerve travels from the base of the skull down through the lungs, heart, diaphragm, and stomach and then up to the neck, throat, eyes, and ears.

The vagus nerve encompasses the ventral pathway and dorsal pathway. The ventral responds to safety cues and feelings of engagement and social connection. The dorsal pathway responds to danger cues that make us feel disconnected, spaced out and possibly heading to some sort of collapse.

As we saw in the trauma and attachment sections, if we have had early experiences that have primed our autonomic nervous system to be highly adjusted to danger, then we may feel on red alert for much of that time in adult life and this can come to feel normal. This may make people quite productive and creative as it gives energy that drives them but can be counterproductive in the long term. These clients may be constantly on and busy and can become distressed if they are forced to slow down long enough to allow emotions to emerge. We sometimes see this with grievers who are encouraged to take time off work and then this downtime creates more distress. However, coaching is about change and this requires calm creative energy. These clients may seek to move onto new things in a search for safety, as we saw in the section about leaving and endings. This over stimulation of the vagus nerve can also create physical problems because "the body keeps the score" (Van der Kolk, 2014). Here we see issues such as chronic fatigue syndrome, irritable bowel syndrome, and autoimmune diseases.

In coaching, we need to set up an environment for our clients that sends a signal to their physiology that says, "you are safe here" and for them to believe it, so they switch from being in the sympathetic system to the parasympathetic system which allows for certainty and insight to occur.

Breathing techniques and mindfulness are known to calm the nervous system and again many activities that have been a traditional part of a coach's toolkit, now have a basis in science.

The grieving brain

Pain and suffering go hand in hand with grief and loss as well as emotions such as anger, sadness and increased levels of anxiety. For clients who already had highly attuned, adaptive survival parts, then bereavement of any sort can tip them into a highly aroused distress state. This is why everyone's experience of grief is unique. It is not purely down due to circumstances and the event but the griever's biological and psychological propensity to respond in a certain way that could already have been predetermined.

From MRI scans it has been discovered that brain areas that experience physical pain are also the same areas that light up for psychic pain (Blakeslee and Blakeslee, 2007). This corresponds with many people noticing that grief can feel as if it is hurting as much as when we are attacked bodily. Our hearts can feel that they are literally aching.

> **Supervisor case study: Not just a supervisor; a sister's loss**
>
> In early 2018, my beautiful, vibrant younger sister, diagnosed with a non-operable brain tumour in 2007 – who had been given a "Two years to live" diagnosis – was in the final months of her life.
>
> My 'new normal' became a 6-hour journey to see her every two weeks, staying for four or five days, caring for her along with her husband and my two nieces. Cooking lots to occupy ourselves and just …. being. My work diary was full on those days when I wasn't with her. Because what I know about myself in times of grief is that I work. My "be strong" driver goes into overdrive. It's been my pattern through the death of my brother and my mother.
>
> I know that my vulnerable, exhausted, grief-stricken self is hiding in there. But she can't come out. Not just yet. There will be time for that later. There must be time for that later.
>
> I 'must' live through it, live with it and then open it all up and let the floodgates open.
>
> Faulty thinking? Maybe. But it's what I do.
>
> Coaching, supervising, team coaching – involves being fully in the moment with a coachee, supervisee or team. It takes the attention away from that raw, helpless, hopelessness.
>
> Besides, I've got a big team event to organise in late July. I can't possibly cancel. Can I?
>
> In the back of my mind: "What happens if she dies then? What will I do?" Shall I mention it to the client? Or not?
>
> I decided not to and to 'play it by ear'. How trite that sounds.
>
> What was I avoiding?
>
> My sister died in the early hours of a beautiful June morning. Two days before my next planned visit. I had team coaching calls booked in that afternoon – they are still in my calendar, and I have no recollection of whether I did them or not. Although I did the event 6 weeks later.
>
> Four weeks after the funeral, I sat with a supervision client whilst he told me about his partner who had been having tests for cancer. No diagnosis yet.
>
> "Have you ever supervised or coached anybody in this situation?" he asked me.
>
> I hesitated. Do I share my personal sadness? Or don't I?
>
> I did. I felt a sense of calm knowing that the focus was on him, not on me.

> I truly realised in that moment what it is to be compassionate – the difference between empathy and compassion had never seemed so huge.
> Had I been an 'amateur' before?
> Four months after my sister's death I sought bereavement counselling. The time felt right. My counsellor held the space for me. Holding the space. The most powerful 'tool' we have.
>
> **Lynn Scott**
> Executive Coach, Team Coach, Coach Supervisor, founder of the Effortless Leader Revolution.
> www.lynnscottcoaching.co.uk

Some brain-based practices we use in coaching that are particularly helpful during times of grief and loss are some that we mentioned in the section on self-care:

Taking breaks: Our conscious brains can only process six or seven key things at any one time whereas our unconscious brains have almost limitless capacity. Taking a break from what feels overwhelming could involve something physical when feeling mentally stressed, for example, walking in nature, gardening, napping.

Reframing: Not one for immediately after the emotion of loss but in time, once unhooked from emotional triggers, a client with lower emotional intensity has great processing power. Also trying to suppress emotion does not work as it can make it more intense and creates a greater threat response by the brain. Rating their anxiety on a scale of 1 to 10, and how they would like it to be gives an opportunity to talk through some actions that might help, for example, listening to music.

Stress: This has been shown to shrink the brain, whereas cardio exercise increases brain volume by neurogenesis (literally creating new neural networks). Exercise also uplifts levels of the neurotransmitters we discussed earlier, meaning clients can impact their own biochemistry and lift themselves out of dark or sad moods. Encouraging clients to exercise even when they may not feel like it, is a useful suggestion to get out of their brain and into their body. This alleviates that oft-quoted numb or disconnected feeling that grievers report.

Sleep: Encouraging the best possible sleep that a coachee can manage at difficult times may be about encouraging napping or even five-minute meditations, to change neurochemistry, especially their serotonin levels.

Coach on what a client can control: Try small simple tasks like desk tidying, sorting files, set a daily schedule, stick to systems and processes each day that don't require too much thinking, as the prefrontal cortex decision-making process may be blunted through 'brain fog' or 'grief brain'.

Change targets and objectives temporarily: If clients are working towards big tasks, break them down and even move the goalposts until they are in a more resourceful state.

Build in rewards: Research shows that people whose brains are intolerant to uncertainty have less of a thrill from rewards, so it is even more important to schedule into their day moments of joy or indulgences for increased dopamine.

Connect with other people: During loss, the instinct is to withdraw; however, from a neurotransmitter perspective, we need to connect with others to stimulate more oxytocin.

Mindfulness or meditation: This quiets the mind and allows the unconscious to take up more of the emotional heavy lifting and provides moments of new awareness. Some coaches will have experienced clients who are resistant to meditation or find that it doesn't suit them. Here are some alternatives:

- Breathing – this can be done within a coaching session without the visualisation component ("Pause for breath" activity (p. 171)) as slow deep breathing will change brain states quickly.
- Muscle relaxing – again, this is a quick activity that can be done in a coaching session together, particularly with an upset client, and many people will be familiar with this process from yoga or other exercise scenarios. It involves tensing for five seconds then relaxing for ten seconds each set of muscles, one at a time, starting from the legs, and moving all the way up to the head and face. Saying "relax" as the muscles are released is helpful and doing it together stops any self-consciousness by the client and enables mirror neurons to fire as coach and client brain activity starts to coordinate with each other (hopefully, the client's rhythms start to slow down to synchronise with the coach's.)
- Walk in nature – this is a form of meditation while in motion (also swimming and cycling because of their repetitive nature). It has been shown that blood pressure falls within fifteen minutes of being amongst trees. It is a reminder that our bodies can take action even if we feel helpless. Coaching outdoors is ideal for this. It is becoming increasingly common for a client and coach to have their session walking in nature.[10]

Keep present focussed: For many grievers, the problem is worrying about the future and remembering the past. Focussing on what is happening right now is a good technique to teach clients. A very accessible way of doing this is the

---

10 For more Information you can visit www.walkingmentorship.com

Rule of Three. Look into the distance and name three things that can be seen, then three sounds, and finally wiggle three parts of the body. This all helps to connect what is happening here and now visually, aurally and kinaesthetically, as well as facilitating a shift from the sympathetic to parasympathetic state.

> ### Supervisor case study: Remaining fit for purpose in supervision
>
> I was offered the opportunity to act as Coach Supervisor with a group of coaches where loss was one of the central themes of the coaching as coaches and our coachees.
>
> In 2020, the year the Covid-19 pandemic started, the manifestation of multiple losses in my life over the previous few years was a challenge for me. I divorced, was diagnosed with Breast Cancer, remarried and moved, lost my dad and mum within a 7-year period. Somehow, they magnified at the point of losing my mum in April 2020. I now reflect on how well I self-managed, showed self-care and compassion and remained "fit for purpose" as a Coach Supervisor.
>
> What I found helpful, working with a team of coaches looking at loss, was our ability to reflect, be open in a way that showed compassion, humour and an honest, ethical stance.
>
> This meant that I could be myself and show feelings and emotions as they arose in our work in full recognition that sometimes I was triggered but tried to remain helpful.
>
> As an empathic person, I find it very easy in the moment to switch of "my stuff" and focus exclusively on the other person/team and feel no interference.
>
> However, what is crucial is to decompress effectively myself. During this time, I did this with my own coach supervisor exploring my thoughts and feelings about grief and how they manifested working as a coach and coach supervisor, we did this using imagery and metaphor.
>
> It was key to allow myself time to just be, do nothing or walk and reflect to allow restoration. I also had some success with self-talk in terms of positive affirmations and saying no to things that I did not feel resourced to do.
>
> What didn't go so well? I view my voyage of discovery about myself with a light touch and humour and usually allow some introspection but not to be overly reflective.
>
> In this time of grief, I felt overwhelmed more easily by the various demands placed on me by my mum's death as well as professionally. Of course, with all my training, education and experience I could talk

to myself compassionately and take the meta view but some days I just did not feel fit for my purpose as a coach supervisor and found it difficult to forgive myself for not showing up in my best shape.

When I think of what I learned about grief and loss, the words "accepting what is" comes up regularly for me in grief and it seems that once I am at peace with whatever loss I have experienced it enables me to be even better at what I do as a coach supervisor.

Another learning is to give a good amount of time to explore the losses as they happen. In retrospect, I have not done that sufficiently. To acknowledge the loss fully, experiencing the light and the dark side of loss.

A friend reminded me that grief is like glitter it shows up when you least expect it; when you thought you had got rid of all the glitter there is still more to hoover up.

It is alright to feel and be preoccupied by grief and I would encourage a fellow professional to self-coach by asking "How do I respond helpfully for myself and my clients at this time?" and "What do I need to add into today's self-care?"

Diane Hanna
Lead Coach and Coach Supervisor
Capel Jones Consulting Ltd

Cultural considerations

The world is a place of richness when it comes to culture. Our planet is home to many different rituals related to loss in general, and death particularly. As bereavement is considered a process rather than an event, it is only natural that in this process many rituals take place. This process is conducted differently for different cultures, religions, educational backgrounds, and customs.

Culture impacts bereavement in many different dimensions: history and roots, geography, nationality, religion and/or spirituality, ethnicity, class, age, gender, symbols and artefacts, mindsets, and beliefs. We know that women grieve differently than men, and elderly people grieve in a distinct way than younger generations. Additionally, some ethnicities have certain death rituals that make perfect sense in their culture, which may be considered appalling to other cultures. Also, across the globe, the various class levels determine how rich the funeral might be: whether there is an edified tomb or a ground burial or whether the family can keep the corpses for longer in their homes or not (as happens with the Toraja culture in Indonesia). There can be different national or cultural approaches to mourning where there is much outward sorrow and expressiveness in certain groups of mourners versus those cultures which are more restrained and mourn individually.

There are various forms of rituals when it comes to death. All of them charged with symbolism. It is not a matter of which one is better. It is a matter of making sense and what people were brought up with. For some migrant ethnicities, it might be more difficult to celebrate their rituals and the conduct of their bereavement ceremonies in their adoptive countries, as these might not have the same customs nor understanding of its meaning in its fullest extent.

As coaching grows worldwide, it is also common that coach and coachee might come from two different cultures and/or backgrounds. Respecting the differences is something that a coach needs to do and to pay attention to when coaching, especially when it comes to this topic.

When coaching someone through bereavement, it is likely that the client when narrating her story details some parts of the rituals they go through.

Listening attentively is important for the coach, as it is the usage of neutral language, as a sign of respect for the partnership existing between coach and client.

Despite the fact many coaches are curious to learn more about other cultures and their rituals when it comes to this topic, others clearly know their boundaries and what triggers them. Another key coaching skill to master when it comes to bereavement is acknowledging with an innocent and compassionate curiosity, not to be in service of our inquisitiveness but rather to be in service of the client. Take care that the curiosity is not just yours for its own sake, that is, you find it fascinating, but does it serve your client? Acknowledge the qualities, the values, and the beliefs the client brings into the coaching session and its relevance for them rather than you.

So, having a heightened self-awareness of our own behaviours or mindsets when it comes to a determined topic is key to understanding whether we are the best coach for that client or not. In some cases, it is worthwhile referring to other colleagues who can continue the coaching programme, maybe even from a similar or the same culture, or who may not have the same issues that we may have.

Likely issues for both coach and client have their source in the way people were brought up, their values and beliefs system, and the influence the cultural traditions had on them, including religion or the lack of it.

Many of these possible triggers are linked with unconscious bias, which Lyon and Parke (2012) describe as the combination of attitudes, experiences, cultural norms, and expectations that everyone holds, and are unique to each of us. Everyone has unconscious bias, including coaches and supervisors. And because they are unconscious, they may be outside of awareness.

An example of unconscious bias is, for instance, when people refer to their boss in a conversation. The chances are that some of the people who are listening picture the boss as a white male. This thought might skew the conversation in a totally different direction had they not had that in mind.

Another common example of unconscious bias happens when people refer to their partner, spouse, etc. the tendency is to picture someone from the opposite gender. Nowadays, with so much focus on this topic, this bias is becoming more conscious, and many people are aware of it.

When it comes to bereavement, an unconscious bias might be that any loss is negative, or death can only be acknowledged with a sad ceremony. Another example lies in the expectations of how someone else 'should' grieve based on their own experience and own cultural norms. For instance in the past there was a very common custom for Catholic women to dress in black after the death of a close family member for a long period of time and this is still the case in some Catholic communities today.

Also, as we discussed earlier, the assumptions made about the various types of death, for example, tragedies, age of the deceased/bereaved, prior illness, or even suicide. It is still common to have strong thoughts and feelings about someone who decides to end their lives. These thoughts and feelings might be projected as well onto the bereaved family members.

Let's pause here for a moment and take stock. What do you notice in you when you read all these examples? What would you like to explore further with your supervisor? What is your conscious bias towards death, bereavement, rituals, symbolism, suicide? What could be your unconscious bias?

It is essential for the coach to be aware of the existence of unconscious bias related to this topic and to be open to explore the coachee's and theirs, either in a supervision setting or with other peers. Understanding the reactions that are triggered by an unconscious bias is instrumental for our enhancement as coaches. Many of these reactions show up as micro-expressions displaying surprise or even disgust about a detail from the narrative being told by our client. An example of that is the reaction to the buffalo sacrifice in the funerals celebrated still in the twenty-first century on the island of Sulawesi in Indonesia. Here buffalos are considered the vehicle for the afterlife. Another celebration that might create some noteworthy reactions is the Famadihana that happens in Madagascar every seven years, where the corpses are taken out of the tombs, wrapped in cloth, and are taken to dance to music. These are not tribal rituals, rather strong cultural traditions that are alive to this day.

Additionally, burial beads are quite common in South Korea, or the recent fashion for ashes to be turned into jewellery that one can wear any time anywhere without anyone understanding the person is carrying the ashes of their deceased ones on their neck or wrist. These have seen a recent increased interest in countries such as the UK and the USA.

The coach who becomes more aware of her own reactions and is open to explore its impact on others, will probably be better equipped to remain loyal to the coaching partnership.

The Global Code of Ethics (see Appendix 3) mentions in point 2.18 the responsibility to set and main culturally sensitive boundaries: "Members are responsible for setting and maintaining clear, appropriate and culturally sensitive boundaries that govern all physical and virtual interactions with clients or sponsors", and in point 3.4: "Members will avoid knowingly discriminating on any grounds and will seek to enhance their own awareness of possible areas for discrimination and bias, including in the use of technology or inaccurate or fake data."

What could be some of your reactions?

One other aspect that it is important to consider is that during the Covid-19 pandemic, many rituals were not allowed and did not take place. Many cultures were not able to respect their own traditions because of the legal obligations required by their local governments. Just to name a few situations that impacted the bereavement process – burials were substituted by cremations; in certain countries funerals were replaced by common burial instead of individual ones; and many corpses were kept in fridge containers for longer periods of time than normal.

Refer to the bibliography for more information about other different types of burials and its ceremonies around the world.

Julia's supervision case study: Family dynamics and dying

Darren went to his supervisor (Angela) wishing to talk about a recently bereaved coachee called Beth.

Beth had recently lost her father. Her mother had died over 40 years ago when she was aged eight and her father had never remarried.

Beth has three brothers and one sister. The last time Darren had seen Beth, she was still upset about the death of her father but not unusually so, and she reported feeling relieved that his suffering was over, as he had had dementia for many years.

However, Darren was taken aback by how tired, stressed, and haunted Beth looked the next time he saw her. As part of the discussion about funeral arrangements within the family it had emerged that there was a family burial plot and that her father had left instructions in his will that he wished to be buried there. The plot belonged to her father's side of the family. Beth had no idea that the burial plot existed or that this was her father's final wish. She had always expected that he would be cremated, and his ashes scattered in the same place as her mother's.

One of her brothers had known about the burial plot but none of the other siblings did. Beth was feeling unhappy and conflicted because she felt "squeamish" about burial compared to cremation. Beth had never been to a burial and found that her imagination ran away with her about what a dead body would look like in a coffin in the ground. As well as the shock of finding this out, there was now conflict in the family as she and a younger brother felt the same, whereas the other siblings were happy to proceed with a burial. Beth felt conflicted about going against her father's wishes. She was now feeling obliged and under pressure to agree with the rest of her family. She had tried to think of the positive aspects of burial such as a grave to visit, but was now suffering anxiety, poor sleep, and concentration at work due to the constant arguments about the arrangements. The family were now under time pressure to have a funeral for their father and the funeral directors had tried to mediate and allay fears, to no avail.

Darren wanted to process his own feelings in supervision. He had never been to a burial before, but his wife had, and they had talked about how different the experience was.

His supervisor, Angela, admitted that she too felt more "pro-cremation" and that they were in danger of colluding together. There were elements of the drama triangle swirling about with Beth in the victim role, Darren her rescuer and the family as persecutors.

Angela decided to start with Darren's feelings: "What aspect of this situation do you recognise as your own emotional reaction"? "What part of it is being evoked by your coachee in response to the situation?"

From this Darren described his vulnerability not only in terms of his own feelings about burials but also about being seen as a good enough coach who could professionally detach from the heat around this issue. It felt good to say out loud the fears that seemed silly whilst still as thoughts. One action he decided on was to become more informed about burials. A quick google search brought up the pros and cons of both burials and cremations. He knew this would be helpful for Beth too and may facilitate an agreement to go with the majority view. However, by the end of his supervision session, Darren was coming to realise that the disharmony in the family was coalescing around the issue of the burial when in fact this could be a smokescreen for tensions that had already been there. He decided to help Beth focus more on exploring the conflict and some of its history so he could establish whether Beth may need more specialist help outside of coaching. A therapist could help on the family dynamics but also with a topic of burial in case it was verging on the edge of a phobia. He also appreciated that he may just have to

> hold her in a supportive safe space through this difficult time in case this was a temporary feature of "this is just what happens in families when they all grieve in different ways".

References

Berne, E., 1967. *Games People Play*. Harmondsworth, Middlesex: Penguin.

Blair, L., 2011. *Birth Order: What Your Position in the Family Really Tells You About Your Character*. London: England: Piaktus.

Blakeslee, S. and Blakeslee, M., 2007. Where Mind and Body Meet. *Scientific American*, [online] (18). Available at: https://www.scientificamerican.com/article/where-mind-and-body-meet/

Bretherton, I., 1992. The origins of attachment theory: John Bowlby and Mary Ainsworth. *Developmental Psychology*, [online] 28(5), pp. 759–775. Available at: 10.1037/0012-1649.28.5.759

Calhoun, L., Tedeschi, R. and Amir, M., 2006. *Handbook of Posttraumatic Growth*. London: Routledge.

Chartered Institute of Personnel and Development, 2021. *The Design and Development of Bereavement Policy and Support for Line Managers*. [.pdf] Chartered Institute of Personnel and Development. Available at: https://www.cipd.co.uk/Images/a-guide-to-bereavement-support-Feb2021_tcm18-81624.pdf [Accessed 7 April 2021].

Higgins, D., 2021. Identifying the Drama Triangle. [Blog] *Medium*, Available at: https://liminalcounseling.medium.com/identifying-the-drama-triangle-63a87dbe0470 [Accessed 11 November 2020].

Karpman, S., 1968. Fairy tales and script drama analysis. *Transactional Analysis Bulletin*, 7(26), pp.39–43.

Lyon, J. and Parke, C., 2012. *Top Tips for Managers of Working Parents*. Leicester: England: Troubadour Publishing Ltd (Matador).

Menaul, J., 2014. Reflections On The Suicide of Successful Women. [Blog] *Spark Coaching and Training*, Available at: http://www.sparkcoachingandtraining.co.uk/blog/be-perfect-driver [Accessed 18 March 2014].

Menaul, J., 2019. *The Coach's Guide to the Drama Triangle*: [ebook] Bookboon. Available at: https://bookboon.com/en/the-coachs-guide-to-the-drama-triangle-ebook

Porges, S. W., 2011. *The Polyvagal Theory: Neurophysiological Foundations of Emotions, Attachment, Communication, and Self-Regulation*. New York: W.W. Norton.

Ruppert, F., 2015. *Trauma, Fear and Love*. Steyning, UK: Green Balloon Publishing. Bridges.

Sarner, M., 2021. Post Traumatic Growth: The Woman Who Learned to Live Profoundly Good Life After Loss. *The Guardian*, [online] Available at: https://www.theguardian.com/lifeandstyle/2021/may/11/post-traumatic-growth-the-woman-who-learned-to-live-a-profoundly-good-life-after-loss [Accessed 21 May 2021].

Sheridan, C., 2019. *People Management*, [online] Available at: https://www.peoplemanagement.co.uk/voices/comment/my-brother-took-own-life-after-being-suspended-work#gref.

Van der Kolk, B. A., 2014. *The Body Keeps the Score: Brain, Mind, and Body in the Healing of Trauma.* London: Penguin Random House.

Vaughan Smith, J., 2016. [.pdf] *Traumatised Psyche: Traumatised Soul.* Available at: http://www.limbus.org.uk/soul/Traumatised%20Psyche%20and%20Soul%20-%20Julia%20Vaughan%20Smith.pdf [Accessed 18 May 2021].

Vaughan Smith, J., 2020. *Why Coaching the Survival Parts in Coaching Doesn't Bring About Change - Coaching and Trauma.* [online] Coaching and Trauma. Available at: https://coachingandtrauma.com/why-coaching-the-survival-parts-in-coaching-doesnt-bring-about-change/

Vaughan Smith, J., 2019. Working with 'Parts' of our selves. [Blog] *Becoming Ourselves,* Available at: https://www.juliavaughansmith.co.uk/blog/working-with-parts-of-our-selves [Accessed 26 August 2021].

Part III

Practical Guidance and Activities for Coaches and Supervisors

In this section, we present several different models and approaches from the world of coaching that have relevant connections to bereavement, loss and grief, which can intensify ability to work more effectively with clients whether coaches or coachees. This list is not definitive, and we would encourage everyone to use knowledge and skills they already have from other sources as well as tune into future continuing professional development with one eye on its use for handling loss issues as and when they arrive.

The list of activities in Part III proves that many current exercises in a coach's toolkit are useful for helping clients with bereavement issues as well as some others that we hope you may not know about or have not considered before in this context. Like most coaches, we also tailor and adapt different tools we encounter throughout our work with clients, so we would encourage you to use, transform, add, alter, convert, translate in a way that suits you and your clients best.

Chapter 7

Tools and Techniques to Work with Grief and Loss

Activities

How to use Part III
To provide consistency we will break each activity into the title of activity, what it is and how to use it with clients (in a step-by-step instructional way), the types of clients who may benefit the most, other considerations or warnings for its use, and further references if you want to explore more from original authors.

Pause for breath

What is the technique?
It is a mindfulness technique that connects breath and body and calms a busy mind. It can be done in person or virtually. The coach can also do this alongside the coachee.

Who is it for?
For clients experiencing anxiety in the moment or emotional overwhelm. To bring someone into the present.

How to use it?
Learn the script in such a way so that you are not purely reading it out. Adapting and changing to your own words is ideal. Slowing your voice down and softening the tone also creates the right ambience for this relaxing meditation. Allow gaps of silence between each step. It should take no more than 15 minutes and can be used at the start of a session or even at the end.

DOI: 10.4324/9781003087502-11

Here is the script:

> *"Sit comfortably in your chair with back upright but relaxed and with feet in full contact with the floor. Put down anything in your hands and rest them palm down onto thighs.*
>
> *Notice the contact between your feet/shoes and the floor. Become aware of the contact between hands and thighs. Also notice the contact between the chair and your legs. Become aware of your sitting bones in contact with the chair. Notice your spine and let it grow to its full length by imagining each vertebrae lifting away slightly from each other.*
>
> *Now…. bring your attention to your breath. On each inhale and exhale notice the rise and fall of the abdomen. Imagine each breath seeping in between each of your vertebrae, allowing them to expand a little bit more. As you exhale imagine your breath softening and cleansing your belly and lungs.*
>
> *Follow your breath for a few moments (silence).*
>
> *As you breathe mentally scan your body, notice any areas of tension and breathe into those. Choose one, and for a few breaths imagine your breath soaking into this area of tension, and taking a longer exhale imagine this dissolving any discomfort, and on each out breath imagine the air carrying it away, so letting you rest.*
>
> *So, after a few breaths………………………start to become aware again of the contact between you and the chair, your hands and your legs and then your feet and the ground.*
>
> *When ready open your eyes. Stretch, move, shift position to break state to be ready to re-engage with the world."*

Considerations
If done virtually and the client chooses to close their eyes, then either the coach or client could also choose to switch off their cameras to avoid distractions.

From: Ridings, 2011

Mindfulness techniques

What is the technique?
A mindfulness technique that switches off the sympathetic nervous system and takes the body into the parasympathetic system. It creates present focus awareness by encouraging clients to focus on minutiae as a

form of distraction. It can enable a switch from an emotional limbic response to a more cortical response when describing five random items in the room. With the raisin technique, it allows a better connection with all five senses.

Who is it for?
For clients experiencing anxiety in the moment or emotional overwhelm especially when first arriving in session. To bring someone into the present. Particularly good for clients who have poor somatic connection and find it difficult to get out of their heads and connect more to their body/emotional responses.

How to use it?
It might be appropriate to settle the client by using a small portion of the pause for breath activity and then guiding with the following:

- Ask the client to look around the room and **slowly** name five things. Optionally you could then ask: "What drew you to X?" and then "What drew you to Y?", etc. By the time all five things have been described, you can then check with, "How are you feeling now, compared to when you came in?"
- Raisin technique. Most of us don't have a handy raisin (a piece of fruit can work well!). However, even in a virtual setting, you could ask your client to just pick something at random within arm's reach of their desk. Ask them to hold it in their hands, feel it, roll it around, look at it from different angles, different distances, feel its weight, bring it up to their nose and smell it. Taking a few minutes to do this creates time for the amygdala to calm down and then optionally you could use the same questions as previously.

Considerations
Some clients may resist this and want to rush through it. Your slow speaking speed is crucial. Due to mirror neurons, it only takes a few minutes for the other person to have to alter their own brain states to align with yours.

Further reading: Williams and Penman, 2014.

Gratitude journal

What is the technique?
This technique is about being thankful and grateful. Thinking about some everyday experiences may help to demonstrate the broadening effect of positive emotions. When things go badly and we get to the edge of panic and

our attention narrows enormously. Positive emotions have the opposite effect. Our thinking and hence possible actions become much more expansive and take in greater range of possibilities. So, with clients facing loss we could help them to broaden this focus leading to the promotion of more flexible thinking and creativity. Essentially you are training their reticular activating system in the brain to notice things that would have been unconsciously filtered out.

Who is it for?
Anyone feeling emotional turbulence who may have dropped into a downward spiral of only seeing the negative events around them. Research has shown that after redundancy or bereavement, people who experienced more positive emotions (note that they still experienced the normal negative emotions associated with such events) had better wellbeing a year or so later.

How to use it?
Ask coachees to keep a gratitude journal of three pleasurable things noticed each day. These can be very small, for example, seeing a robin hopping about on the lawn, taking a first sip of coffee in the morning, receiving compliments, etc. This enables people to pay attention to all the positive things around them that they may be filtering out. The discipline of the exercise means that they will start looking out for things to be able to fill out their journal. Once they have achieved the target of three things, at the next session step up the target to five, and then ten. Clients can then look back on their journal entries in the future.

Considerations
Assure the client you don't need to see their journal and they won't be required to fill it out. Encourage them to buy a beautiful journal as a keepsake rather than use one of the myriad of 'gratitude' apps (especially if you have a client who spends too much screen time anyway).

Build up the number gradually without the client knowing that the target will be increased. This builds their confidence in being able to achieve the task initially.

Further reading: Seligman, 2003

Taking best care of self: Nourishing versus depleting

What is the technique?
This is a simple list that clients can do on a weekly basis in order to separate into two columns events/situations that drained them of energy and thus were depleting, versus those activities that nurtured and nourished them.

Who is it for?
For clients who have an imbalance between the amount of items they weave into their day that nourish versus those that may be depleting items that they cannot change. Rather like a set of scales, if there are depleting items that can't be removed because they are a permanent situation, for example, caring for an elderly parent or a disabled child, then the scales cannot be tilted in favour of the nourishing side by the removal of depleting factors alone. The balance can only be tilted by the addition of more nourishing activities.

How to use it?
Encourage your client to draw up a simple table or provide them with a template. Over a set period they list nourishing activities and depleting activities. At the end of the week and before the next coaching session they can then reflect on the following questions whilst looking at their list:

- What do you notice as a result of this exercise?
- How might you increase your Nourishing list?
- How could you approach the Depleting activities in a different way?

Considerations
Some clients will need to be encouraged to become more creative in their list of nourishing activities, which can be pleasurable or give a sense of satisfaction. Once they have a larger list, they can draw on this list easily without having to think too much about doing something when times are stressful. Pleasurable examples might be taking a long bubble bath, going out for a walk, phoning a close friend, cooking something special. However, it is best to guard against barriers or 'killjoy' thoughts that make them think ahead and decide beforehand that they won't enjoy it. Achievements tasks can be things like clearing a cupboard, paying a bill, taking some exercise. Again, ensure that clients don't approach this with high standards and engage in thoughts like "it should be better/faster/easier". Break down tasks into small steps and celebrate minor milestones.

From: Chapman-Clarke, 2015.

Identifying triggers

What is the technique?
A simple way for clients to gain awareness on areas that they have total control over (T), partial control (P), or no control (N) at all.

Who is it for?
This is useful for clients who are experiencing stress, and anxiety by worrying over many items that they actually have no control over.

How to use it?
Ask clients to list all their current, stressors/things that trigger their anxiety and worry.

Then next to each item on the trigger list to give a score out of five for how much it throws them off balance. One is the lowest, five is the highest.

Next to each they write T, P, or N. A coach would be looking to see if their client had marked N next to many items as well as how high they score it.

Take each one that they are totally in control of. Take one at a time, perhaps one each day or one a week.

1. Ask them: "What is the worst that can happen? What's the best? What's likely?"
2. Ask them: "If the worst happens, will it kill you? Will you or anyone else get physically hurt?"
   Note: If it genuinely could kill, what are they going to do about it to prevent death? That's something worth worrying about and worth taking positive action for!
3. Ask them to verbalise and then write a statement resolving to accept the worst should it occur.
4. Consider what specific steps they will take to begin immediately to improve upon the worst possible outcome, working on one stressor or anxiety factor at a time.
5. Now do the same with "For the best outcome" and work out what actions they can take to bring this about.
6. And then do the same with "The most likely outcome" and work out what actions they can take to bring this about.

Considerations
It may be helpful to provide examples from a coach's own experience. For example, if we are late for work because it has snowed then that's an example of having no control; if we are later for work because of a traffic jam then we may still see some partial control as we could have left home earlier.

Further reading: Tracy, 2006.

Lifelines

What is the technique?
This helps clients to stand back and take a meta view of key events in their lives to draw insights into how they have handled difficult life events in the past. It can enable identifying previous strategies to use for current difficulties or just to gain a more optimistic perspective,

Who is it for?
For clients asking existential questions.

How to use it?

1   Ask clients to create a lifeline on a large sheet of paper (landscape). Perhaps do your own or an example as an illustration.

    Draw a line through the centre of the page from left to right. Start with birth (0 years) to the left and end up to today (age now) to the right.

    Mark positive events above the line and negative below depending on whether the event was happy, neutral or challenging.

    Once completed, look back at each event and place a symbol next to each event:

    ! – Important learning for me
    R – Did I take a risk?
    X – Did I choose this?
    ? – Did I have no choice?

2   Now ask clients to answer some of these questions while looking at the results:

    a   What does this account of your life so far, say about you and how you have lived your life?
    b   Does anything surprise you?
    c   What are the most important elements of your peak experiences?
    d   What have you learned about yourself from the peak and trough points?
    e   To what extent do you take risks? How did they turn out?
    f   Does your life divide into themes and what unfinished themes are there?

Considerations
This can bring up examples for the clients to draw strength from when they have had difficult events happen before and how they have coped. What resources could they bring to today's challenges?

From: Mumford, 2007.

Nine box grid

What is the technique?
It is a simple activity that asks, "How balanced is your life?"

Who is it for?
It is helpful for clients exploring their work-life balance. For a client after a loss, it may help to facilitate a conversation about what else they need to surround themselves with if a large percentage of their boxes are empty. Particularly for clients who have over invested or overidentified with limited aspects, for example, they lose their job and it was a big box on their grid.

How to use it?
Draw an empty nine box grid and ask clients to name different elements in their life to fill each box (use the example below). This can be done within a session or as pre-work in between sessions.

"Here are two (male and female) examples of the different areas that make up someone's life. For ultimate balance, all nine areas could be full; this can be very helpful when one box becomes empty, such as death of a loved one, loss of job, kids leaving home, etc. If all your boxes are earmarked with something and one disappears then you will be able to cope with the loss as you have other things in your life that are important. This will reduce stress and enable you to take action to fill your boxes again!" (Table 1).

Table 1 Nine box grid. Susan Jeffers, Ph.D. (1987)

Male Example		
Relationship with my wife	Relationship with my kids	My Job
Main hobby: Climbing	Developing an internet business sideline	Supporting Nottingham Forest FC
Member of Choir	Show Dog Competitions	Pub once a week with best mate
Female Example		
Being with my partner	Looking after my disabled daughter	Yoga classes
Part-time work in call centre	Studying for MBA	Walking our dog
Organising charity events at church	Volunteer at hospital	Reading crime fiction

Considerations
Care may need to be taken on when to use this activity especially if you already know that your client has poor work-life balance. If they are suffering a serious loss that removes one of their 'squares' then this may confront them with something extremely difficult at a time of great vulnerability. This activity may be better used with someone who has good balance overall but could do better, or for the longer-term period after loss when they are able to reflect on how they need to change their lives in order to become more resilient for future life events.

From: Jeffers, 1987.

Time to Just Think in 10 steps

What is the technique?
Sometimes clients just want to verbalise the swirling thoughts and emotions in their brain without some well-meaning person giving advice, sympathy, or interrupting.

Who is it for?
This mini activity is based on Nancy Kline's *Thinking Environment*™. It can be a precursor to the clients deciding to take some action afterwards or for the coach/supervisor to then use another tool or technique depending on what emerges for the client.

How to use it?

1 Explain to your client that sometimes a download of what they are thinking and feeling can be useful. Use your usual contracting guidelines to establish with client that this is not therapy, but they may find it therapeutic.
2 Agree a set time frame. Use your judgment initially on how emotional your client seems and how long your session is scheduled for. You can agree uninterrupted time between 20 and 45 minutes.
3 Say to your client that you will not interrupt them for 'X' minutes; however, you will be listening.
4 Some clients may be doubtful they can talk that long (they will!) so assure them that if before the allotted time is up if they feel they have said everything they can say to you the phrase "I'm done".
5 To facilitate them talking just start with the question: "What do you want to think and say right now about this?" Allow plenty of silence to encourage them to open up.
6 If there are gaps still maintain full presence and hold the silence. Don't leap into pauses with additional questions, summaries, reflections or observations. 'Stay easeful', sit comfortably, and quietly. Using body

language to show presence is crucial here and a few 'mm-hms' and 'okays' will show you are listening empathetically.
7 If they say, "I'm done" before the allotted time, give them a supplementary question such as: "What more do you think, feel, want to say?" Remember to pause and invariably they will continue and more will emerge. You may need to say this question a few more times to really 'overdrive' anything that may still need to be voiced.
8 If they are still talking when the time is up, use your professional judgment on whether you need to wait for a good pause to remind them that they have had the time you agreed. This is your opportunity to check if they want to continue. Most will not.
9 A good way to finish off this section of the session is to ask content-free questions such as: "How are you feeling now?" "What has emerged for you from this?" "What has been most important for you?" "What are you now aware of?" "What do you know now?"

Considerations
From this may emerge another stage for them. For some people, it may be a sense of wanting to take some action and you can help them with this as a goal for the rest of the session using your usual tools or approach. Some people may want to just sit with what has emerged and reflect so it may be useful to draw the session to a close ensuring a duty of care to your client without over-rescuing but offering support before the next time you see them. A good way to close may be to offer a brief appreciation of a quality or strength you have observed as you have listened. Note this is not a comment on the content, narrative or actions.

Further reading: Kline, 2003

Self-care wheel for coaches

What is the technique?
There are two stages to this activity which can be done individually and alone, or with a supervisor.

The first stage is to work with the overall wheel called "Coaching excellence" and then the "Self-care Wheel for Coaches" which 'sits' underneath.

This should ideally be done with a supervisor who can help you uncover areas you may not see.

Who is it for?
This is for coaches in supervision but can be adapted easily for coaching clients. It is ideal as a structure for a conversation on self-care as many clients have a limited idea on what constitutes self-care (and not self-indulgence).

How to use it?
Both wheels can be seen on page 116, 117

"Coaching excellence".

Examine each quadrant and review a coach's processes and procedures in all areas using some of the example questions here.
The quadrant "Check wheel of self-care" takes you onto stage two.

"Self-Care Wheel for Coaches"

You can use this generally to assess how well you have balance across your own life that will ensure fitness to practice. You can also use it more quantifiably by scaling each quadrant 1 to 10, with 10 being at the outer edge of the wheel and 1 in the centre. By awarding yourself a score for each you can see where you may have to commit more time and development. Again, it can lead to the identification of specific topics to take to a supervisor to explore further.

Considerations
This wheel can also be adapted to use with coachees by changing "Supervision and therapy", to "Coaching and therapy/and support" or whatever feels appropriate for your particular coachee.

From: Wonfor, D., and Ross, M., 2019 (Wonfor and Ross, 2019).

Using attachment theory in supervision

What is the technique?
It is an enquiry into a supervisee's early relationships, their attachment pattern, and connections to the attachment pattern of clients.

Who is it for?
This is ideal for maturing coaches who have been in a supervision relationship for a while, trust and rapport have been built up and they wish to explore more continuing personal development. This will enable a deeper biographical enquiry by the supervisor and help coaches to connect patterns and themes from their early life to how they behave as coaches inter- and intra-personally. It also enables an opportunity to discuss death and endings very specifically due to the emphasis on family relationships. (Table 2).

Table 2 Using attachment theory in supervision. Campion (2020)

Relation and First name	Alive (Y/N)	Age (on death)	Briefly describe (a) what they are /were like, and (b) how is/was your relationship with them?
Maternal Grandfather			
Maternal Grandmother			
Mother			
Paternal Grandfather			
Paternal Grandmother			
Father			
Self i.e. how you see yourself (in relationship to others)			
If applicable:			

(Continued)

Table 2 (Continued)

Relation and First name	Alive (Y/N)	Age (on death)	Briefly describe (a) what they are /were like, and (b) how is/was your relationship with them?
Sibling 1			
Sibling 2			
Sibling 3			
Add more if necessary			
Other significant figures, e.g. teachers, club leaders, friends			

How to use it?
The questions can be asked simply and verbally in a session or laid out in a table for supervisees to complete as intersession work and then explore in more detail.

Considerations
This activity should be used sparingly with coaching clients and only those who have done a great deal of personal development work over a long period of time in coaching. It requires a reflective coachee who is seeking big transformational shifts and feels safe with the coach to explore more emotive topics. Coaches should be aware that the conversation may highlight areas that would be better served in therapy rather than coaching.

From: Campion, H., 2020 (Campion, 2020).

321 reflective writing

What is the technique?
It is a timed reflective writing exercise that allows thoughts and feelings to emerge to assuage interference and give more clarity. The timings are in stages: three minutes, two minutes, and one minute and should take only ten minutes in total.

Who is it for?
It can be used for coachees and supervisees at the start of a session when a client is overwhelmed with too many things and feels unfocussed. It can lead to the client recognising what is a priority to focus on by getting thoughts down onto paper.

It can also be used at the end of sessions to provide a quiet period of reflection on learning and an opportunity to step back from the content of the session to list actions.

How to use it?
It can be done face to face or virtually and just requires a paper and pen. The supervisee/coachee decides what to reflect on (client, an enquiry, a feeling, etc.)

The coach/supervisor coach or supervisor sets a timer for three minutes and the coachee/supervisee is to write constantly for that time. Instructions should be to keep writing even when there feels nothing to say, not to censor, or check spelling or punctuation (it will not be seen by anyone else).

When the three-minute timer sounds they must stop immediately and briefly read back to themselves what they have written.

For the two minutes of writing provide a prefix for the coachee/supervisee to use. Propose one or give a choice of some of the following (whichever feels suitable):

> I notice...
> Am aware of...
> I am curious about...
> I'm surprised by....

After the two minutes timer sounds, they must stop writing again
For the final one minute they must write a list of either:

a   Items they are still curious about.
b   Items they want to discuss in the session.
c   Learning identified.
d   Actions they want to take.

Considerations
A longer timed segment is an option however it is recommended that the three stages are still conformed to. The second two stages are crucial for teasing out strands of clarity and removing stuckness.

From: (Ford, 2020).

"Who are you?"

What is the technique?
It is a short (two-minute) activity for supervisees and coachees to explore their approach and attitude to identity and self-concept. It also underpins resilience building as "resiliency comes from the discovered self and not the constructed self" (Siebert, 2005)

Who is it for?
It is an ideal exercise for clients who may over-identify with some roles to the detriment of others. Often, we are rooted in external things, for example, our role, our seniority, our social network. The activity enables experiential learning for the client about how they see themselves and what they value. Clinical Psychologist, Al Siebert, suggests that if we root ourselves in internal insert dash here things - our personal qualities, values, abilities - we are less prone to identity anxiety when things change. A good example would be the mother who over identifies with her maternal role who then struggles with who she is when her children have left home. It is therefore particularly helpful for clients whose losses have created a crisis of identity as it helps them to see that they are more than the external label that they ascribe to themselves.

How to use it?
Invite the client to playfully engage with the activity. Explain a little about Seibert's three gatekeepers of good resilience – self-confidence, self-esteem and self-concept.

This activity will help them explore their self-concept.

Set a timer for two minutes. During the two minutes you will constantly repeat the question "Who are you?" and they must reply "I am............" for the next two minutes. The repetition is crucial so prepare them for that, as you may have to encourage them to keep going until the time runs out. Take a playful light approach (it's not a test) and note down all the words the client says to the repeating question.

When the two minutes is completed, the coach/supervisor reads back their words.

Then facilitate an exploration of what emerged for the client with questions such as: "What did you notice about the sorts of words that came out initially and later? "What surprises were there? "What was difficult/easy about doing that exercise? And why?"

Considerations
Often clients will start off by quickly listing external identifiers such, as husband, brother, son, job role, and then as time progresses and the question repeats this leads to more subtle qualities like attributes and behaviours, for example, "I am clever, I am warm, I am angry, I am loyal, I am tenacious, I am stubborn......". There are no right, or wrong answers and they don't have to be positive words.

Further reading: Siebert, 2005

Farewell letter

What is the technique?
Write down a farewell letter using pen and paper, or simply using your computer, addressed to the person/pet/thing you have lost. There is no limit on words or styles. One can also use creativity and draw.

Who is it for?
For everyone who needs and likes endings, as the writing symbolises a termination of a cycle. Many clients find comfort in writing down a letter for their deceased ones or simply for the thing they have lost.

How to use it?
The idea is to bring out and put onto paper or screen the emotions one is going through, the memories one cherishes and unload some of the charge one is feeling. At the end of the exercise, many clients find themselves feeling lighter and, to some extent, more ready for the next move forward.

Considerations
Some clients decide to burn the letter afterwards or float it out on open water such as a lake or the ocean. Many prefer using social media; we have also seen these types of letters in posts in Facebook, Instagram, etc. It really depends on personal style and what they would like to disclose, knowing that once it is out there it will be almost impossible to erase it from digital memory.

From: Course Materials - Medical Coaching – www.medical-coaching-institute.com

Talking out loud with the person who has left

What is the technique?
It is a one-way conversation with the person/pet/thing lost.

Who is it for?
This is a very simple activity everyone can do that gives instant release (even if slightly), as we unload what is going on inside.

How to use it?
The client is to imagine themselves in conversation with the lost person (or even item). Posing questions, answering, even using a different type of tonality in different parts of the conversation. Some people using this tool decide to make requests like: "Please help me with son/grandchild." "Please put in a word for me there where you are." "Take care of me.", amongst others.

Considerations
It reassures the connection is still existing, despite the fact that the person/pet/thing is no longer here. It helps to craft a 'new' relationship, particularly with a lost loved one. It grants some comfort for the person who is talking aloud as they may feel they are actually in a conversation. With time, the conversations might be less frequent, or less intense, as acceptance starts to take place and it becomes more a routine or a ritual. It is more commonly used for people rather than things.

Characterising the pain/emotions/suffering

What is the technique?
This exercise has its roots in NLP. For some clients who want to grasp the concept of pain or suffering, sometimes it is helpful to help them in describing and characterising the pain itself.

Who is it for?
This is a very simple activity everyone can do that works like an indicator that they can assess.

How to use it?
Ask the client to describe the pain using the five senses, for example, colours, smell, shape, size, dimension, texture, etc. This can also be done for the deep emotions they are feeling or even the suffering they are going through.

Considerations

Interestingly over time, these characteristics might change, fading for instance, and the person can immediately notice that which in turn might help them to move on or to strengthen their confidence in their present, instead of continuing living in the past. It is important to mention that some clients even though they experience the lower end of the intensity pain/emotions, etc., they are sometimes not yet prepared to let go. So, it would be relevant to work with that and even challenge the client about what is making him/her hold onto something that no longer exists with the same intensity? What is their secondary gain? What are they saying no to, by clinging to that remnant?

What is making him hold to something that no longer exists with the same intensity, what is their secondary gain, what are they saying no to by clinging to that remnant. Get curious!

Adapted from: Course Materials - Medical Coaching – www.medical-coaching-institute.com

References

Campion, H., 2020. Use of attachment theory in supervision. In: M. Lucas, ed., *101 Coaching Supervision Techniques, Approaches, Enquiries and Experiments*, 1st ed. Routledge.

Chapman-Clarke, M., 2015. *Mindfulness at Work Pocketbook*. [ebook] Alresford: Management Pocketbooks Ltdp. 90. Available at: https://www.pocketbook.co.uk/product/mindfulness-at-work-pocketbook/

Ford, L., 2020. 3-2-1 Reflective Writing Technique. In M. Lucas, ed., *101 Coaching Supervision Techniques, Approaches, Enquires and Experiments*. Abingdon: Routledge.

Jeffers, S., 1987. *Feel the Fear and Do it Anyway*®. London: Penguin

Kline, N., 2003. *Time to Think*. London: Cassell Illustrated.

Mumford, J., 2007. *Life Coaching for Dummies*. Chichester: Wiley & Sons.

Ridings, A., 2011. *Pause for Breath*. London: Troubadour Publishing Ltd (Matador).

Ross, M. and Wonfor, D., 2019. *Self Care in Coaching Supervision* [Webinar]. Association of Coaching Supervisors. Available at: https://www.associationofcoachingsupervisors.com/community/aocs-april-2019-webinar-self-care-in-coaching-supervision

Seligman, M., 2003. *Authentic Happiness*. London: Nicholas Brealey.

Siebert, A., 2005. *The Resiliency Advantage*. San Francisco: Berrett-Koehler Publishers.

Tracy, B., 2006. *Eat That Frog!*. 2nd ed. San Francisco, CA: Berrett-Koehler.

Williams, J. and Penman, D., 2014. *Mindfulness. A Practical Guide to Finding Peace in a Frantic World*. London: Piatkus.

Summary

It is fitting that we find ourselves at the end of a book that examined endings and the ultimate end.

At the start, we set out to explore the dearth of knowledge and practice around bereavement, grief, and loss within the coaching and supervision sphere.

Perhaps this is not the end but only the beginning. New research, books, articles, and postings are appearing almost daily on this most universal topic. Even more so since the Covid-19 pandemic. There are many other angles and opinions we have not been able to incorporate due to time and space.

We wanted to test whether coaches and supervisors were handling grief and loss issues in coaching and what was happening when they did. From our research with a small group of coaches and supervisors, and through our reading around the subject, we established there certainly was a place for coaches to handle grief and loss in coaching and supervision whether it was their clients or their own. We have seen that the line between counselling and coaching on this topic is not easy to define, and that there are many considerations when it comes to embracing grief and loss discussions in the coaching and supervision room. Some of these considerations have been shown to be about culture, upbringings, defining normal versus mental health issues, as well as seeing grief and loss in a broader context than just bereavement from death. For us, the huge number of losses that encroach on our lives was an unexpected discovery on our journey in bereavement, that made us more convinced than ever that this was certainly a coaching topic.

As supervisors we were already banner bearers for coaching supervision (and supervision of supervision); however, this topic has cemented our commitment to the importance of having a supervisor in your corner for when clients (and your own life) throw curved balls into your path.

We wish we could have written more as there was more to say but are happy to hand over the baton for the time being and hope that our effort here is now a catalyst for others to develop bereavement, grief, and loss in coaching further.

We offer this book as a starting point for coaches and supervisors to reflect on their professional practice and personal journey incorporating past events and those still to come.

Go well.

Bibliography

Barnes, J., 2008. *Nothing to Be Frightened Of*. London: Johnathan Cape.
Beard, R., 2017. *The Day That Went Missing: A Family Tragedy*. London: Penguin Random House.
Becker, E., 1997. *The Denial of Death*. New York: Free Press paperbacks.
Brown, P. and Brown, V., 2012. *Neuropsychology for Coaches*. McGraw-Hill: Open University Press.
Byfield, R., 2016. *Where There's a Will, There's a Way*. [online] Bacp.co.uk. Available at: https://www.bacp.co.uk/bacp-journals/private-practice/spring-2016/where-theres-a-will-theres-a-way/ [Accessed 4 April 2019].
Cancer.Net, n.d. *Understanding Grief Within a Cultural Context*. [online] Available at: https://www.cancer.net/coping-with-cancer/managing-emotions/grief-and-loss/understanding-grief-within-cultural-context [Accessed 23 February 2021].
Clarke, R., 2020. *Dear Life: A Doctor's Story of Love and Loss*. London: Little, Brown Book Group.
Compassionate Inquiry, 2021. *Compassionate Inquiry | Course Outline*. [online] Available at: https://compassionateinquiry.com/online-training/course-outline/ [Accessed 2 February 2012].
Dent, G., 2021. British Grief Centres Mainly Around the Making of Sandwiches. *The Guardian*, [online] Available at: https://www.theguardian.com/food/2021/feb/19/british-grief-centres-mainly-around-the-making-of-sandwiches-grace-dent [Accessed 30 March 2021].
Funeral Guide, 2016. *How People From Other Cultures Cope with Grief*. [online] Available at: https://www.funeralguide.co.uk/blog/how-cultures-cope-with-grief [Accessed 23 February 2021].
Gawande, A., 2015. *Being Mortal*. London: Profile Books.
Gould, P., 2012. *When I Die, Lessons from the Death Zone*. London: Little Brown.
Govender, R., 2015. Coaching Through the Frame of Neuroscience. [Blog] *International Coaching Federation*, Available at: https://coachingfederation.org/blog/coaching-through-the-frame-of-neuroscience [Accessed 15 October 2018].
Gregory, A., 2021. At-risk' Families to Get Support After Suicide of Relatives. *The Sunday Times*, [online] Available at: https://www.thetimes.co.uk/article/at-risk-families-to-get-support-after-suicide-of-relatives-9p3k95nsz [Accessed 15 October 2021].
Hitchens, C., 2020. *Mortality*. London: Atlantic Books.
Joao, M., 2018. Coaching: *O Guia Essencial Para Coaches e Líderes*. Lisbon, Portugal: Lua de Papel (Leya).

Joao, M., 2011. *101 FAQs About Coaching*. Milton Keynes, UK: AuthorHouse Publishing.

João, M. and Menaul, J., 2020. *As the tears dry*. [online] Coaching at Work. Available at: https://www.coaching-at-work.com/2020/02/29/as-the-tears-dry/

Kalanithi, P., 2016. *When Breath Becomes Air*. London: Penguin Random House.

Kets de Vries, M., 2009. *Sex, Money, Happiness, and Death*. Basingstoke: Palgrave Macmillan.

Lewis, C., 2013. *A Grief Observed*. London: Faber & Faber.

Machado, J., 2017. *Funerais Curiosos Pelo Mundo | Chicken or Pasta?* [online] Chickenorpasta.com.br. Available at: https://chickenorpasta.com.br/2017/funerais-curiosos-pelo-mundo [Accessed 1 September 2021].

Mannix, K., 2019. *With the End in Mind: How to Live and Die Well*. Glasgow: Williams Collins.

Mannix, K., 2021. *Listen: How to Find the Words for Tender Conversations*. Dublin: Harper Collins.

McCrum, R., 2017. *Every Third Thought*. London: Pan Macmillan.

McKay, S., 2020. *The Uncertain Brain. A Guide to Facing the Fear of the Unknown.* - Dr Sarah McKay. [online] Dr Sarah McKay. Available at: https://drsarahmckay.com/the-uncertain-brain-a-guide-to-facing-the-fear-of-the-unknown/ [Accessed 4 April 2021].

McKay, S., 2021. *When Meditation Fails. Alternative Ways to Calm an Anxious Mind.* - Dr Sarah McKay. [online] Available at: https://drsarahmckay.com/meditation-fails-alternative-ways-calm-anxious-mind/

Menaul, J., 2017. *Compassionate Coaching in the Corporate World*. Copenhagen: BookBoon.

Napton, S., 2017. Depression is a Physical Illness Which Could be Treated With Anti-inflammatory Drugs. *The Daily Telegraph*, [online] Available at: https://www.telegraph.co.uk/science/2017/09/08/depression-physical-illness-could-treated-anti-inflammatory/ [Accessed 15 October 2021].

Relational Dynamics Ltd., 2019. *Safeguarding for Coaches*. [.pdf] Available at: https://cdn.ymaws.com/www.associationforcoaching.com/resource/resmgr/articles_&_handy_guides/coaches/articles/rd1st_safeguarding_2019.pdf [Accessed 20 May 2021].

Rowe, D., 2007. *Beyond Fear (20th Anniversary Edition)*. London: Harper Collins.

Samuel, J., 2019. *Grief Works*. New York: Shribner.

Samuel, J., 2021. *This Too Shall Pass – Stories of Change, Crisis and Hopeful Beginnings*. London: Penguin Random House.

Siegel, D., 2015. *Mindsight: The New Science of Personal Transformation*. New York: Bantam Books.

Ware, B., 2011. *Top Five Regrets of the Dying: A Life Transformed by the Dearly Departing*. the. Bloomington: Balboa Press.

Whittington, J., n.d. Organisational Health: The unwritten rules. *Life Love Leadership*, [online] Available at: https://lifeloveleadership.com/organisational-health/ [Accessed 24 November 2020].

Williams, C., 2015. Is Depression a Kind of Allergic Reaction. *The Guardian*, [online] Available at: https://www.theguardian.com/lifeandstyle/2015/jan/04/depression-allergic-reaction-inflammation-immune-system

Yalom, I., 2008. *Staring at the Sun: Overcoming the Dread of Death*. London: Piatkus.

Appendices

Appendix 1

Coaching niches

Personal/Life Coaching

"A collaborative solution-focussed, results-orientated and systematic process in which the coach facilitates the enhancement of work performance, life experience, self-directed learning and personal growth of the coachee".

Executive Coaching

"As for personal coaching, but it is specifically focussed at senior management level where there is an expectation for the coach to feel as comfortable exploring business related topics, as personal development topics with the client in order to improve their personal performance".

Corporate/Business Coaching

"As for personal coaching, but the specific remit of a corporate coach is to focus on supporting an employee, either as an individual, as part of a team and/or organisation to achieve improved business performance and operational effectiveness".

Speciality/Niche Coaching

"As for personal coaching, but the coach is expert in addressing one particular aspect of a person's life, e.g. stress, career, or the coach is focussed on enhancing a particular section of the population, e.g. doctors, youths".

Group Coaching

"As for personal coaching, but the coach is working with a number or individuals either to achieve a common goal within the group or create an environment where individuals can co-coach each other".

Source

Grant, A., n.d. *Coaching Defined*. [online] Association for Coaching. Available at: https://www.associationforcoaching.com/page/Coaching Defined [Accessed 18 September 2004].

Appendix 2

Our research findings

As part of the research for the writing up of this book, the authors created a survey that has been circulated internationally over many months. Up to the date of this book's publication, 102 answers have been collected, from which approximately 76 were female coaches and/or supervisors, 20 were male, and 6 preferred not to say.

From the 102 answers, 2 answers came from the Americas (USA, Canada, and the Cayman Islands), 3 answers from South Africa, 2 answers from Oman, and the rest of the vast majority from Europe, being 86 of the answers from the UK (including England, Scotland, and Northern Ireland).

Regarding age groups, 14 respondents belonged to the age between 35–44, 26 between 45–54 years old, 43 people were between 55–64 years old, and 19 of the respondents were 65+ years of age. No one from the age group up to 34 years old answered this questionnaire.

51% of the respondents confirmed that bereavement has been a topic in their supervision sessions.

With regards to the question "If you have had a bereavement experience yourself, how does that impact the way you supervise?", many responses were in line with:

- Having a heightened self-awareness of own interferences they might bring into the supervision session.
- Giving greater sense of perspective.
- Being empathic, attentive.
- Being more focussed on self-regulation and self-care.
- Listening actively more.
- Rescheduling appointments and stopping for a while.
- Getting their own bereavement and its impact on the client to supervision.
- Being even more present.

Similar answers were given to the question "If you have had a bereavement experience yourself, how does that impact the way you coach?" with the following additions:

- Being more consciously challenging in the coaching session.
- Building more rapport quicker.
- Being more aware of own emotions during the coaching session.
- Not sharing with the client.
- Requiring more effort and focus to be in the mind space.
- Avoiding 'solutionising'.
- Exploring more deeply self-care both at a conscious and a subconscious level.

The ideas that the coaches and supervisors shared in this question "What do you become aware of that you start and/or stop doing/being while coaching/supervising?" are as follows.

Stop:
- Talking.
- Challenging the coachee.
- Remembering own experiences.
- Sympathising with coachee.
- Making assumptions of what might be happening.
- Parallel processes.
- Coaching for longer than two hours.
- Thinking on outcomes and how to make a difference.
- Disclosing less about self.
- Being spontaneous.
- Coaching/Supervising if not feeling resourceful.
- Presuming people feel the same way they felt.

Start:
- Keeping detached and stay in the moment with the client.
- Focus more on the person than the question.
- Listening for longer before moving into action planning.
- Being more watchful whether a professional therapy referral is required.
- Being more aware of somatic responses.
- Bringing a sense of urgency, as life is finite.
- Naming things.
- Offering resources.
- Being gentler with self.

- Holding some of the other objectives for the coaching programme more lightly until the client mentions what they need to deal with regards to the bereavement.
- Re-contracting 'compartementalising'.
- Reflecting back the words the client uses.
- Reframing.
- Being more candid.
- Providing more space.
- Being less self-critical.
- To slow down.
- Practising mindfulness before a coaching session.
- Making sure they are in the right state before coaching or supervising.
- Having more supervision.
- Being more silent.
- Passive listening.
- Plan for longer sessions.
- Being more open to other experiences.
- Encouraging self-care.

Below you will find an *ipsis verbis* list of the best practices the respondents highlighted as their response to the question "What best practices would you like to share, when coaching someone through bereavement or supervising a coach whose client is going through bereavement?"

- "Take the time, give time and space for sorrow, listen and be there for the other. Help them embrace their loss and find strength in the relationship they had and continue to cherish. This sounds like the obvious. There is no best practice for approaching such an exceptionally personal event as losing someone through death, is my view."
- "Meet people where they are. Let go of the need to frame everything in 'positive' terms. Some things are just ****ing hard and deserve to be acknowledged as such. Also let go of assumptions - the other person might be hugely relieved and even glad this person has died."
- "I have suggested people seek counselling – either in parallel to the coaching or before continuing the coaching."
- "Do own bereavement work ideally with therapist. The learning from that comes through on many levels. Deep recognition that everyone is different, but that the Kübler-Ross curve is still useful. Be very OK with tears. Be very OK with silence. When supervising particularly coaches who have not been bereaved but working with bereaved clients explore loss in other forms if appropriate. As ever own self-care, self-compassion."
- "You can't fix the problem and you can't be in their shoes, but you can be there and can help validate how they feel."

- "Hold steady in yourself. Don't assume because it's death that it's the worst thing. Ask how they are doing but don't over sympathise. Listen and encourage self–care."
- "Listening and letting them say what they need to say."
- "Staying aware of the difficulty some people have. The tension between acting 'normally' and letting themselves be sad and express their feelings. Particularly in work situations. Having a black book with contacts for bereavement (and other) types of counsellor/therapist for referring clients."
- "Disclosing if you have been bereaved too (without hogging the airspace), sharing models of how men and women can grieve differently, sharing good books on bereavement, e.g. book by Julia Samuel, Grief Works and another by Sheryl Sandberg, Option B. If the bereavement involves a child or baby, I direct them to child bereavement great resources."
- "One of the main things might be to help others identify when therapy may be more appropriate. The other thing might be to equip yourself with some specialist tools alongside any usual coaching tools / techniques."
- "Ask yourself why you are 'coaching them through bereavement' – you are a coach, not a counsellor. Be mindful of their situation being unique to them – please do not use the expression, "I know how you feel." You don't! This is the time to use unconditional positive regard - how the individual deals with bereavement is their right. Be conscious of boundaries - you are not performing the role of a bereavement counsellor. Be conscious of the drama triangle - otherwise you may become their rescuer. Entering this script may lead you to them becoming your persecutor and you becoming their victim. Then, you may end up using your supervisor as a rescuer, in a parallel process."
- "Think it is just that it is an OK space to occupy and keep the context of the coaching in mind – how does the coachee's outcome relate to the bereavement."
- "A bereavement has served to heighten the importance of the 101 s of coaching: (i) acceptance that you have no idea of what is going on for someone else; (ii) remaining judgement free: different experiences impact different people in different ways; (iii) acknowledging that people have different support mechanisms; as a coach I have not brought my bereavement to my supervisor, I've sought support elsewhere. And that has no bearing on my supervisor."
- "Take the extra time to reflect - both pre- and post-session. And don't be afraid to postpone sessions if emotions are too raw."
- "The importance of empathy and support over driving for any other outcomes. Putting a halt to existing contracts and re-contracting around this issue specifically and its impact elsewhere in their lives."
- "Give them space, permission to be as they are, presence."

- "If a client has just been bereaved, say something along the lines of: 'I cannot imagine how you are feeling .... if you feel up to it, can you explain? And no worries if you'd rather not at this point'."
- "I referred them to further coaching and counselling. This had been unspoken and not fully acknowledged within them for many years and it was quite a big thing for them to say it aloud to another person. Just be with them in their space and emotion."
- "Making sure the client is in the right frame of mind to be coached or supervised; exploring what support they have in place; give voice to safety to practice (supervisee); pacing the client carefully."
- "Some Gestalt techniques with clients have helped in the past."
- "An awareness of the change / bereavement curve."
- "Work on your own experiences of loss first, it doesn't have to be exactly a 'bereavement', significant loss appears in many ways in our young lives. Then in the current situation always work in competence. That's our responsibility as coaches. Know where your competence ends. Know your skills. Keep your confidence. Bereavement is a natural part of life ... and yet we are sometimes poorly equipped to hold it."
- "Listening; acknowledge the grief process (e.g. Kübler-Ross); working through coping strategies to manage the grief and balance this with living."
- "Re-contract."
- "Time - can't rush the process! Acceptance even if unexpected feelings come up...relief, blame, freedom, guilt, etc."
- "Do not make assumptions. Stay with the coachee. Ask their permission about challenge if I felt appropriate to challenge to gauge their thoughts."
- "For the coaches...bring these issues to supervision and access supervision regularly. The same applies for supervisors. Explore relationships, what you notice at times that interfere with your thought processes. Recognise that these are helpful and need to be explored in a safe space."
- "Don't rush anything. Remember it's different for everyone and they need to go at their own pace. Let them fully set the agenda and go over and over the same emotions if necessary. Be alongside as far as possible. Remember that the W of GROW might not be applicable for some time and that this will depend on the individual."
- "Handling self/what to say to a person."
- "Holding the space can be very powerful. To just acknowledge the feelings of the client and remain grounded can really help them."
- "Be person-centred. Listen and demonstrate core coaching skills (empathy, etc). Don't try to solve."
- "I think there are boundary and ethical questions about whether the Coach or supervisor feels equipped, and sometimes need to seek help elsewhere as well and instead, although having said that the coaching space may be where they feel most comfortable as everyone responds differently."

- "Stay curious and away from sympathy."
- "Be mindful of pace, recontract for what's need now, discuss workloads & cases (possible impact on client work), wellbeing."
- "Firstly – listen & empathise. Secondly – understand impact of the bereavement on them & their world. Thirdly – (if possible & appropriate) find positive actions they can focus on."
- "I think if had personally been recently bereaved, I would decline to coach or supervise someone who was going through bereavement to avoid the risk of my own feelings getting tangled up with theirs."
- "Awareness of Kübler-Ross change curve; noticing and supporting self-care needs of the coach; the coach needs to be more aware of their own emotional state working with others, so increased focus on that aspect in supervision."
- "Co-creation of boundaries, role of coaching in creating a space to share context of bereavement when coaching at work. Multi-dimensional perspective on client resources."
- "Being still, completely attentive to the client's needs and allowing whatever space and time is necessary for the emotions to speak."
- "Just listen."
- "Be led by client requests and be flexible."
- "Intuitively go where the client goes in coaching and check boundaries and resilience in a supervisee."
- "Maybe the simple things such as acknowledging, attending, not assuming, helping people know (if they need this) what the range of 'normal' is when grieving and mourning – if they are worrying about themselves or clients. Quite a few things not to say about how they 'must' be feeling or 'was probably for the best' and so forth."
- "Normalising the need to take time and deviating from previously agreed agenda."
- "Depending on where they are with their bereavement, is to hold the space for them, pacing is important as they go through the different stages of grieving, checking in."
- "Respecting their experience and being open to hearing what they are saying in a way that is supportive and non-judgmental."
- "Listen & don't push for responses. Ask if they'd welcome me to 'check in' with them in a day or two."
- "Remembering that every bereavement and every response to it is unique, with some features that our similar. Respect for the individual differences and offering of reflective space, specialist referral or whatever is important for the client and ethical for the helper in the moment."
- "To develop softness."
- "I think mindfulness (something I use in coaching and supervision anyway) could be helpful here. Perhaps a writing exercise."

- "As a coach listening at a deep level is so important as it can be so hard for a coachee to share their true feelings. The safe, non-judgmental, listening ear of the coach can be very important."
- "My experience (personally & with others) is people go a little distorted after the death of someone close... or in the face of a traumatic death, or an unexpected one. The circumstance of the death, the preparedness of the person for that death. These things impact how people respond and deal with the loss. There is a lot to unpack. I'd say be aware of which parts are supervision and which might be therapeutic. Calmness, detachment, kindness, gallows humour, treating the client as if they are not broken."
- "Really stay present with the vulnerability!"
- "All ideas of body/breath work – coming back to centre, working from the heart."
- "I think the usual points apply – to be open to explore, be compassionate, share experience if appropriate, but not be drawn into the point of being almost immobile. To sit with and not feel you have to do anything. There may be silence and tears, and that is ok. It is a being time, not a doing time."
- "Being gentle, kind, compassionate and making sure to go at the coachee's own pace."
- "Knowing and recognising when one (as a coach or supervisor) should not coach or supervise if our own experience is too raw, asking ourselves the question 'What can I do to be of service to my client?' and take time if time is needed. Also, I would take this to supervision myself."
- "Silence and space. Showing compassion and empathy and listening."
- "Disclosure at the right time is ok."
- "Listen without intervention."
- "To check-in on the self-care, support and practical things that the coachee is doing. As coaching is a future-focussed space, the client can often want to move forward at the expense of their wellbeing, especially if not fully aware of the impact that grief and grieving is having on them."
- "Attend to what is said and not said, attend to what is emerging."
- That the bereavement process varies from person to person, and across and between cultures.
- "Go with the person's story, know there may not be a tangible outcome. Listen and be aware of the persons coping strategies – are they healthy? Not to assume that bereavement affects everyone in the same way and that the person's emotional response needs time, even if they don't like it! Some coaches may want to fix or cure the unwanted emotions – however the process is a natural one, even if the client/coach/supervisor are not comfortable with it."
- "Listen + observe + feel + 'clean(er) language questions'."

- "Patience. Use the deceased person's name as the coachee would use it."
- "Empathic listening is more important than practical suggestions."
- "Respect for distress but stay professional."
- "Being willing to sit with distress. Listening. Curiosity."
- "Listen and be in the moment fully."
- "I use Lois Tonkin's model of loss and restoration. I would want coaches to be aware of the importance of allowing space for loss but also supporting the client in finding ways in which they can experience any degree of restoration. I would also want them to recognise that grief is never in a vacuum. It also needs to be considered in terms of the impact on the system the coachee is part of, whether in their family or at work."
- "Check they have other professional support, if necessary. Have shorter supervision sessions."
- "Validate feelings and listen."
- "In supervision, 'best practices' might include inviting the coach to reflect about their own experience of bereavement and how this may be showing up with their clients; we may explore the bereavement cycle (Kübler-Ross) so that the coach understands what may be happening to their client; we consider whether the coaching assignment need to be put on hold, we consider how the coach can be human with their client - acknowledge and sit with their client in their grief."
- "Stay with where they are. Allow their experience to be what it is without judgement. Be aware if they need counselling or therapy not coaching. Sense when they're ready to move forward."
- "First, take some time for yourself, to deal with the situation so it does not affect the coach-coachee relationship and process. After the experience is processed it can be of added value as it will allow you to better relate and emotionally connect to a person in the same situation."
- "The same for any other coaching topic. Plus, raise your self-awareness of your own thoughts, feelings, and assumptions regarding bereavement. You may be holding limiting and untrue assumptions that could unintentionally impact the other persons' experience of your coaching and/or supervision."

For the question "What practical provision have you made as either a coach or supervisor in the event of your own death whilst still running your coaching and supervision practice?", the vast majority had never thought about the matter. Approximately only 17% had put some thought to it and already had or were in process of doing a coaching will and/or made provisions with next of kin or close colleague/business partner providing them with details of what to do and who to contact in the event of a sudden death or illness.

Appendix 3

The Global Code of Ethics

Introduction and Purpose

All the bodies ("the bodies") mentioned in section 5, as signatories to this Code of Ethics ("the Code"), wish to state the following:

As membership bodies, we are committed to maintaining and promoting excellent practice in coaching, mentoring and supervision, a field that is becoming increasingly professionalised. All our members, in their roles as coaches, mentors, supervisors, trainers and/or students, as part of their continuing membership, agree to adhere to the elements and principles of this Code of Ethics.

The Code aligns with the content and requirements set out in the Professional Charter for Coaching and Mentoring. The Charter, drafted in accordance with European law, is registered on the dedicated European Union database, which lists self-regulation initiatives in Europe.

The Code is a guidance document rather than a legally binding one that in detail spells out what a member can and cannot do. The Code sets the expectation of best practice in coaching, mentoring and supervision promoting the development of professional excellence. Its purpose is to:

- Provide appropriate guidelines, accountability and standards of conduct for all our members
- Set out how our members are expected to act, behave and perform when working with clients
- In conjunction with our respective bodies' professional competences, guide our members' development and growth in the profession
- Serve as a guide for those individuals who do not necessarily identify themselves as a professional coach or mentor, but nonetheless use coaching or mentoring skills in their work
- Be used as the basis of any complaint or disciplinary hearing and action following our bodies' respective complaints procedures.

Each signatory to the Code may decide that – in creating a complete ethics-related framework specific to their membership – it needs additional ethical principles and/or a code of practice (to reflect context, activity, membership criteria, membership structure, etc.) to complement the Code.

Such additions must not contradict the essence of the Code, nor carry an obligation for the other co-signatories to adopt. Such additions may be shared with the other co-signatories as part of the ongoing collaborative exchanges between professional bodies.

The Code of Ethics

The Code is arranged into five sections and covers the bodies' general expectations of professional behaviour and conduct as well as the list of all the membership bodies that have signed up to this Code of Ethics:

1. Terminology
2. Working with Clients
3. Professional Conduct
4. Excellent Practice
5. Signatories to the Global Code of Ethics

1. Terminology

For reasons of brevity this Code where appropriate refers to:

- Coachees, mentees, supervisees and students as "clients"
- Coaches, mentors, supervisors and trainers as "practising members" or "members"
- Coaching, mentoring and supervision work as "professional work"
- Coaching, mentoring and supervision as "profession".
- The signatories to this Code acknowledge that the terms "profession" and "professional" are being used for activities that are not under statutory regulation but are being increasingly professionalised and self-regulated.
- The signatories to this Code acknowledge that the titles "coach", "mentor" and "supervisor" are not protected and may be used by anyone in the field of practice, member or not member of a professional body.
- Each signatory will define exactly which of its members and other stakeholders are expected to abide by this Code (who are hereafter collectively referred to as the "members").
- For proper understanding of this Code members should be aware of their respective professional body's definitions and terminology for the precise meanings of key words used in this Code e.g. coach, coaching, client, member, mentor, mentoring, sponsor, supervisor, supervision and training

2. Working with Clients

Context

2.1 When professionally working with clients in any capacity members will conduct themselves in accordance with this code, committed to delivering the level of service that may reasonably be expected of a practising member.

Contracting

2.2 Before they start working with a client, members will make this Code available to their client, and explain and make explicit, their commitment to abide by this Code. Members will also make their clients and sponsors aware of their respective bodies' complaints procedures.
2.3 Before starting to work with a client, members will explain and strive to ensure that the client and sponsor know, and fully understand, the nature and terms and conditions of any coaching, mentoring or supervision contract, including financial, logistical and confidentiality arrangements.
2.4 Members will use their professional knowledge and experience to understand their clients' and sponsors' expectations and reach agreement on how they plan to meet them. Members will also try to take into account the needs and expectations of other relevant parties.
2.5 Members will be open about the methods they use, and on request will be ready to supply the client and sponsor with information about the processes involved.
2.6 Members will ensure that the duration of the contract is appropriate to achieve the client's and sponsor's goals and will actively work to promote the client's independence and self-reliance.
2.7 Members will ensure that the setting in which any coaching, mentoring, supervision or training takes place offers optimal conditions for learning and reflection and therefore a higher likelihood of achievement of the goals set in the contract.
2.8 Members should always put their client's interests first but at the same time safeguard that these interests do not harm the interests of the sponsor.

Integrity

2.9 Members will accurately and honestly represent their relevant professional qualifications, professional body to which they belong, experience, training, certifications and accreditations to clients, sponsors and colleagues.

2.10 In communication with any party, members will accurately and honestly represent the value they provide as a coach, mentor or supervisor.
2.11 Members will ensure that no false or misleading claims are made, or implied, about their professional competence, qualifications or accreditation in any published, promotional material or otherwise. Members will attribute ownership of work, ideas and materials of others to the originator and not claim it as their own.
2.12 Members will act within applicable law and not in any way encourage, assist or collude with conduct which is dishonest, unlawful, unprofessional or discriminatory.

Confidentiality

2.13 When working with clients, members will maintain the strictest level of confidentiality with all client and sponsor information unless release of information is required by law.
2.14 Members will have a clear agreement with clients and sponsors about the conditions under which confidentiality will not be maintained (e.g. illegal activity, danger to self or others) and gain agreement to that limit of confidentiality where possible unless the release of information is required by law.
2.15 Members will keep, store and dispose of appropriate and accurate records of their work with clients, including electronic files and communications, in a manner that ensures confidentiality, security and privacy, and complies with all relevant laws and agreements that exist in their country regarding data protection and privacy.
2.16 Members will inform clients that they are receiving supervision and identify that the client may be referred to anonymously in this context. The client should be assured that the supervision relationship is itself a confidential relationship.
2.17 If the client is a child or vulnerable adult, members will make arrangements with the client's sponsors or guardian to ensure an appropriate level of confidentiality in the best interests of the client, whilst also complying with all relevant legislation.

Inappropriate interactions

2.18 Members are responsible for setting and maintaining clear, appropriate and culturally sensitive boundaries that govern all physical and virtual interactions with clients or sponsors.
2.19 Members will avoid any romantic or sexual relationship with current clients or sponsors. Further, members will be alert to the possibility of any potential sexual intimacy with the aforementioned parties and take

appropriate action to avoid the intimacy or cancel the engagement in order to provide a safe environment.

Conflict of interest

2.20 Members will not exploit a client or seek to gain any inappropriate financial or non-financial advantage from the relationship.
2.21 To avoid any conflict of interest, members will distinguish a professional relationship with a client from other forms of relationships.
2.22 Members will be aware of the potential for conflicts of interest of either a commercial or personal nature arising through the working relationship and address them quickly and effectively in order to ensure that there is no detriment to the client or sponsor.
2.23 Members will consider the impact of any client relationships on other client relationships and discuss any potential conflict of interest with those who might be affected.
2.24 Members will disclose any conflict openly with the client and agree to withdraw from the relationship if a conflict arises which cannot be managed effectively.

Terminating professional relationships and on-going responsibilities

2.25 Members will respect a client's right to terminate an engagement at any point in the process, subject to the provisions of the coaching, mentoring or supervision service agreement.
2.26 Members will encourage the client or sponsor to terminate the coaching, mentoring or supervision engagement if it is believed that the client would be better served by another practising member or a different form of professional help.
2.27 Members understand that their professional responsibilities continue beyond the termination of the professional relationship. These include:
- Maintenance of agreed confidentiality of all information relating to clients and sponsors
- Safe and secure maintenance of all related records and data that complies with all relevant laws and agreements that exist in their country regarding data protection and privacy
- Avoidance of any exploitation of the former relationship, which could otherwise call into question the professionalism or integrity of the member or the professional community Provision of any follow-up that has been agreed to.

2.28 Members are required to have a provision for transfer of current clients and dissemination of records in the event of the member's incapacitation, or termination of practice.

3. Professional Conduct Maintaining the reputation of the profession

3.1 Members will behave in a way that at all times reflects positively upon and enhances the reputation of an increasingly professionalised service.
3.2 Members will demonstrate respect for the variety of practising members and other individuals in the profession and for the different approaches to coaching, mentoring and supervision.

Recognising equality and diversity

3.3 Members will abide by their respective bodies' diversity statements and policies.
3.4 Members will avoid knowingly discriminating on any grounds and will seek to enhance their own awareness of possible areas of discrimination.
3.5 Members will be cognisant of the potential for unconscious bias and seek to ensure that they take a respectful and inclusive approach, which embraces and explores individual difference.
3.6 Members will challenge in a supportive way any colleagues, employees, service providers, clients or participants who are perceived to be using discriminatory behaviour.
3.7 Members will monitor their spoken, written and non-verbal communication for inadvertent discrimination.
3.8 Members will engage in developmental activities that are likely to increase their self- awareness in relation to equality and diversity.

Breaches of professional conduct

3.9 Members accept that any breach of the code that is upheld in a complaints procedure may result in sanctions including loss of accredited status and/or body membership. The bodies may share details of such breaches between them in the interest of client safety, upholding quality standards and maintaining the reputation of the profession.
3.10 A member will challenge another member if they have reasonable cause to believe that the member is acting in an unethical manner and, failing resolution, will report that person to the body.

Legal and statutory obligations and duties

3.11 Members are obliged to stay up to date and comply with all relevant statutory requirements in the countries in which their professional work takes place and work within any organisational policies and procedures in the context in which they are working.

3.12 Members will have the appropriate professional indemnity insurance to cover their coaching, mentoring and supervising work for the countries in which they operate.

4. Excellent Practice

Ability to perform

4.1 Members will have the qualifications, skills and experience appropriate to meet the needs of the client and will operate within the limits of their competence. Members should refer the client to a more experienced or suitably qualified practising member where appropriate.

4.2 Members will be fit and healthy enough to practice. If they are not, or are unsure if they are able to practice safely for health reasons, they will seek professional guidance or support. Where necessary or appropriate, the practising member should manage the termination of their work with the client and refer the client to an alternative practising member.

On-going supervision

4.3 Members will engage in supervision with a suitably qualified supervisor or peer supervision group with a level of frequency that is appropriate to their coaching, mentoring or supervision practice, the requirements of their professional body and the level of their accreditation, or evidence engagement in reflective practice, ideally with peers and/or more experienced colleagues.

4.4 Members need to ensure that any other existing relationship with the supervisor does not interfere with the quality of the supervision provided.

4.5 Members will discuss any ethical dilemmas and potential, or actual, breaches of this Code with their supervisor or peer supervision group for support and guidance.

Continuing professional development

4.6 Members will develop their level of coaching and/or mentoring competence by participating in relevant and appropriate training and/or continuing professional development (CPD).

4.7 Members are expected to make a contribution to the professional community that is appropriate to their level of expertise. Forms which this may take include informal peer support to fellow practising members, contributing to advancing the profession, research and writing etc.

4.8 Members will systematically evaluate the quality of their work through feedback from clients, their supervisor and other relevant parties.

Source

With permission from the AC (Association forCoaches). Available online at: https://www.associationforcoaching.com/page/AboutCodeEthics.

Resources

Grief in the workplace

UK guidance

https://pdf4pro.com/view/managing-bereavement-in-the-workplace-a-good-practice-5af161.html

A good practice guide on managing bereavement in the workplace has some pragmatic tips and useful case studies on handling the death of employees.

https://www.cipd.co.uk/Images/a-guide-to-bereavement-support-Feb2021_tcm18-81624.pdf

A Guide from the Chartered Institute of Personnel and Development covering the design and development of bereavement policy and a support for line managers.

USA guidance

https://www.shrm.org/hr-today/news/hr-magazine/0917/Pages/how-to-support-employees-through-grief-and-loss.aspx

"SHRM, the Society for Human Resource Management, creates better workplaces where employers and employees thrive together. As the voice of all things work, workers and the workplace, SHRM is the foremost expert, convener and thought leader on issues impacting today's evolving workplaces. With 300,000+ HR and business executive members in 165 countries, SHRM impacts the lives of more than 115 million workers and families globally."

https://www.insperity.com/blog/how-to-help-employees-through-grief/

"Since 1986, Insperity has been showing companies how to harness the power of HR to improve business success. We've grown from two people sharing a one-room office to a $4.3 billion company with more than 70 offices across the U.S."

https://www.thebalancecareers.com/bereavement-leave-sample-policy-1918879

Interestingly – perhaps not surprisingly – you can find articles like the one above for employers advising them how to avoid or manage the onerous requirements of the new bereavement laws and also doing the right thing so that you'll be seen as a good employer.

Suicide

Further Information and Support in the UK

https://uksobs.org/

Survivors of Bereavement by Suicide (SOBS) (including a very useful booklet for individuals and professionals Support After a Suicide).

Cruse Bereavement Care https://www.cruse.org.uk

Support After Suicide https://supportaftersuicide.org.uk/

The Samaritans https://www.samaritans.org

Zero Suicide Alliance www.zerosuicidealliance.com

Global

https://www.befrienders.org/

A charity that helps people who are considering suicide or experiencing general emotional distress. Befrienders Worldwide evolved from the Samaritans in the UK, some of its centres use the name Samaritans, while others use Befrienders or similar. The primary aim of all centres is to relieve distress and thus reduce deaths by suicide. A good search engine relating to all countries in EU and the States and Australasia.

Organisations in the USA

https://suicidepreventionlifeline.org/

The National Suicide Prevention Lifeline provides free and confidential emotional support to people in suicidal crisis or emotional distress 24 hours a day, 7 days a week, across the United States. The Lifeline is comprised of a national network of over 180 local crisis centres, combining custom local care and resources with national standards and best practices.

https://www.iasp.info/resources/Postvention/National_Suicide_Survivor_Organizations/

Post-suicide bereavement resources akin to the Samaritans in the UK.

Carers

https://www.carersuk.org/help-and-advice/practical-support/when-caring-ends/bereavement

Bereavement when caring ends

https://www.caregiver.org/resource/grief-and-loss/

Bereavement charities and support groups

https://www.bereavement.eu

European site for Covid-19 bereavement.

http://nationalgriefawarenessweek.org/

Grief awareness week in the UK is the first week in December.

www.deathcafe.com

Networking and community support whilst exploring themes of death and dying.

www.griefspeaks.com

USA based grief specialist with extensive blog postings on all types of grief and loss.

https://www.professionalexecutors.co.uk/

The Professional Executors Service for Psychotherapists, Counsellors and Coaches in the UK.

www.medical-coaching-institute.com

Medical Coaching, training, and consulting.

Index

Page numbers followed by f indicate figure and by t indicate table

Abortion 59–60
Acceptance 48
Acknowledging 162
Advisory, Conciliation and Arbitration Service (ACAS) 81
Ageing 59
Anger 48
Angry victim 131–132
Anxious avoidant 134
Anxious style 135, 136
APPEAR model, stages of 108–109
Attachment
 bonding and 153
 loss and 137–139
 loss and grief through 134–139, 139–150
 secure and insecure 134–135
Attachment theory 134, 136
 using in supervision, technique of 181–183, 182t
Automatic nervous system, impact of 155–156

Baby loss 44–46
Bargaining 48
Behaviours 36
Bereaved employees 80
Bereavement
 approaches to 18
 of coach 63–78
 coaching program 39–42
 culture impact on 161–166
 definition of 13–14
 of employee 80
 helping the coach with 109–110
 life coaching *vs.* executive coaching 31–32
 signs of 16–18
 suicide 147–148
Bonding 153
Brain, human 151–152, 151f
Brain system 153
Breathing 159
 breathing techniques 156
Bridges model 92–94
Broken Heart Syndrome 37

Carer's grief 52–54
Characterising the pain/emotions/suffering, technique of 187
Child death 46–47
Client-centered stage of development 121–122
Coach(es)
 bereaved coaches 63–78, 75–77
 ill coach 71–73, 72f
 mental health 30, 30f
 myths 28
 return-to-work support 88–89
 self-care 65–71
 survival self 143–144
 therapy 118
Coaching
Cognitive Behavioural therapy (CBT) 12
Compassion 23–26
Concentration 36, 65
Confidentiality 208
Conflict of interest 209
Connect with people 159
Context 207

Continuing Professional Development (CPD) 120
Contracting 207
  coaches and 84–85
  coaching and 28
  psychological 28–29
Counselling 12
Counsellor 67
COVID-19 pandemic
  coaching for job loss during 126
  disengagement from activities during 92
  generations working in organisations 80
  loss for some clients 91
  rituals during 164
  rituals in the workplace 127
Culture 161–166

Death
  Child 46–47
  of client 124–125
  of spouse as top stressor 49
Denial 47–48
Depression 36, 66
Development 101
Disenchantment 93
Disengagement 92
Disidentification 93
Dismantling 93
Disorientation 94
Diversity 210
Divorce 49–51
Drama Triangle 129–134, 131f
Drone Zone 39
Dysfunctional attachment 136
Dysfunctional suffering 30f, 35–36

Emotions 36
Empathy 24–26
Employee Assistance Scheme (EAP) 33
Empty nest syndrome 50, 54–57
Endings 125–127
Equality 210
Ethical practices 104–109

Faith 27–28
Farewell letter technique 185–186
Fearful style 135, 136
Feet on floor; bottom on chair (FOFBOC) 144

Flow Zone 38f, 39
Focusing technique 159–160
Frustration 48
Functional suffering 30f, 31

Gestalt 12
Global Code of Ethics for Coaching 63, 73, 104, 164
Gratitude journal 173–174
Grief
  carer's 52–54
  as crisis of meaning 20–22
  definition of 14
  in executive coaching 10–11
  growth through 45f
  in supervisor room 110
  symptoms of 16–17, 81
  tools and techniques to work with 171–187
  unresolved 17
  in workplace 80
"Grief-ball," 46
'Grief brain,' 17
Grieving brain 156–161
Group coaching 195
Group vs. individual supervision 101
GROW model 33, 34f

Health loss 51–52
Healthy self 140, 140f, 142
Historical loss 43–44
Hobby 68

Ill coach 71–73, 72f
Illness-wellness continuum 72f
Insecure attachment 134–135
Integrity 207–208
Interactions 208–209

Job loss 47–49

Kandel principles 152–154
Knowledge, cultivating on certain topics 67
Kübler-Ross Curve 47–48, 50, 55, 92, 93

Language 26–27
Legal and statutory obligations and duties 210–211
Level of challenge 66
Lifelines technique 177

Line managers 82–83
Listening 24, 162
Loss(es)
  abortion as 59–60
  attachment and 137–139
  of baby 44–46
  coaching and types of 42–43
  as crisis of meaning 20–22
  divorce as 49–51
  Drama Triangle and 132–133
  grief and 14
  of health 51–52
  historical 43–44
  of job 47–49
  offspring 54–55
  relationship 49
  of reproductive capability 55–57
  response 118–120
  retirement and ageing 57–59
  in supervisor room 110
  tools and techniques to work with 171–187
  types of 15–16
  unresolved 18, 125–127

Mediating 69
Medical coaching 37, 51–52
Meditation 159
Memory 36
Memory systems 153, 154
Menopause 55–58
Mental health 30, 30f
Mental illness 30f, 36–37
Mindfulness
  during loss 159
  nervous system and 156
  technique 172–173
Muscle relaxing 159

Neuro Linguistic Programming (NLP) 12
Neuroplasticity 153
Neuroscience
  coaching and 154–155
  field of 151
  Kandel principles 152–155
  loss and grief through 150–161
Neurotransmitters 152, 154
Nine box grid technique 178–189, 178t
Non-disclosure agreements (NDAs) 126
Nourishing 174–175

Objectives 159
Offspring 54–55
Ongoing supervision 211
Organisational Machine 79–96, 132
Organisations
  game playing in 132
  generations working in 80
  lack of HR guidance for bereavement 81
  mishandling loss and grief of employees 79–80
Outplacement coaching/counselling 47

Pain 16
Panic Zone 38f, 39
Parallel process 103
Parasympathetic 156
Pausing 65
Performance 81
Persecutor 130
Physical signs 36
Polyvagal theory 155
Procrastination 36
Professional conduct 210
Professional development 211
Psyche trauma 139
Psychological contract 28–29
Psychologist 67
Psychology of Flow 38f

Reciprocity 99
Recognise, Allowing, Investigation, Nuture (RAIN) 46
Re-contracting 107
Redundancy 47
Reflective writing 183–184
Reframing 158
Relationships 15, 49
Rescuer 130–131
Research findings 199–204
  survey questions 197–199
Resilience 114–118
Retirement 58–59
Rewards 159
Rituals 164

Secure attachment 134
Self-care 65–71
Self-care wheel 115–118, 117f
Self-criticism 36
Self-reliance 135, 136

Seven eyed model 100f
Signs of crisis 22–23
Skills 29–30
Sleep 158
Sponsor 86–87
Stress 158
Suffering
  dysfunctional 30f, 35–36
  functional 30f, 31
Suicide risk 146–147
Supervision 99–104, 100f
  as defined by Hawkins and Smith 99
  functions of 101–102, 102f
  group *vs.* individual 101
  ongoing 211
  pain and suffering in 9
  as place for reflection 120
  resilience building through 114–118
  stages of development through 121–124
Supervision of supervision 100
Supervision process 99–100
Supervision triangle 101, 102f
Supervisor
  grief and loss in room of 110
  helping in loss and attachment 137
  to help the coach 67
  privilege as role of 109
  tips to help in unexpected loss during programme 83–84
  working with coach experiencing loss 110–112
Support
  to client within and outside the organisation 87–88
  of coach in normalising grief 105
  as function of supervision 101

organisations and lack of 80
Survival self 140, 140f, 141–142
Sympathetic 155
Sympathy 24
Symptoms 16–17, 81
  perimenopause and menopause 56
  retirement 58

Targets 159
Techniques 69, 156, 173, 174–175, 177, 178–189
Terminating 209
"The new normal," 93
Therapy 12, 118
Thoughts 36
Transactional Analysis (TA) 12, 130
Transition 92
Trapeze 76f, 77–78
Trauma
  connecting to coach and loss 142–143
  definition of 139
  informed coaching 139–140, 140f
  loss and grief through 139–150
  Psyche 139
Trauma model 139, 140f
Trauma self 140–141, 140f
Travelling 68–69
Triggers 175–176

Unconscious bias 162–163
Unresolved grief 17

Vagus nerve 156
Victim 131–132

Workplace 80

Milton Keynes UK
Ingram Content Group UK Ltd.
UKHW022150171023
430811UK00006B/57